SIX LIGHTED WINDOWS

SIX LIGHTED WINDOWS

Memories of Swamis in the West

SWAMI YOGESHANANDA

Available through Vedanta Press
1946 Vedanta Place
Hollywood, CA 90068

All Rights Reserved
Second Edition
Printed in the United States

ISBN 0-87481-410-3

Library of Congress Cataloging-in-Publication Data
Yogeshananda, Swami.
     Six Lighted Windows: Memories of Swamis in the West/
by Swami Yogeshananda. — Rev. ed.
     Includes bibilographical references.
     ISBN 0-87481-410-3 (alk. paper)
     1. Ramakrishna Mission — United States. 2. Spiritual life
— Ramakrishna Mission. 3. Spiritual biography. I. Title.
BL 1280.235.U6Y65 1997
294.5'55'0922 — dc21
[B]   97-18229
                                                   CIP

CONTENTS

vii | Preface

xi | Introduction

1 | Philadelphia Story — Swami Yatiswarananda

35 | High Above Hollywood and Vine — Swami Prabhavananda

91 | A Buddha At the Golden Gate — Swami Ashokananda

151 | Mother's Parkside Patrician — Swami Nikhilananda

209 | "Except Ye Become As a Little Child ..."
— Swami Madhavananda

251 | "London Is a Man's Town - There's Power In The Air..."
—Swami Ghanananda

287 | Appendix A: Addendum on the Philadelphia Center

291 | Appendix B: Notes on the worship of Sri Ramakrishna

293 | Appendix C: Notes on worship

296 | Appendix D: Puzzle solution

297 | References & Bibliography

PREFACE

I used to think that I knew what spirituality was. At least the books — *The Practice of The Presence of God, Tales of the Hasidim, The Buddha-Charita* — were in some agreement about it. Living beside the extraordinary souls of whom I speak in *this* book, I had to revise my conceptions. Spirituality seems to take many forms and surprising shapes. The temptation to put people on scales in order to gauge their spiritual weight or judge one against another is to be resisted. Applying an illustration used by Sri Ramakrishna may be our best course of action: "In a great chandelier, the lamps are of various shapes and sizes, but the light shining through each one is the same and from the same source."

Whatever spirituality is, or rather whatever I could comprehend of it, has been revealed gradually and continually as I lived with these men.

These accounts are not biographies, but they are more than cameos. The monks discussed here were true pioneers of the work of the Ramakrishna Order in the West, and whatever can be preserved of their words and actions is of value.

The particular situations faced by these men may seem unique, but they are not without historical precedent. Whenever exporting or transplantation of a great world faith has been undertaken, the tides of multicultural interplay have been set in motion. We do well to recall in this connection the lives of de Nobili in India, Ricci in China and St. Francis Xavier in Japan. Swami Vivekananda, his two tours of the West completed, ended his brief life leaving guidelines of sorts for workers in the West, but certainly not a handbook.

Agreeing from the start to make the sacrifice of working in the Occident, these men needed to establish new frameworks of monastic living. Readers will look in vain here for the orthodox *tapasya* of Indian monks: the austerity of fasts, vigils or protracted contemplation. Their austerity was of a different kind: As they came to serve us, the curious Western devotees, their food became whatever was cooked for them; their sleep, a brief respite from community, doorbell and telephone; their *japa* and meditation superimposed over the public work itself. They alone could know the impact of *that* austerity.

My focus here has been on the swami. Those around him have been brought into the picture where they reveal him, as dictated by memory and interest. And, as Swami Prabhavananda told us, "The swamis are all very different, it appears, but remember that if you just scratch the surface a little, you will find Sri Ramakrishna as the base of every one."

Generally in our life we have but one period in which our minds, like blotting paper, soak up the ink of strong impressions. This may account for my dealing with one figure at greater length than the others. These portraits of the monks are presented in the order of my initial encounters with them; thus, although the bulk of my Hollywood experience followed the San Francisco episode chronologically, Swami Prabhavananda's is the second chapter rather than the third because I initially encountered him before I made my way to San Francisco.

In the Indian tradition, monks do not write autobiographies. The "old life" is dead, burned up in the "funeral fire" kindled before final vows. Unlike Thomas Merton, who said he was commanded by his superiors to write and publish the story of his life (for what were undoubtedly good reasons), my only excuse for using autobiographical material here is to set the stage for a cross-cultural experience from which others may learn —

as well as to provide the continuity which such a book requires.

In the accounts to follow I have tried to portray my experience of the dignity, expertise and exaltation of these teachers. Readers may understand that I was not blind to, nor unaffected by, the darker side of monastic life. It is by no means all sunshine and roses, and black flecks have speckled my canvas here and there. As the subject of the book was their lives, not mine, nor monastic life, I did not feel it necessary or appropriate to deal with either of these in greater detail.

I am much indebted to William Buchanan, former Professor of English at Olivet College in Michigan and Dr. Beatrice Bruteau, formerly of Fordham University, New York, who read the manuscript and offered many helpful suggestions. The late Swami Anamananda of Ramakrishna Monastery in Trabuco Canyon, California; Dorothy Madison of Alameda, California; Kurt Friedrichs of Hamburg, Germany; Betty Robinson of New York and Barbara Foxe of Bristol, England, each read at least one chapter for me, correcting factual errors and offering useful opinions and suggestions. Finally I thank Lucas Carpenter, Emory University, for encouraging and very ably assisting me in putting the work into published form, Kath Beasley for her careful and helpful preparation of the typed manuscript, and Jon Monday, Ann Myren and Gail Gregory for invaluable assistance in preparing it for publication.

Swami Yogeshananda
Atlanta
1995

INTRODUCTION

One of the first things I recall seeing is the attendant with the wooden leg hobbling down the railroad track toward the station. Old Pegleg had been fired. He was not needed — now that all these young men had come to be "tendants," as the patients called them, at Pennhurst. Moreover, they said, that leg could bruise and hurt you when he used it as a paddle. The "patients" were the mentally handicapped, 1500 of them, divided by gender into two encampments: women and girls on the hill, men and boys in the valley.

But this was 1944 and we said "mentally deficient" in those days; later it became "retarded," and today one says "challenged." The new young men were the 30 members of Civilian Public Service Unit #129 who had arrived, some with their wives, to serve out their time in service alternative to the armed forces. In fact it was they who were challenged — their ideal of nonviolence was to be put to the test as they handled the inmates and mixed with the staff.

Housing for patients was in "cottages," long dormitories each with a large common sleeping room and a dayroom, sequestering the hundreds of men and boys. The cottages were scattered across the slopes of grass and trees which dropped down to the Schuylkill River and were named by letters of the alphabet: U 2 meant the second floor of "U" Cottage. This was the lockup. It had special attendants, like Pegleg.

When you're sitting on a bench in a dayroom most of the day — facing dozens of others, equally misshapen, who are mirroring your grimaces and pleasantries — mealtime is momentous. Fed in shifts at wooden tables in vast kitchens where the cabbage, potatoes, and ground round were cooked in huge vats and cauldrons, patients slavered with anticipation as they marched in military formation to the hall. In the winter or in rain, this thrice-daily trough tramping took place underground. Through long concrete tunnels decorated with the molds and rivulets that spread along seeping walls, one found one's way to one of three dining halls, each with its own menu: patients', attendants', management's.

The odors of Pennhurst were in a class by themselves.

Yet if it had not been for a nearly forgotten, tireless woman whose astonishing achievement this was, these unfortunates would still be wading in pig mud, feared and despised, kept in animal pens, caves and hovels run by mercenaries imprisoning their bodies and souls. For such was the case in 1843 when Dorothea L. Dix began her crusade to wake up the conscience and dispel the ignorance of the American people regarding the nature of insanity and retardation.

It was not difficult at all for us to look over the Pennhurst scene and deplore it; very few of us seeing it had any idea how vastly improved had the lot of "inmates" become during the preceding hundred years, through her skillful agitation in one state legislature after another. Miss Dix served her country well. Appointed superintendent of women nurses at the outbreak of the Civil War, she not only managed that responsibility, but — because of her national prominence — she was now able to influence and further her campaign for state and federal legislation providing guidelines for institutionalizing the mentally ill. I often think, now, of how little the country has known or cared to remember this national hero (her face finally appeared on a one-cent postage stamp), and of how little she ever valued credit for her achievements.

Pennhurst was a monster of a state school. There was the

bumbling bureaucracy with its proverbial blindness to abuses; the aging doctors who might or might not take seriously cases such as these; the paltry attempts at school classes, sports and recreation; the dirt, the vermin, the heartless scrimping; and, most of all, the physical and mental abuse dished out by hard-boiled and mercenary caretakers and supervisors.

We, teachers and preachers, nurses and scholars, farmers and clerks of C.P.S. Unit 129, had come from all parts of the country, direct from outdoor camps. During that initial induction period we had dug ditches, reclaimed soil, cut trails and fought forest fires under the direction, sometimes benign, more often scornful, of the Forest Service and other bureaus of the Department of the Interior. Now we had won the privilege of submitting our convictions to the regimen of life in a state-run full-care institution. Administrators made use of our special skills — replacing, ironically, men who then went off to war. Most of us worked as wardens, caretakers of this broken, pitiful and overlooked segment of humanity.

A tremendous ferment took place, both in Pennhurst and in our lives. Each man (and woman, for there were half-a-dozen) was now plunged into unfamiliar work with new demands, hostility from the employees, along with ridicule from the brighter patients who picked up on the employees' disdain, all in addition to the usual displacements of war service. Our work shifts, six or more days a weeks, were often twelve hours long, our "allowance" fifteen dollars per month.

As for the institution itself, there was a profound shake-up. One can only wonder if, in the end, it did not regret having accepted the "free" labor of the objectors. Partly as a result of this wartime involvement, Pennhurst went on to become of historical importance. It was chosen as a pioneer in the pilot program for transfer of the patients deemed suitable to halfway houses or hostels where, from the security of small, home-like urban centers, they were gradually to approach integration into normal public life.

That program failed notoriously, for various reasons. But by then the state hospital had virtually shut down (saving the taxpayers millions of dollars), while the mentally incapacitated fell among the homeless we find on our streets today.

There were happier moments; memory tends to drop much unpleasantness. I recall the light in the eyes of a boy finding someone to play a new game with him; the sheer novelty of being cared about, on the part of some man who had been left here long ago by bitter and forgetting parents; or getting administration finally to do something about an abusive situation. But our richest compensation may have lain in the fellowship to be found in this extraordinary company of very bright, sensitive and diversely talented draftees.

We were received in third-floor quarters which had just been renovated and painted, then crowded by twos into rooms intended for one. The long halls led to a common room — the focus, now, of what social and recreational life we could have. We did our best to gather books and jigsaw puzzles and to make it look and feel "homey," inventing activities and meetings to stimulate a corporate intellectual life. In this we met with some success, as in that dayroom we met such influential people as Norman Thomas, A.J. Muste, Douglas Steere, Muriel Lester and Bayard Rustin. The Peace Churches, responsible for the off-duty dimensions of C.P.S., were of the greatest help here in trying to take care of their people just as they had in the camps.

War is famous for heightening religious interest and feeling, some of it conventional, conservative or fanatical, some of it idealistic, progressive, "spiritual". And we were not exempt from the power of that *Zeitgeist*. Though the men of Pennhurst Unit were pacifists from diverse origins — Quaker, Mennonite, Methodist, Jewish, humanist — we found much common ground. In the light of all the foregoing and considering the strain we were under, it should be no surprise that four or five banded together to use their free time for the study and practice of what could only be called "the spiritual life." I belonged to this group, the Gemeinde, as the most learned of us chose to nickname it — perhaps a fancy word for club.

Two pairs of roommates, in adjacent rooms, we made a common pool of our books and began to read and study together; during long walks on half-holidays, or on picnics near the river, we read from "The Garden of Proserpine" or *Time Must Have a Stop* or *Four Quartets*. Aldous Huxley and Gerald Heard for us became first-name friends, as it were. We watched, from our own isolation and confinement, the entry into monastery life of Merton and Isherwood. When a weekend retreat in New Jersey under the leadership of Gilbert Kilpack was announced, we saved holidays and experienced it together.

As a Friend (not by birth but of some years' standing) I was familiar with meditation as understood by Quakers. The word was used in connection with Meeting for Worship (silent), which took place usually once a week on First Day (Sunday) morning. It was the practice to sit in silence until the meeting became "gathered" in an undistracted, focused communal rapport. And this required something of the nature of meditation. Only then was the time ripe for individuals to be, perhaps, inspired to speak out on something of benefit to the gathering, a concern that was on the heart; otherwise the silence only deepened for the remainder of the hour. Never had I known or heard of Friends who "meditated" daily or privately.

Yet the American Friends Service Committee, the social action arm of Quakerism, had us meditating in "work camp" in 1941. I recall how a dozen-and-a-half of us, college students, spent a sultry summer in Michigan as volunteers helping a Chicago Cooperative build recreation facilities in a camp at Circle Pines. Before work began in the morning we went out daily to the big oak in the front yard of the farmhouse and sat under it for twenty or thirty minutes of silent meditation. No methods were taught or suggested; perhaps we were mulling over Hegel or Kierkegaard, residue of our bull sessions.

So at Pennhurst the inner need intensified. After a few weeks of working in the medical ward I lost all my previous projections of becoming a doctor or psychiatrist: the "miseries of the world" were all too real in the miseries of "Tom" and "Shorty" and "Red." All the mystics were telling us, "Physician, heal thyself," and that made sense. I saw that our failings, as ministers to these benighted souls and their keepers, were the failures of our own self-mastery. We could put patches on wounds or even on a mind — but to heal? A soul?

Of course they had souls, didn't they? How does one know? Before coming east I had often gone out alone in the California camp and sat on a hillock to ponder the dictum of Keats: "Beauty is Truth, Truth Beauty — that is all / Ye know on earth and all ye need to know." Was he right? I had found that Beauty was Truth, I thought; no questioning that. But is all truth beautiful? What did it mean? Here I was, about to embark on an adventure in the care of "Mongols, morons and idiots;" there was Truth for you! Would it be beautiful?

One of our Gemeinde, the eldest and so the leader, had been a professor of literature; another was a Protestant youth and church worker; the third was Jewish by upbringing but fresh from college, brightly agnostic. All of us had served in the camps operated jointly by the three peace churches, so we had some acquaintance with meditation. None was imbued with Roman Catholic or oriental mystical traditions. The world of St. John of the Cross and Meister Eckhart, of St. Bernard and the two Teresas, of Veda and Gita, Buddha, Ramakrishna and the Sufis, fell suddenly upon us as if from storage bins high in the heavens.

For me there was additional incentive. My eldest brother and his wife, also Friends, were visiting the retreat set up by Gerald Heard in Trabuco Canyon, California. They were sitting in awe as quotations from the mystics fell in profusion from Heard's learned lips. They were joining others in silence and prayer in the spherical oratory. They wrote to me about it.

Supported by this, we four decided to learn to meditate. We thought we could learn it from books such as *Raja-Yoga* of Swami Vivekananda or *Autobiography of a Yogi* by Yogananda. Impressed with the importance of regularity, we sat together each evening — setting a half-hour as our target. This, mind you, after 12 hours of duty, much of it wearying and stressful. Problems quite naturally arose. One of us regularly dozed off, inspiring others to do the same; another could not, for the life of him, concentrate his mind; another, forcing himself, might have subsequent nervous twitches or headaches.

Books were not enough. A master was needed.

And this is where my account really begins — in the search for a spiritual teacher. With *guru* a word hardly known, and even "yoga" spoken of in muted tones, the search began on the part of this tiny band of like-minded truth-seekers huddled in an unlikely place, who eventually abandoned group meditation and went their separate ways — but who, because of the grace of their initial experiences, were altogether convinced of the reality of the life of the spirit and committed to its practice.

How I became the one who went out to look for a teacher, I am not sure; I believe the others urged me on their behalf. It took a long time. I had leave every month of one-and-a-half days and the journey to Philadelphia was time-consuming. One would have thought that among our Friends at the meetings there in the heartland, someone might be found to help us with our quest, but I did not at first discover one. No one there knew of any habitual meditator. From previous experience I was sure we would get little help on spiritual matters from the professionals in psychology of that era. I turned to the clergy and began knocking on ministerial doors. In turn I tried the pastors of Lutheran, Episcopal, Methodist, Congregational and other denominations. When I described what we were after, some said harsh things: "anachronistic," "medieval," this practice of meditation. Others knew nothing of it. Occasionally I would describe it as mental prayer — a phrase which would have pleased Dorothea Dix. She, a Unitarian, had spent the first hour of her day in "prayer and meditation" and kept this up to the end of her life, saying it was what kept her up, through illness and despair.

Still I had no luck. One minister admitted he had heard of meditation but knew naught of how to go about it. In later years there were those who asked why I had not tried the Catholic church, where there might have been some expertise. They forget that the church was in those days much more dogmatic and demanding than now. With our backgrounds, none of us could have paid that price. As it was, the master we found fit only me: Two of the group never had interviews with the swami, and my roommate, although he did so, did not become his student.

At long last we turned up the name of a Joseph Wilson, a Friend who was said to be a daily meditator. I approached this man. He kindly agreed to see me and our meeting led me to Swami Yatiswarananda.

I did not know then that my quest had ended. I found the teacher of spirituality — for me. What I found in him and in subsequent teachers as well (*upaguru* is the Sanskrit word) is the subject of this book.

Swami Yatiswarananda about 1945

PHILADELPHIA STORY

SWAMI YATISWARANANDA

He lived in the first-floor flat of a two-storied frame house, on Pine Street just off Rittenhouse Square in downtown Philadelphia. Not the likeliest place in the world to find someone who is going to turn your whole life upside down, but there it was. That is where I found him, on a late summer's day in 1944, for a brief encounter spread over a scant six months. I was a bird on the wing — pausing in the area for only a year — and his Vedanta Center was to become a refuge of only seven years' duration. But of that I knew nothing at the time.

"If you really want to know about meditation," Joe Wilson (see Introduction) had said, "there is a swami of the Ramakrishna Order living in Philadelphia. I can give you his name and address. All I know about it I've learned from him." Wilson was a Quaker whose name I had obtained, after a long search, as that of "one who meditates every day." We had sat in Joe's yard in Swarthmore, discussing the purposes of meditation. The group to which I belonged had read the books of Gerald Heard and Aldous Huxley and we were out for big game. Nothing less than the Mystical Way to the Ultimate Union with the Ineffable Godhead, was how we saw it. Joe had more modest aspirations; an inventor by profession, he used the technique before going to work in the morning, to dream up new machines. The books we had read did not answer all one's questions, and when specific difficulties arose, we scarcely knew what to do. How long at a time should one sit? Does it have to be the lotus posture? On what should one concentrate? Or should the mind be made blank? What do you do if headache or other, stranger, sensations arise? These were questions this Quaker businessman could not, or dared not, answer. But at last, after knocking at the doors of many, both lay and clergy, I had found someone who meditated daily. Few in those days knew even what we were talking about. When I would broach the subject, I would refer to it as mental prayer or meditation, trying to guess which term the listener's ear might like better to hear. People had all sorts of reactions — ridicule, jest, bafflement, frank unknowingness.

It was something else Joe Wilson had said that clinched it: "One thing I can tell you: For every step you take experimentally you must take two steps ethically." I pondered this; yes, Joe was all right; he could be trusted. Maybe I should look up this swami after all. I noted the address and took leave of my friend.

A couple of hours' joggling on the Paoli Local train to Pennsy's Twelfth Street station, then a smoother run downtown, and one came out on Broad Street. Making my way through the pigeons in the square, I tried to imagine how Swami Yatiswarananda might look: surely a respectably flowing beard, eyes of honey, crowned with a high and sweeping brow; glistening hair — rather like Rabindranath Tagore, one might think — seer, poet, litterateur, venerable but romantic. Well, there was nothing romantic about this gray wooden house on Pine Street. With not a few misgivings, I rang the bell opposite his name indicating the ground floor. Shortly a door opened and there appeared a rather short, middle-aged Indian in a gray business suit, balding and looking out in a kindly way through very plain, circular eyeglass frames, old-fashioned even for those days. His ears were prominent, giving his face an altogether owlish look. Had I pressed the wrong doorbell? My second thought was that perhaps this was someone who serves the great man. Yet there came to my lips the question, "Are *you* Swami Yatiswarananda?" No doubt I murdered the pronunciation.

"Yes," said he. "What can I do for you?"

There was a sinking feeling in my heart; how could I over-come my discomfiture enough to unburden it? Providentially, a thought struck me. "Do you have copies of *The Gospel of Sri Ramakrishna* for sale?" I asked. A year or so before, I had made a brief acquaintance with this volume when I encountered it in a library.

"Yes," said the swami, "please come in." He led me through a hall to his sitting room in the middle of the flat, which was also his office and reception room, and there we began to get acquainted. Adjoining, at the front of the house, was a lecture hall formed by having thrown together a living room and dining room. "The Truth is One; sages call it by various names" — this and an Om decorated the fireplace, as I remember. Books were displayed on a table, and when it emerged that I had not sufficient money with me to acquire the *Gospel*, yet felt I should buy something, a small blue book about Swami Brahmananda, *The Eternal Companion*, caught my eye and I bought it. Was that eye caught, I sometimes wonder, on a strand of hope spun out by the swami standing close by my side? Who knows?

But there was no air of the psychic or mysterious about Swami Yatiswarananda. He was all common sense. We talked that day of the mystics and saints and their common refrain. It was perfectly obvious from the start that he could quote as readily from the Bible or St. John of the Cross or Meister Eckhart as from the Upanishads, the Gita or Shankaracharya. Buddhists, Sufis, Lao-tze or Maimonides, he knew about them all. Two qualities of this teacher now stand out for me above all others: the *catholicity* of his knowledge and the *balance* of his personality — his level-headedness. Action was not to be stressed at the expense of contemplation. Devotion should set aflame the candle oft-dipped in knowledge and renunciation.

Some of the other talk in that first interview comes to mind. It was his cool affability, totally devoid of pressure, that eventually won me. One felt that in approaching him one need have no fear of hooks or barbs, hidden motives or a yen for gain. And gradually I told him of our meditation group and our several problems. When he inquired about the nature of my work I told him I had been drafted to do "work of national importance

under civilian direction," and was attending the mentally handicapped in a large institution. His instant comment was, "Oh,
you have a good job." This was a surprise. Ever since being assigned that work I had hugged around me a slight mantle of
martyrdom and self pity, and never would I have thought of it as
a "good job." I dared to ask him why. He replied, "Because it
gives you the opportunity of directly serving man" — or something of that sort. "Nurses and teachers are fortunate in this way."

He spoke to me that day about the body, about how one
should not be attached to it — for after all, is it not filled with
unsavory things? Does it not last but a few years? And so on. All
along I had been thinking that the body is something quite valuable, even rather beautiful at times, and generally to be well kept-
up. My settled ideas were being seriously disturbed.

When it came to the difficulties in meditation we were
encountering as individual beginners, swami offered on this first
day only a jar of molasses. It was a parable of Sri Ramakrishna. If
one attempts to hold molasses in a jar with holes in the bottom,
it is obvious what will happen. "Lust, anger, desire, distraction
— these are the 'holes' through which spiritual power leaks out,"
said the swami. He asked about my health, complaining that my
face looked dark. He said little else, but left me with the conviction that he had diagnosed my "case" all right, and I knew I
would return.

The price of *The Gospel of Sri Ramakrishna* was then $7.50,
and with a salary of fifteen dollars a month it was difficult to save
the money, but on the second visit I was able to purchase the
book. Swami told me to note down questions which arose as I
read it and to put them to him at the next visit. It turned out to
be an excellent method of study. He asked of me what I think he
asked of many others, that I memorize the words to one of the
songs Sri Ramakrishna used to love, "Thou art my All in All, O
Lord." He suggested I meditate in the "heart," which, through
japa (continued repetition of a mantra, a name of God or the
like) and meditation the seeker comes to feel is the point of contact between the individual consciousness and the cosmic Divine
Consciousness. The true meaning of the heart center is revealed
to the aspirant in due course, so one must have patience, as Swami
Brahmananda, beloved disciple of Sri Ramakrishna and the

swami's teacher, used to tell his monks. Let me quote from a letter of later years to make it clearer:

"The point of consciousness that we feel in the region of the heart where we have reaction of our emotions is a part of the infinite consciousness which you may liken to light. To give another analogy, the heart is like a landing stage on the stairway to a flat, through which we contact the infinite consciousness. There is a plane of consciousness corresponding to the heart in which the devotee sees the holy forms. The point between the eyebrows is also a gateway to a higher plane of consciousness in which the soul, freed from body and mind consciousness, feels its union with the infinite spirit. It is always better to begin with the heart."

It was clear from the outset that Swami Yatiswarananda was not a teacher of *hatha yoga*; yet the simple basic exercises of *pranayama* were a part of his instruction. I ventured one day to ask if there were any physical exercises which assist us in our spiritual practice. He was silent for a few moments. Then he mentioned certain muscles which should be made strong and proceeded to demonstrate simple exercises for them.

More of our conversation at the book table is coming back to me. Gerald Heard's book *Preface to Prayer* had just been published, and our little spiritual *Gemeinde* had read it together admiringly; we were fans of Gerald and Aldous. Here was the book, on the sales table, and I asked swami if he had read it. He had. What did he think of it? "Yes," he replied, "it is good. But we wish he had said more." However he may have intended it, this was the perfect answer for me. Without casting any aspersions on Heard, my current ideal, it hinted of more to be learned about prayer — and that the swami knew what it was.

Prayer was pursued in one of his later conversations, which, like most of the others, was replete with quotations and stories. He told of a little girl whose older brother made a trap for catching birds. The girl grew angry and disgusted whenever the trap was successful, and she berated her brother. One day the family pastor came to tea, and inquired kindly after her brother, who was not at home. She described him as a very naughty boy because of his persistence in catching birds despite her vehement protestations.

"Pray for your brother, my dear," had been the clergyman's

advice. "Pray earnestly to God to make your brother a better boy, more gentle, more merciful. God answers prayer." When the pastor called again after a few months he remembered the predicament and asked the little girl about the bird trapping.

"Oh, he doesn't catch any birds now," she answered.

"No?" smiled the visitor.

"No. For several weeks I prayed to God to make Claude a better boy, but he went right on. Finally I just went out and kicked that old trap to pieces."

Naturally the ending took me by surprise. But it was some years later that I realized how it distills a very basic difference in the approaches of East and West.

Probably it was at the second interview that I explained to him how I seemed to be able, in meditation, to reach only a certain level of concentration or absorption before some kind of barrier would arise beyond which there was no further penetration. "One day I went into a building here," was his comment, "where I had business on the seventh floor. A lady got into the elevator with me and pushed the fourth-floor button. The elevator went up but stopped just short of the floor and the door would not open. So we went down again and started up once more. The same thing happened. After the third try, a thought occurred to me. 'Look, I want to go to the seventh floor. Why don't we both go up there, and if I can get out, then you approach the fourth floor from above, and see if that works.' And it did. After leaving the car I listened to hear that she had opened her door successfully. Sometimes we just don't aim high enough."

At the next visit, when we were on other topics, swami began again the elevator story. "Yes, swami," I interrupted, "you told me that story last time."

"Did I?" said he, unfazed, and went right on telling it. How subtle! What a deft way of saying, "I did not forget I told it; but you have not absorbed its meaning." These sessions took place at perhaps three-week intervals over a period of five or six months at most. Then it came time for me to leave the Philadelphia area, for I had received a medical discharge from C.P.S.

Swami Yatiswarananda had left India in 1933 to preach Vedanta in Europe. His invitation had been to a home in Wiesbaden, Germany, where he gave no public talks but held classes daily in the house for a handful of earnest seekers. After that had come work in Switzerland, then Paris, Holland and finally Sweden and Norway. War had driven him from Europe and he came at last to the United States. After visiting his brother monks he had decided to work in Philadelphia where he found facilities for a temporary center. All this too was unknown to me at the time. Managing to attend one of the Sunday lectures and one of the evening scripture classes, I found that Swami Yatiswarananda did not appear to be teaching Hinduism or any "ism" but religion, mystical and essential. His views on spiritual matters were practical, broad and always well-balanced. He was not a remarkable lecturer. He told me that he did not care about attracting a crowd, that he preferred to guide to a higher level of being the lives of a few sincere individuals. Hindsight shows us how superbly he did it.

In meditating to begin the class, swami would settle down by gently moving his head back and forth a few times, perhaps to relax neck muscles; then he would seem to become absorbed. After the allotted fifteen minutes or so had gone by he would give a deep sigh and turn easily again to the group assembled. He used to tell us that a spiritual person should enter into meditation as eagerly as a worldly one gets into his bath. Swami at one time assisted the aging Swami Bodhananda in the Vedanta Society, New York, by taking the train in time to give an evening class there. He would return the next day.

Since our meeting, things had moved quickly for me, and I now began to feel jolted by the contrast between customary thoughts and pursuits, and the values and subtleties swami's life and teaching were revealing to mind and heart. Talk about cool! He was unwilling to draw or to be drawn, and where concerns arose there was an almost contagious detachment concerning them. "See the fun!" was one of his favorite phrases for looking at problems. Here were no vested interests, no bank account or property, family or wife — nothing to compromise his utter dedication. Before long one realized that if one wanted to be like him, this is what it would entail. I now came to the swami with the astonishing proposal that I renounce the world and live with him and serve him.

Swami Yatiswarananda beamed broadly; one can almost

say he laughed — and at once grew serious. "I cannot start a
monastery here. See, there is no place for anyone." He opened
the doors behind to display his tiny bedroom and kitchen. Besides, I was still afflicted with wanderlust and would later visit
other centers and monasteries before settling down in San Francisco. I told him I dreamed of going to India some day. He was
not very encouraging. "Someday, perhaps, you may go," he said,
" — for a visit." Much later, in a letter of the year 1957, he would
have much more to say on this subject, as we shall see.

Meanwhile I had become addicted to japa, and I informed
him with more bravado than realism that on the train to California I would try to sit up all day with my rosary. He nodded knowingly. "You may also doze sometimes, like this," he said, showing
a drooping head. (I am glad he gave permission in advance!)
Now he grasped my shoulders in a half-embrace and, looking
intently into my eyes, he touched my chest, over the heart: "Always remember, He is *here*."

Of course the original idea had been to go out and find a
teacher of meditation for our little band of four. We all met him.
I arranged a joint meeting, bringing swami to Pennhurst one
day. He gave us a talk, answered questions and concluded with
the simplest of breathing exercises. "I was deeply impressed,"
one of the group wrote to me years later. "Nowhere in my church
have I found so gifted a 'spiritual director'. I used the exercise
subsequently in guiding college students." Only one other in the
group sought further contact with the swami, and he adds from
his experience a measure to our estimate of Yatiswarananda. At
college a brilliant scholar, Jewish, this young man had fallen away
from or rejected the customs and expectations of his faith and
seemed as good a candidate for the perennial philosophy as any
of us. To me, then in California, he wrote:

> I asked Swami Yatiswarananda about whether ritual and orga-
> nized religion was necessary for *bhakti* [approaching Truth
> through the heart]. He didn't think so. He said one must never
> try to divert anyone from his own tradition, but some people
> are able to do without any tradition. The important thing is to
> follow one's own light.
>
> We had a fine talk of about an hour-and-a-half. He gave me

a chart, which you probably have, showing the progress of the devotee from the anthropomorphic conception of God to the formless. The Incarnation, he said, is the link between man and the Absolute. He didn't seem very sympathetic to traditional Judaism, which we discussed briefly, and he confirmed [L. Adams] Beck's idea that the Essenes were a quasi-Buddhistic sect. He pointed out that monasticism had been foreign to Judaism prior to that time, and that Buddhism had by then spread itself to the Near East as well as the Far East.

Swami spoke very highly of the San Francisco Center, at which he stayed for some time, and that it was the place he had in mind for you originally... He spoke of Swami Ashokananda as *jnana* (the approach to truth through the intellect) on the outside and deep bhakti within.

He spoke of the need of choosing between the celibate life and that of the householder. The life that he outlined for the householder sounded infinitely more difficult, and to have no attraction but that of getting rid of one's desires if one is not strong enough to control them by oneself. He said that the celibate life is very hard and spoke of the necessity of controlling the desires on the subtle level even after having controlled the gross manifestations. He rather pooh-poohed the idea of a 'spiritual' relationship with a girl while one was still on a low level. Too much danger of being dragged down. But, said he, if you don't think of yourself as a man, you will not think of girls as women. Speak to them just as to a man. Regard them as sisters. (I was curious as to whether one should avoid any and all associations with women.) He said that wasn't necessary, since what counts is the inner attitude.

My friend was not destined for the monastic life. Probably we can assume that the swami clearly saw this, in saying what he did.

One can see from this correspondence the swami's typical way of responding to a Western intellectual, Jewish in this case, fully prepared to challenge him on every score. In another letter the truth-seeker continues:

But what has worried me most has been the question of accepting one tradition. Swami Yatiswarananda has helped me on that by saying that only some people need first to grow in one tradition and then broaden out to others. Others are able to dispense with such initial concentration... I was puzzled as to why monastic life should be harder (than life in the world) for one who was already committed to the life of the spirit, which demands freedom from distractions and thrives best when one's whole schedule can be oriented toward the spiritual search. Swami smiled when I asked him that question and said that we have external obstacles only because of internal obstacles; that when the external obstacles and stimuli are removed, we then start on the real struggle with ourselves.

Swami encouraged me to continue with my intellectual reading, so long as it related to the Way. He said one's mind cannot always be on the spiritual or mystical plane, so that it is better that when it falls, it falls to the intellectual rather than the physical. He said that one ought to acquaint oneself with the ideas of one's day, the latest trends in theological insight.

This, by the way, was something Swami stressed to all his students: the habit of daily study. "When you are unable to meditate, and the mind is tired even of japa, fall back on study." He encouraged me to make a practice of writing.

It is said of Sri Ramakrishna that when anyone came to him, of whatever stripe or persuasion, that person would leave his presence proclaiming to others that the sage was one of his own sect. I have always felt that much the same could be said of Swami Yatiswarananda: He never pushed or pulled, but simply tried to boost you up on your own particular ladder. This close friend subsequently plunged into a surprising rediscovery of his own roots and became a professor of comparative religion, a specialist in the Hasidim and Martin Buber.

For the next 21 years I saw Swami Yatiswarananda only twice, on both occasions only for a day or two. Other swamis, abbots of their monasteries, took over the immediate responsibility for me. There was a good bit of moving about. One would arrive at a center and find one's estimate already set up. "You are a disciple of Swami Yatiswarananda? Oh, that's great! Next to Swami — (their own teacher) we like him the best of all!" It happened again and again, and helped to smooth the way. Correspondence thus became the only recourse, the last resort, and as the years went on I was both impelled and compelled to use letters more and more. Many have attested to his power to wield the guru influence fully as competently by post as in person. In view of the vast number of his students around the world it is a wonder that I heard from him as often as I did. He even altered my mantra by mail — twice.

His letters were always intimate, consoling, encouraging; helpful just on the point where help was needed. "You had places you wished to visit. It is good to see other places before one discovers what is likely to suit one best," he wrote when I had finally begun monastic life. "The San Francisco Center has a wonderful atmosphere helpful to spiritual life... association and atmosphere which cannot be found in any of our centers in this country. So all good wishes to you in your new life."

He came to San Francisco on a visit in the summer of 1947, I believe it was, and after an evening discourse in the Old Temple the devotees went up to greet him. Next morning he and I had a long walk together in the city's Marina district. Long a vegetarian, Swami depended on nuts as a staple of his diet. I remember how we walked from hot-dog stand to vending machine in search of his preference — pistachios. Peanuts galore! Even almonds, but nowhere a single pistachio. I felt a deep sense of regret not to be able to give him, my teacher, on this golden occasion, just the item which would have pleased him most.

Then he passed through the bay area in 1949 on his way back to India, never again to return to the West, and we met at a philosophy lecture at the University of California campus in Berkeley. T.M.P. Mahadevan was the visiting speaker. After the lecture Swami grasped my left elbow firmly in his hand as we went out the doorway together. The gesture seemed eloquently to say, "Though I may be far away, I am looking after you. I have taken your spiritual responsibility. I will be your guide, for you are my child." I also thought of the symbol of the Good Shepherd. I will never forget that sensation.

After delivering a lecture in the Berkeley temple, Swami was given a reception in the center's library. He had a great stock of funny remarks and stories, particularly about the foibles of

married life; so he shared some of these with us. He had asked
me to join the men now taking over the facilities of Trabuco
College and forming a nucleus for the Southern California
society's new monastery. That was like a frightening mask looming up before me and stirring me to anguished internal debate.
From the Gretz ashrama near Paris in France, where he was then
staying, this is what he wrote:

Why don't you think this way? When a swami asks a person to do a practice, he may give him also some power. But much
of that power is lost through the leakages in that struggling soul.
Through struggles more power comes. Pray to the Master for
strength.

Like others of Swami Brahmananda's disciples, he loved
to quote his master, Sri Maharaj. The next message was, "For
one who is up and doing, failures are steps to success... I am
touring in Europe. I am writing you from The Hague. From here
I shall go to Copenhagen and Stockholm. Finally I wish to visit
Italy and then get myself ready for sailing to India. Things will
be done as the Lord wishes."

Swami well understood the hurdles being encountered
at the new foundation in Trabuco Canyon and the cactus spines
of human relationship. No pasture so green as the one you left
behind! Memories of past unpleasantness fade out, psycholo-
gists tell us, and a mist of nostalgia is allowed to veil from us the
eternal spontaneity underlying every present moment. "The San
Francisco Monastery has a spiritual tradition of its own, established through many years," he reminded me. "The Trabuco
Monastery is new and so are all the boys. I am sure a fine spiritual atmosphere will be created there also in due course. Go on
doing your japa as well as you can." This came again from Gretz,
where he must have been staying for some months. He would
advise us repeatedly to read *The Eternal Companion*, Swami
Prabhavananda's classic on the life and teachings of their Master. "Read it constantly, including Chapter XIV which was mostly
addressed to me. Try, try, try again. The breeze of Divine Grace
is constantly blowing. Unfurl your sail."

It was 1950 by the time he arrived on Indian soil. What it
meant to him, after so many years abroad, and to be once again
in the midst of brother monks and friends, we can well imagine.

With characteristic understatement he wrote in May: "I am adapting myself nicely to my present conditions and am enjoying the unique spiritual atmosphere of the Belur Math, with its countless associations with the great disciples of the Master. In spite of the heat, I am doing very well mentally." The spiritual value of the experience was the emphasis — not personal satisfactions. "The Master is keeping me busy. I am holding two weekly classes for our *Brahmacharis* [novice monks in training] and also meeting quite a few spiritual seekers every week. I am doing some serious literary work also. There are very many letters to write, but for this I do not find time enough. There is talk of my going to the South, from where I have received many invitations."

This was the first hint to me of the true stature of Swami Yatiswarananda. Sri Ramakrishna used to say that only an expert in diamonds can estimate the value of a large diamond. How could I have any picture, then, of his place in an Order of several hundreds of monks? I had known him as the leader of a tiny mission lost in the heart of a large city. How could I know that this invitation to the South of India was a portent of his role as traveling spiritual guide all over the area, and as such, guru to hundreds and hundreds in South India, Ceylon, Burma and Singapore? That he would later be elected by virtual unanimity to be the Order's President — of this I could not dream.

Probably he did not give out rosaries in the Philadelphia days; I had bought mine in a Catholic shop. Hollywood students had Indian rosaries. So I requested him to send me one through Swami Prabhavananda, who was just returning from a visit to India. "I am glad to know that you received the rosary," he responded. "Use it regularly and you will find what a friend it is. Whenever the mind is disturbed, sit in a quiet corner, take up the beads, repeat the Lord's name and meditate on Him. Offer yourself, body, mind and soul, to Him without reserve. This is the best way to keep the mind uplifted."

In this same letter — a very important one — he outlined the principle which it is taking the remainder of this life to realize: no environment will ever be ideal. This was embedded in how he saw my immediate situation. "The restlessness of your mind seems to be creating some troubles. It is natural and you can certainly overcome it with an amount of intelligent effort.

The mind plays many tricks with us. It gets tired of one place, finds no end of faults with it and idealizes another...

> There is no such thing as an ideal place. Each place has its advantages and disadvantages. What suits one person does not suit another, owing to difference in temperament and other causes... The San Francisco Center has its tradition of monastic life since the time of Swami Trigunatita. At Trabuco the Swamis and the rest of you have to create the tradition, following the ideal as lived and preached by the Master, Swamiji, Maharaj and the other great disciples of the Divine Incarnation. You have got the privilege of doing something of a pioneering work by your life and thought and activities. May the Divine Mother and the Great Ones bless each one of you boys... Be of good cheer. Make others happy by your happiness.

Such a message could sustain one's spirits for months to come.

It was the firm conviction of Swami Prabhavananda, founder and head of the monastery, that an opportunity to try out the monastic life should be granted to anyone who appeared earnest and sincere about wanting it. This must have been true even when he himself felt it probable the individual would soon give it up. Great for the individual, but hard on the management! We seemed to be forever re-arranging work schedules, choir parts, living quarters, as men would come and go. I was grumpy about it, and must have let Swami Yatiswarananda, then at Belur Math, know of it. His eventual answer was revealing: "It is indeed a very hard job to help in establishing a new monastery. The greatest difficulty lies in getting fellow-workers, for very few are fit to live a celibate and disciplined life." He quoted the words of Jesus, "Many are called, but few are chosen." "So you three try to do what all you can, leaving out what is beyond your powers. I am sure Swami Prabhavananda will understand you fully. Do everything following his guidance. The great task before you boys is to form a good nucleus which will attract new additions in due course. You have the blessings of the Master and the guidance of the Swamis, and so you have every chance of succeeding in due course. Give up all depression and always be of good cheer."

And he closed the letter with an exquisite prayer: "The Master is the embodiment of Bliss. May a little of this Bliss sweeten your life and make you discover the source of Infinite Bliss lying in you and everybody, far and near." After another six months, the same message: "Without caring who comes or who goes, you cling to Sri Ramakrishna and offer yourself to him wholeheartedly. Our real stability lies in surrendering ourselves unconditionally to the Supreme Spirit — the Soul of our soul, the Divine Director of the Drama of Life."

Given charge, in 1951, of the Bangalore ashrama in Mysore State, he made this his headquarters, and in addition to running a multifaceted program for this center in a big city, he traveled out to other places, small and large, in various directions. Trivandrum, Ootacamund, Mangalore, Madras city, were but a few of his "ports of call." Usually he replied from Bangalore. Years later when traveling in India I was shown the cottage near his room in Bangalore where he used to give his personal interviews. A similar structure was pointed out in Nettayam, near Trivandrum.

"Recently our General Secretary and some of us flew to Singapore," he told me in December of 1952, "in connection with the opening of the new temple and also visited Malaya and Bangkok. I wonder if my wish to go outside India is going to be fulfilled with this trip — which left me tired and indisposed. So my wish to make a world trip seems to be disappearing just like the amount I reserved for such a trip. It may be many of those I would like to meet in Europe and America would themselves be visiting India sooner or later. So why should I waste both energy and money unnecessarily." Well, that seemed to leave me out, and a lot of others. But sometimes we manage to read into the teacher's words things which are not in his intention. This information agitated me considerably, as I had asked him, "Aren't you due to visit the West again now?" So it seemed that he wanted to, had planned it, knew that his students scattered world-wide were longing to see him — yet the hope of it was fast dissolving. Did the letter imply that all of us should somehow perform the unimaginable feat of making our way over there to Bangalore?

Certainly in my case it did not! Later letters will make his attitude amply clear. As for his money reserve, not everyone at that time knew he had a lively interest in seeing started the parallel Order for women envisaged so long ago by Swami

In India

Vivekananda. This was a controversial project to the authorities of the Ramakrishna Math and Mission; he was firmly on the side of its being established as soon as possible and took an active part in bringing this about. I cannot verify it, but it is quite possible that some of the funds he had saved for the trip West he invested in this cause. Increasingly Swami Yatiswarananda was in demand everywhere in India as well as outside. In the year 1954 he was able to send me only one letter. He said that he was in better health than before, and wished he were younger and had greater energy at his command to cope with the ever-increasing demand for service, as there was an unlimited scope for it in India.

Two of us in the monastery now became eligible in the view of Swami Prabhavananda for the vows of *brahmacharya*, the novitiate. He intended to hold the ceremony at Trabuco as he had for two others the year before. But I was wrought up within myself at the prospect, feeling that as a vow is a very solemn affair, perhaps I shouldn't yet be able to live a life of such dedicated purity. Moreover, of what importance are such formalities, thought I, if one is a brahmachari at heart anyway? It is interesting to look back now and see these two rather contradictory objections existing in the same mind, but it seems typical of the kind of tricks our mind plays. Here is what Swami Yatiswarananda had to say about the matter:

"I have seen in many cases, including mine, that vows sincerely taken with appropriate ceremony positively help to strengthen the will-power." And he asked if I had read Gandhi's autobiography. "The Soul which is a part of the Sat-Chit-Ananda, Infinite Existence-Consciousness-Bliss, has cut itself off from the Infinite Source and is yearning for Infinite Bliss. But having lost its way to the Infinite, it follows a wrong direction and tries to have satisfaction through sex enjoyment etc., but eventually it fails. Not finding the pure spring water it goes to the gutter and drinks the poisonous gutter water and falls ill. Sex urge is perverted yearning for Infinite Bliss. So Sri Ramakrishna says, 'Turn its trend.'"

So I took *The Story of My Experiments with Truth* by Mahatma Gandhi and read it through. It was disarmingly candid and truly inspiring. Nevertheless, after the lives we were accustomed to reading about, of the Master and the Holy Mother and their disciples, intent on high mystical experience and perfumed with the deepest essences of devotion, Gandhi's account seemed pallid and quite different, and that is what I wrote to Swami. "It is good you read Gandhi's autobiography. You are right in thinking that you miss in his life the deep spirituality you find in the disciples of Sri Ramakrishna. But, apart from that, what a remarkable personality he is to be able to control his passions and live a life of brahmacharya in the midst of the temptations that surrounded him. He is an object lesson to the modern world in this respect and also in living a life of devotion and dynamic service."

Then — clearly unconscious of the fact — Swami
Yatiswarananda went right on to mount before our eyes the portrait of just such an object lesson in himself: "We are doing fairly
well here. The Master's work is increasing and a larger number
of people than ever — men, women and children — are participating in the ashrama activities. We are now busily engaged in
the construction of a students' hostel which will ultimately house
some hundred college boys. This and other preoccupations have
compelled me to cancel some of my tour programs."

One day at Trabuco some frustrated young monk commented that although there are a great many books in our tradition dealing with the individual's spiritual struggles, there are
very few treating of the problems of community living. Swami
Prabhavananda's new assistant, Swami Vandanananda, was
present and acknowledged the truth of it. Hear, then, the letter
which follows. I cannot now remember what problem of mine
drew this rejoinder, but we recognize in its beauty and mastery of
statement exactly the sort of spiritual counsel referred to:

"You need not feel junior or senior to anybody. Recognize the Atman in everyone and treat everyone with dignity. The
result will be that you, too, will be treated as such. The longer
one stays as a monastic member, undergoes the necessary struggle
and finds the ideal still far off, the more one should become
humble. Those who for some reason or other develop the 'senior' mentality come to grief. If you be a little careful you will
naturally avoid this superiority complex which is really an expression of the inferiority complex. With your prayer and spirit
of self-surrender to the Lord, you can steer clear of both." It is a
most significant pronouncement, the like of which I have not
seen in any other place.

It was 1956, the year in which worldwide centenary celebrations of the birth of Sri Sarada Devi, the Holy Mother, were
being inaugurated. The Vedanta Society of Southern California
would hold a dedication service for its newly constructed temple
at the convent in Santa Barbara during this auspicious period,
and Swami Prabhavananda had invited two eminent trustees of
the order to come over from India and participate in the function. There was an air of suspense and excitement when Swami
Madhavananda (longtime general secretary of the order) and

Swami Nirvanananda (a future vice-president of the order) arrived, visited the limbs of the center, and took their part in the august and colorful dedication. Swamis from other centers were of course included. The new temple was a distinctive creation of great beauty and simplicity, in its rustic setting nestled in the hills of the Montecito district of Santa Barbara. I took the opportunity to sound out these swamis concerning my teacher's welfare, and wrote to him an account of the whole festival.

"You must have been delighted to meet Swamis Madhavananda and Nirvanananda and get direct news of India," he commented. "I wish that some day the Master would bring you to the land of His birth and enable you to come in close touch with the spiritual current, which also is flowing in the West, but which can be contacted more easily here than there." The language used was very careful here. The "spiritual current" is flowing everywhere, but one can "contact it more easily" in India. Why? Because for centuries the subcontinent has been geared to that — through its lifestyle, its music, rituals, poetry, nursery tales, even its varied malfeasance. Hundreds of thousands of Westerners, coming to realize this, have, wisely and unwisely, scrambled over to touch its vital nerve.

Anyway, for me this was a first, a first hint that he might one day welcome me if the chance to go should ever come.

In addition to the problem of frequent shifts in personnel, life in a complex spiritual community offered other problems. One would, for instance, somehow get into a position of responsibility and a little power, then realize that some of the newer members would be quite happy to let you go on doing those chores forever, and suddenly the cream turned sour. One of our favorites among the popular desk signs of the day read, "Are you looking for someone with a little authority? Nobody has less than I." Swami lifted a bit of this burden with the insights in two other letters of this period:

"It is a universal phenomenon that when people find someone is managing things nicely and efficiently, they want to take advantage of it without sharing the responsibility and trouble," he noted. "To cook food for persons who are fastidious about their food is very difficult. Somehow or other, I have to a great extent solved my problem of food. I take boiled vegetable,

lentil and milk or curd. These agree with me very well... What all
thoughts you have to give to your duties, by all means give. But
minimize the wastage of mental power. Develop the consciousness that the Supreme Spirit dwells in you and you dwell in Him,
the Soul of all souls. Feel that through Him, you are in tune with
everybody." He went on to remind me that not all spiritual teachers work in the same fashion. I needed that reminder; the methods of Swami Prabhavananda and those of Swami Ashokananda
were vastly different, and as the twig is first bent, so tends the
tree to grow; this inflexibility was a long-standing obstacle.

"There are various methods for training probationers,"
Swami Yatiswarananda now explained. "The path that some of
us follow is to give them plenty of freedom and opportunities.
Those who do not profit by it are taken away and given other
chances elsewhere. A tremendous Divine Power is working for
the good of mankind. Through your spiritual practice come directly in touch with that and grow in spirituality and also in the
spirit of service. I am sure that both Swami Prabhavananda and
Swami Aseshananda will understand you very well." Long ago
he had told his students that he wanted them to love all the swamis. Then there was this self-revelation: "My time is fully occupied in the Lord's service. The older I grow, the more enthusiastic I feel in serving the God-in-man in various ways. May He ever
protect and guide us, and fill our hearts with His divine Presence
and Peace, and may we be able to share these great boons with
our fellow-beings!"

When I reported to him that I was taking recourse to
barbells and the like, with the hope of building up a body which
seemed too weak, I felt a bit nervous about his reaction. But he
said it was an excellent idea, and that I should indeed wish to
develop the "muscles of iron and nerves of steel" demanded by
Swamiji. "I wish you all success," he said.

Emboldened by his having mentioned, a year earlier, the
possibility of visiting him in India, I suggested that I might now
be more useful to the movement in the Indian context, serving
him directly as an attendant or secretary. Especially for his English correspondence, I thought. With unusual alacrity he replied in unequivocal terms that his present secretary knew good
English. "I fear you will not find proper scope for this. Our cli-

matic and other conditions are such that I cannot advise any
Westerner to come to India and try to get settled here and ren-
der active service. We have not succeeded in a single case. Swami
Atulananda's case [perhaps I had mentioned him, the first West-
ern-born swami of the order, *a.k.a.* Gurudas Maharaj] is different. He has been living a retired life for years, moving to a cooler
place in summer and to a temperate one in winter. It is my clear
conviction that your place of service should be the USA After
years of service there, you may visit India later on. But the present
is not the time for you to come over." And he added, "It may be
romantic, but not practical." Ah, well. We can all dream! This
was now many years ago, and Indian conditions have changed
somewhat; still one feels that the judgment given here by the
swami represents wisdom at several levels.

He reported on a tour he made in 1959 to Hyderabad
and Madras, when he was forced to rest in the latter, due to a
cold and cough. From this he had rebounded. "I am feeling well
enough for my age, which has already exceeded the Biblical one
of three-score-and-ten.

"Always remember that our past, present and future rest
with the Divine Master and the greatest joy in our lives should
be to feel the Divine Presence within and outside and love and
serve Him as manifest in the many. Every day at the end of your
prayer offer your body, mind and soul to Him and pray to Him
to guide your understanding and enlighten your consciousness."

In June of 1959 Swami Yatiswarananda, writing from Bangalore, reveals the way in which, in his own thinking, he consis-
tently turned the spotlight away from himself as personality and
guru, and let it fall on the figure of Sri Ramakrishna, his ground
and wellspring. Though this extract is rather personal, I quote it
at length that the reader not be deprived of its richness. The
time was one of those periods in my life when the Divine Mother
was, as we used to put it, "playing rough!"

> I was greatly touched by the quotation you have given from *The
> Eternal Companion*. You have noted: 'Even if you make mistakes,
> the Guru in whom you have taken refuge will wipe out all your
> mistakes.' We have all been taught to look upon Sri Ramakrishna
> as the Guru par excellence. A little of His grace may flow through

a human agency but He is the source. We really are not gurus.
We bring the message of the Guru of gurus. What all service you
can get from me you will. But please turn to Him for light and
guidance, for peace and blessedness. As you yourself are finding,
human beings are not good enough. The Lord, the Guru of gurus,
alone can give us the shelter, the illumination and the bliss we
need.

   In your present state of evolution it is natural for you to get
quite lonely now and then. Human companions are not always
available. But as distinct from these we always have the Eternal
Companion, the Supreme Spirit, the Soul of our souls in whom
we live, move and have our being. As a soul you are like a little
ray of light, part of the Infinite Light interpenetrating and perme-
ating your being and shining everywhere. Instead of depending
on human beings who fail, turn to Him who ever exists in you
and you in Him. Do you know a saying of Kabir? 'How strange it
is for the fish in the water to feel thirsty!' May the Divine Master
so waken your inner spiritual consciousness that you — your soul
— may feel the eternal relation with the Eternal Supreme Spirit.

   Today when one visits the Bangalore ashrama one finds
at the heart of its physical and spiritual activity the temple of
which he now spoke: "We are busily engaged in completing our
new prayer hall which may seat from 400 to 500 people. If everything goes well, we propose to have the opening on 2nd August,
the birthday of Swami Ramakrishnananda [a disciple of Sri
Ramakrishna], the founder of our center here as well as the
movement in South India."

   Over here on the other side of the world another grand
opening was about to take place. The New Temple in San Francisco, badly needed for some years, was ready at last, and in the
presence of ten swamis was dedicated to God at the Durga Puja
season, in elaborate ceremonies inaugurating its use. I was back
in Northern California by this time, and had a role to play in
hosting the visitors. I wrote all about it to Swami Yatiswarananda.
He lost no opportunity to lift the glamour of this occasion right
back up to its genesis: "Thank you," he wrote, "for the description of the opening of the San Francisco Temple. I fully understand that the visit of many swamis to the center and the open-

ing function of the new prayer hall there was very inspiring and uplifting. Certainly the Divine Presence you all felt on that day and also may be feeling hereafter, is really the source of all inspiration and also the real cause of the grand manifestation which you recently witnessed. If we are a little introspective we discover what Sri Ramakrishna sometimes sang, 'O Mother, all is done after Thine own sweet will... Thou workest Thine own work; men only call it theirs.'"

When Swami's letter came from a place called Jalpaiguri, in May of 1961, I was at Thousand Island Park, N. Y., as nurse to Swami Madhavananda. For a long time the General Secretary of the Order, this swami required serious and expert medical attention just now. It was being provided and financed by Swami Nikhilananda in New York. The latter had asked the swami in San Francisco to lend him an attendant to care for the patient

In Europe

during his recovery. But all that is a story for another day. Swami Yatiswarananda said in his letter, "I am sure you are feeling happy to be in close touch with Swami Madhavananda who is certainly a *sadhu* of a rare type. Probably you will be fortunate in continuing to serve him all during his stay in America." Now being drawn into an ever-expanding role of ministry and responsibility, Swami had more details of this to offer than usual. After coming to Belur Math to see Swami Madhavananda off to America he had participated in the opening of new temples — one at the birthplace of Swami Shivananda, the other at Jalpaiguri in North Bengal. The latter spot was in view of the Himalayas and he made a point of saying that on one day they were fortunate in getting a good view of Kanchanjangha and other peaks.

"Both the President Maharaj (Swami Shankarananda) and the Vice-President Maharaj (Swami Visuddhananda) being unwell, I have to meet a very large number of devotees seeking initiation. This is no doubt keeping me very busy. But it is also giving me the opportunity of finding out how the Master is drawing many souls towards Him and installing Himself in their hearts. May his glory spread more and more and may He also fill our hearts with His divine presence, purity, love and bliss." Subsequent to this he was elevated to the vice-presidency.

Temples were sprouting up all over the place. The "sixties" played host to the expanding energies of the Indian spiritual seekers, just as those years did for us in the West. The next temple was in New Delhi, the capital. From there Swami wrote that he was busy going from one to another, meeting large numbers of devotees, new and old. "In the last six months," he reported, "in Bengal alone I met thousands of them, out of whom more than 1300 people received spiritual instructions and the special blessings of the Divine Master in the form of initiation. Here too [i.e., New Delhi] more than a hundred have been favored in a similar way. Through His grace and the prayers of you all, I am maintaining good health in spite of the heat and the strain." Anyone who has known Swami Yatiswarananda even slightly will perceive that this citing of figures is no self-glorification.

Slowly, however, it became too much. The whole picture became different. Had he altered the logistics of his method of initiation and remained seated for most of the time, he might possibly have prolonged his life. But such hazards have a way of creeping up without our becoming aware of them, and Swami's one letter of the year 1962 explains.

> During winter I was quite ill owing to a severe pain in the back. I had to undergo ultra-sonic treatment for several weeks. As a result of the treatment the pain has left me but I have to wear a heavy belt to support the back and avoid further trouble. Having stayed in the West for a long time, my muscles had become stiff and the sitting on the floor and getting up with jerks brought on this back pain. I had to initiate more than 1500 people and that involved my sitting and getting up again many, many times. Now I am not allowed to bend, sit on the floor or walk on uneven ground. But my general health is good and I am able to attend to routine with regularity. I too am taking the old body as it is, depending on the will and grace of the Master.

In that year the senior brahmachari of the San Francisco monastery had been sent over to take the vows of *sannyasa* and spend a year in the favorable Bangalore climate, under the care and affection of the swami. That great day had come, and this is what he wrote: "You must have already learned that Bhrigu Chaitanya has now become a Swami. He arrived here on the 14th instant and is accommodated in our hostel for the college boys, in a ground-floor room with a Western-type bathroom practically attached. The terrible heat of Belur Math, although he stood it very well, seems to have affected him somewhat. I am sure that he will be fine after a few days' rest."

Bhrigu Chaitanya (later Swami Chidrupananda) wrote to me from Bangalore that Swami's stay at Belur Math through the summer heat, while Swami Madhavananda was in New York, was a pretty grueling ordeal, "not the least detail of which was having to sit cross-legged for long periods during meetings of various kinds. This he cannot do since his long stay in the West. Meeting an endless stream of devotees and answering an unending flow of letters (150 were awaiting him when he returned from Belur several months ago) constitute the main elements of his routine. He no longer lectures: one or two younger monks do that. He holds one class weekly for a limited group of women devotees. I try to see him every afternoon when I go to the main ashrama area to attend evening prayers. He is the same quiet, cordial, affectionate person we knew in America, though somewhat heavier."

When, from the ranks of our American monks a prominent member resigned in the following year, none who knew the man was prepared for this surprise. Having been a good friend of his, I was much struck by this event. Swami Yatiswarananda's was always the sympathetic reaction. "I am very sorry to learn of the defection... In this world of maya, sometimes most unexpected things happen and we have to accept them in a spirit of resignation and if possible, profit by them."

My interest in visiting India now grew, and as it grew, Swami's capacity to respond and reply diminished. Watching his health fail even from such a distance, I could not restrain my anxiety lest he give up the body before I had the chance to meet him again. His lack of enthusiasm for receiving and looking after another Westerner was understandable. It is partially reflected in the following: "It has become a problem with me to cope with my voluminous correspondence, even with the help of more than one assistant. Further, with the advance in age, I am losing energy and interest in keeping up correspondence. I have not replied to many letters, even though some have written to me regularly for more than a year. Please do write to me whenever you like; your letters are always welcome — but do not expect an early reply. Whether I write you or not, you are always in my thoughts and prayers."

Swami Madhavananda had also graciously responded to my letters. He had succeeded to the Presidency of the Order, and with him I pressed my case for making the long pilgrimage. Two elderly Swamijis, both quite ill! The hazards of life in India, sometimes a restraining influence on my zeal, began to recede quickly before the strong impulsion to have again their *darshan* (the blessing or purification felt in the presence of holiness), as we say.

It was, in fact, becoming urgent.

"As you already heard, I fell seriously ill in Belur Math last February," acknowledged the vice-president, "due to the at-

tack of a virulent type of virus. After continuous tours and strenu-
ous activity for five months in connection with the Centenary
Celebrations of Swami Vivekananda in different parts of the country and Calcutta, as also the initiation of a large number of people,
I was feeling very tired, and then this virus laid me completely
flat. I had to stay in Calcutta proper [at the Sevapratishthan, our
large hospital] for necessary treatment and medical check-up. I
returned to Bangalore at the end of March. At present I am feeling a little better, but I cannot hope to be young again. Let the
Lord do with me as He pleases." (October, 1964.)

It was 1965, the autumn, and arrangements for passport,
visa and soon for the move to India, were well underway. President Maharaj saw no reason why I should not come and stay at
least until I could take the sannyasa vows. Moreover he was becoming quite affected by various ailments and who knew when
the body might give out? Swami Yatiswarananda's hesitation in
the matter was at first puzzling; seen now in the light of later
developments, it was his motherly concern for my physical welfare and how hampered he would be in looking after it.

> I duly received your letters... but could not reply to them and
> many others due to my ill health. Though I am walking a little and
> taking normal food, I feel very weak and depressed. Age seems to
> be against any substantial improvement in my health. I soon get
> tired and very often I have to lie in bed. I am not able to reconcile
> myself to this sort of semi-invalid existence. All my life I had been
> so independent and self-reliant; now I have to depend on our
> brothers at every step. Now the main trouble is not the back pain
> (which the doctor says can never be cured, but is not so acute as
> to make me an invalid), but a sort of nervous breakdown which
> means the end of my active life. However, there is no use of wor-
> rying about it. Everything is happening according to the will of the
> Lord. Through His will I served Him actively for many years, and
> now through His will I am broken down in body and mind. Please
> do pray for me as I do for you all.

This was totally unbearable. The reader will well understand the shock of this role-reversal, as well as the urgency I felt
about making my trip immediately. The letter said more; after

wondering aloud whether I would be allowed in India under the present political turmoil, he submitted this caution: "If you do come and stay in this country, please be very careful about your diet etc. You should never try to adopt Indian food *in toto*. So far the only American who has stayed in India for a pretty long time is Swami Atulanandaji. He too made many experiments and at last found that he should be very careful about his diet to maintain his health.

"You must have also got the news about Swami Madhavanandaji. His present state of health is causing anxiety to all of us."

While the bureaucracy of governments dallied with the application for a residential visa and the days went sailing by, it became obvious that this would be a real race to get over there for the darshan of the president. As a matter of fact the visa arrived so late it was mid-December before the flight was possible. Swami Madhavananda had considerately waited until the Durga Puja festivities were concluded in October and then given up the body. He could not wait for me.

As for the Guru, his final letter asked me to follow the instructions of the General Secretary. If he asked me to come to India I was to go straight to Calcutta and the Belur Math. "Please do not come to Bangalore now" was underlined for emphasis. It sounded harsh, and so he explained: "My health has greatly deteriorated in the past one month. My back pain has increased and practically I am bed-ridden and confined to my room. So far the doctors have not been able to give me any relief and it seems that it will take months before I can resume my normal activities. In this state of health I would neither be able to take care of you nor the other inmates of the Bangalore Ashrama be able to look after you, as they are very much preoccupied with me. I am feeling very sorry to write to you in this strain, but I cannot help it. I hope you will understand my position and not mind this reply. Although I am unable to help you physically or materially, yet please remember that I am ever with you in spirit and would continue to pray for you always."

Preparations for travel helped to dispel the gloom of hearing from him that he felt his nerves had given way and that his active life was over. None of us could believe it, but, alas, it proved to be true. That he could feel "depressed," however, was so unlike all else we had known about him that I was not at this point prepared to accept it.

Sacramento, goodbye! My plane landed at Dum Dum in that inimitable atmosphere which constitutes one's first descent into the air of Calcutta, on the 13th of December 1965. On arrival at the Math I found that Swami Yatiswarananda had been flown there from Bangalore just the day before. All the monks were wishing and expecting him to assume the office of president of the order so recently left vacant by the passing of Swami Madhavananda. Swami had the greatest respect for his predecessor. They had known each other through many years, and although their opinions had sometimes differed, they remained fast friends. Sri Maharaj, Swami Brahmananda, had told them when they were students, "You two are both very dear to me; you will have to live together and get along." And on a day to follow, Swami told me solemnly, "I can't bear to use these quarters which belonged to Revered Madhavanandaji."

On my first coming into his presence he gave me a long look through those famous spectacles and said, "So at long last you have come." It was the first time he had ever seen me in Indian clothes, and I wondered about his impression. I found a changed and broken man, one whom I scarcely knew. Almost gone were the twinkle in his eye and the cheerful lilt in his voice. It was clear that moving his body was painful. No position was really comfortable for him, whether he was walking, sitting or lying. In spirit he was solemn, disinclined to talk, indrawn and fluctuating in mood. He appeared to be ill-at-ease when monks and devotees approached him to pay their respects. There were few persons he expressed any wish to see, or to have near him. Only in the evening did he sometimes seem to relax; then the old familiar smile and teasing jest might come once again to his lips. Swami had a habit of drawing his right thumb and forefinger across his lips, and this was still in evidence — at least one note of familiarity. Some of the other brahmacharis of the Training Center and I used to sit by him and sing or chant hymns in our various amateur ways. We used the *Universal Prayers*, of course, and *Divine Life*, two small, well-appreciated compilations and translations of his. Occasionally I was able to read to him remi-

niscences about the great disciples of Ramakrishna from magazines or from my own notes.

     During this one month I had the good fortune to visit
Swami Yatiswarananda every day for about an hour or more, and
although most of the time we were silent, just walking as prescribed in his medical schedule, his mere presence satisfied my
heart, and altogether I saw more of him in this period than I had
during the whole previous portion of my life. He would lean on
one of my shoulders when we walked together. If he spoke it was
in a low, soft voice, and I never felt like raising anything controversial or intricate. As long as he was able, he made the daily
morning "presidential walk" with his regular attendants to the
temples of the Math campus, where he would offer his salutations in each one.

     I also took this opportunity to get acquainted with his
other monastic disciples. They were quite a bit younger than I,
but very interesting as they had come from widely scattered parts
and communities — south, north — and had diverse talents. We
attempted to relieve each other's gloom. It seemed somehow
characteristic of the swami's wide human spirit that he should
have drawn to him a company of colorful and assorted natures.

     There were flashes of the old highly concerned interest
in everything around him. He was careful, for instance, to see
that the musicians who sang for him and those who were coming
from distant parts to see him were all given *prasad* (food offered
to the deity in the worship service and to the congregation after-
wards). The welfare, both spiritual and physical, of his attendants was an ever-present concern to him: whether each was
wearing warm clothing, getting sufficient rest etc., though sometimes this was quite beyond his control. To one of them he one
day expressed this fear: "The trustees are insisting that I take up
the presidential chair and I am refusing. I may be punished for
this disobedience." He was perfectly serious. His attendants were
remarkable souls themselves. I would never have imagined the
kind of exhausting service and dedicated vigil these men kept
up over him; it put my own nursing talents to shame.

     One evening when he had felt too ill to sit up, I sat in his
darkened room near his bed for some time, in silence as the sun
set. The dimness in the room slowly increased and the only sound

was his breathing and occasional clearing of the throat. When at last I had to leave, I approached the bed. "Maharaj," I asked, "is there anything you need?"

"No," he whispered; then, "Did they ask you to sit in here?"

"No, Maharaj," I replied, "I myself wished to sit in here." He extended his right arm and laid the back of his hand against my chest. "May the Lord bless you," he said.

But the following week the whole picture changed. The authorities of the Math and Mission decided to send me, just after the festival of Swami Vivekananda's birthday, to Narendrapur, the educational complex south of Calcutta, to teach school. I was dismayed. But of what use is reluctance when the general secretary himself is standing at your elbow asking you to go?

I made final pranam to Swami, and it was the last time we spoke. In my new place I naturally felt the loss of the opportunity to have his physical presence. Still I did not dream that this was to be the permanent state of affairs. Scarcely ten days later we received the shocking news that Swami Yatiswarananda was in the Sevapratishthan hospital and not expected to recover.

His disciples were summoned there to see him, where he lay in a private room, breathing with the aid of a glass tube. It could give us small satisfaction — rather it made us sadder, for we found him in a condition in which he alternated between discomfort and apparent unconsciousness. He had many times warned his attendants in various way that this illness would be final; but we all found ourselves unprepared to accept it. Even in this condition, two days before his death, he continued to be a channel of spiritual power. That power, the *guru-sakti*, continued to operate. The guru-sakti is a sometimes tangible force emanating from a world-teacher which works in the life of a disciple even after the teacher's death. For example, Jesus said "power" had gone out of him when someone held his robe. When I returned home from the hospital I lay down to rest, but fell into a strange sleep in which I had an indescribable spiritual experience. I can only say that the mystery of death seemed altogether solved. Whether Swami was revealing to me his own condition at the time, or whether this was a preview of some future experience in store for me, I cannot say: I know only that I was completely at peace when the final word arrived.

According to custom his body lay for a few hours in the courtyard of the Math so that as many as possible of those four thousand disciples whose burdens he had lifted might pay their last respects, along with the multitudes of friends and admirers. The procession seemed endless. As hand after hand came by to caress the crimson-smeared soles of those tired and holy feet, I tried to absorb as openly and simply as possible the mood and meaning of a sacred *deha-tyaga* in the loving bosom of the Lord and His devotees. Cremation took place with due ceremony on the plot reserved for presidents of the order. I tried to witness it for a while, but then gave up.

It is easy for me to believe that that power I glimpsed in Swami Yatiswarananda surely will continue to work, in those who came under his influence, for their present and eternal welfare.

Swami Prabhavananda at the Convent

HIGH ABOVE HOLLYWOOD AND VINE

SWAMI PRABHAVANANDA

"I am in Hollywood but I am not *of* Hollywood," Swami Prabhavananda said many times. The first time I heard it we were sitting in the "Green House," the oldest portion of the center, which had been the home of Sister Lalita. Sister was Mrs. Carrie Wykoff, one of the three Mead sisters, hosts and helpers of Swami Vivekananda in 1900.

Sometimes one wondered if Swami Prabhavananda were even of this world. His immersion in Elsewhere was of longer duration and more evident than in most persons of spiritual eminence. It was simply that he had practiced being absorbed in God until it had become natural, spontaneous.

In those days there were streetcar tracks through streets of Los Angeles and huge red cars that clanged along them. After meeting Swami Yatiswarananda but before joining the Ramakrishna Order in San Francisco, I had made arrangements by mail for an interview early in 1945, possibly for three in the afternoon. Somehow I found my way to that picture-postcard Indian temple on the hill, a white gem of a Taj Mahal-in-miniature.

Early for the appointment, I was asked to wait on one of

the folding chairs which filled the sanctuary. Things were happening on the platform in front of me. Here was an American girl dressed in a full-flowing Indian print, about to enter the *sanctum sanctorum* — a recess upholstered in gold fabric and featuring an Oriental hardwood shrine which held familiar framed pictures: Sri Ramakrishna, the Holy Mother, Swamis Vivekananda and Brahmananda and more. The girl bore the vase of flowers in her hands like some Minerva, and what with the aroma of incense pervading the hall, I had a distinct impression of the exotic.

My first acquaintance with Vedanta had been among the sedate Philadelphians who were getting accustomed to Swami Yatiswarananda. Crossing the country, and stopping for a few hours to meet the Chicago swami in his apartment, I gradually realized the great variety that characterized this movement. Different places, diverse faces. So when a door on my left opened and a slight figure of a man with a good shock of hair, and a complexion which could best be called a warm gray, fairly floated across the dais and opened a door on the right of the shrine room, I thought it must be the swami.

Swami Prabhavananda now called me into his interviewing office. What first struck me was the remarkable physical beauty of the man; no feminine quality is implied, but beauty is the only word sufficient to convey the air of grace, lithe elegance and charm he exuded. I always felt this way about him; through the years I lived in his company he was a delight to look at. To watch him move, laugh, frown and especially perform worship, was in each case a profoundly rewarding experience. But on that first afternoon, initial attraction gave way to dismay and embarrassment. Why? Because I had to do all the talking! After introducing myself as a "friend of the Swami in Philadelphia" (a beloved monastic brother of his), and now back in California to see my relatives, I sat back to await the usual pleasantries — inquiry of my swami's health, my background, etc. Nothing. Silence. I managed to produce questions about the Hollywood monastery I knew he had started, a statement of my intention to visit Gerald Heard's place, Trabuco College, where I had some connections. Was not Heard his student? Yes. Wasn't Trabuco Canyon a beautiful place? Yes, it was. Swami Prabhavananda evidently spoke mostly in monosyllables. He seemed to know everything in advance. One question I remember I asked: Can there be, in spiritual transformation, a change of consciousness without a previous change in conduct and character? No, the Swami said, it was impossible. More silence. It was beginning to get quite warm in that little room. This was not quite what I had expected; when his replies were so brief, I would look at him in surprise; from that handsome impassive face the eyes would stare back at me with a blandness almost Chinese, and the discomfort was mine. It was a staredown.

Now there was not much left but to pull out some faltering courtesies of farewell and excuse myself. Looking back at the twin rows of Italian cypress framing the approach to the temple, I walked down the hill. As I rode back in the clattering old streetcar, something physical happened. My throat was seized by an overwhelming, almost choking, tickle. The sensation went on and on, as if it were going to bore right through my neck. And as I remember it, the one thought that came to me was something like this: "*That* is one powerful swami. The encounter was working on my ego without my knowing it! I've just met a tool in the hand of God." The strange part of it was that I had gone into the interview with a prejudice, for someone had told me this swami was a chain-smoker. *How could he then be enlightened?* I had thought; hence the question about consciousness and conduct. However, no cigarettes had appeared at the interview.

Not knowing what to expect and failing also to understand what I had found, I can only regard this introduction to the swami as abortive. I did not see Swami Prabhavananda for the next four years. There had followed, first, a fascinating two-week "trial period" at Trabuco College, an experimental foundation whose history must some day be written. By the end of it I had listened, engrossed, to its founder — one of the most brilliant and learned men of the day, Gerald Heard —and decided that he was not yet an illumined teacher. I had met the European woman who had become Sister Dhammadinna, Buddhist nun from Sri Lanka, one of my life's most unforgettable characters. And I had gleaned the gossip from the spiritual "field," tidbits about Huxley, Krishnamurti, Yogananda, the Ramakrishna swamis *et al.*

Then I had made my way up to San Francisco and, in the

Vedanta Society of Northern California, begun the first chapter of my monastic life (see Chapter Three). It was much later, in September of 1949, the College property having been purchased by the Southern California Society for use as a monastery, that I returned to Trabuco at the suggestion of Swami Yatiswarananda.

Swami Prabhavananda had written a letter accepting me and mentioning that he might be in India when I arrived, but not to mind; his assistant, Swami Aseshananda, would look after us well and on his return we would meet. Arriving in Hollywood I was just in time to see the figure of Tantine, Miss Josephine MacLeod, lying in her coffin, before the lid was closed: She had passed away a day or two before and Swami Aseshananda was performing her funeral. Past ninety, this famous friend of Vivekananda had ended her days living "in the house of the Lord."

My life at Trabuco Canyon, where Swami Aseshananda now joined with the five other men in launching the new monastery, will be dealt with in due course. But since the story I've embarked upon is about six particular swamis I have known, and since life at Trabuco, in any case, was punctuated by trips "into town" — i.e., to the Hollywood center, where one would go for special occasions, on an errand or for a change of pace, staying for a day or a week — I'll resume my account of Swami Prabhavananda where he might be seen at his most typical: in the Hollywood center, his home since 1930.

I. COMPLEX ENVIRONMENT, SIMPLE MAN

Look to the left of the white temple and behind it, and you see the domestic house of the center. In its kitchen we cooked and in its dining room we all ate together — old and young, women and men. Swami called us his family, his monastic family; he wanted us to feel that way about it, too. One is tempted to say this was a principle with him, expressed in his method of training. But did he actually have a *method* of training? Isn't it rather that soul consciousness, replacing body and gender consciousness, deep at the heart of his philosophy and his realization? And wasn't the way he conducted his center just the natural consequence of this?

This family mentality gave birth to one of the choice stories in the center's history. An older devotee, a woman who often came on Saturday to help in cleaning, was on her way one day, trudging up the steep hill, when she fell into conversation with a woman with a heavy shopping bag making the same trek. This proved to be one of the housekeepers of the neighborhood, who confided to our friend that she worked for a minister with three children. The devotee responded cheerily, "Well, I'm on the way to work for our minister, myself!"

"Is that so? And how many children does he have?"

Making a quick mental head count, and remembering another about to join, the devotee replied, "Eight, and a ninth is on the way." The shopping bag hit the pavement as the housekeeper stopped dead in her tracks.

"And him a minister!"

Swami Prabhavananda's ground-floor room lay farther back in this same building, with a separate entrance. It was ample and gracious, with windows on three sides, the main elements his bed, desk and overstuffed chair. It was there that the family gathered on most evenings. After the supper had been cleared away, and if there was no public class, one-by-one the residents would quietly slip into the room and sit on the carpet around the big chair. What would Swami's mood be tonight? Difficult to predict. Sometimes he would be lighthearted, animated, full of fun; often the evening would go in chit-chat about seemingly trivial matters: plans for festivities, garden or household problems, taxes and properties (the Society owned an orange grove), something bordering on gossip, regarding new devotees or old. At other times Swami could be serious, silent or extremely withdrawn, the atmosphere so lofty one hardly dared even to think. The boys sat in one group, the girls in another. This afforded opportunities for teasing. One *brahmacharini* (female novice) in particular was forever being scolded for sitting too close to the boys. Of course she was one about whom no one entertained any suspicions. It was an old trick of India, called "scolding the daughter to teach the daughter-in-law." One was reminded of the scenes in the life of Swami Brahmananda in which the great disciple of Sri Ramakrishna — and Prabhavananda's guru — would chat away about all sorts of things not religious, yet leave indelible effects on all those around him. Then, too, Swami Prabhavananda might at any moment in all this palaver enunciate some spiritual principle which would hush everything.

Scolding was not the purpose of these sessions, but if it came up, so be it. I well recall the night when he was explaining something to me which seemed elementary and I was so brash as to say, "Oh, I know all about that." He pulled me up abruptly.

"Never say that you know all about something. That is not a good sign. Thakur [Sri Ramakrishna] said, 'So long as I live, I learn.'"

Often he would teasingly play off the men against the women as if, understanding the human tensions that naturally arose, he might somehow neutralize them by an airing in his

Performing worship, Hollywood Temple

own presence. Did the technique work? Most of the time.

How did we feel about all this? For some it was surely the high point of their day. Others were easily embarrassed. Some, men who described themselves as allergic to "women's chatter," rather dreaded it. Those who could not profit by such freedom and exposure would not stay long in residence. It was not exactly compulsory to come to Swami's room, but otherwise one felt left out. It was part of that peer pressure or family pressure, of which we shall have more to say in other contexts. Certainly for most of his students such opportunities were never to be missed.

In the midst of it all, one senior brahmachari would be furiously scratching out on a notebook every word of Swami's, until tape recorders became available — and even after. Or snapping at apparent random with his insatiable candid camera. He had his own good reasons.

Occasionally such sessions could be true discourses or discussions, covering erudite or esoteric spiritual topics, proceeding step by step and "poking the honeycomb" — the traditional Indian expression for drawing out spiritual wisdom and experience from the teacher. I happened to note down only one such conversation, but it is practically *verbatim* and may reveal to the reader something of the swami's mind and demeanor.

Swami: We are *jivakotis*, ordinary souls.

Question: Can a jivakoti get a glimpse of *nirvikalpa samadhi* (consciousness in which all duality, world and otherness vanish and Atman alone abides).

Swami: No. Well, yes; but then they die. Within 21 days, they die. Not that they have to live 21 days, but that is the maximum; but these cases are very few.

Question: Are they continually in the samadhi while the body is lasting those days?

Swami: I don't know (smiling).

Swami Aseshananda: Is it not because they don't care to take care of the body at that time, that they die?

Swami: Not merely that, Swami. You see, they find the bliss so great they cannot bear to return to this plane. Only the incarnations and *isvarakotis* [souls with special spiritual qualities, who come to earth usually with a divine incarnation and show some of their characteristics] can return from the *nirvikalpa*. With

Sri Ramakrishna came only six isvarakotis. But by his grace, other disciples *became* isvarakotis, as Swami Shivananda tells us himself. So it *is* something that other souls who did not begin as such can become.

Question: Then did all of his monastic disciples become isvarakotis?

Swami: I cannot vouch for that. Probably more than one did.

Question: Could any of us — so long after — become isvarakotis?

Swami: I don't think so. I don't want to limit, so I'll not say it could not be; but it's not likely. *Savikalpa samadhi* [in which a slight distinction remains between the individual and the universal] also makes one free, a *jivanmukta* [one who has been freed from ignorance, karma, etc., even before death].

Question: Is it possible for a person who's had savikalpa samadhi to return to a life in the world, and even have children?

Swami: Not as a general rule; but there are many such cases. Look at the ancient rishis.

Question: But did they have children after realization?

Swami: Apparently some did. Then there is *prarabdha karma* [that portion of karma which has already begun to be reaped in one's life — even if one is a jivanmukta], which causes many strange things to happen which are inexplicable from the ordinary standpoint.

Question: What about after nirvikalpa? Is it possible then?

Swami: Well, I don't know. We have the case of Totapuri. Not that he lived a worldly life — but he *lived*. Isn't that a wonder in itself? You see, he lived on simply because he had to teach Sri Ramakrishna; he had that mission. It is not that those whose prarabdha makes them temporarily overcome by bad tendencies are affected by those events; they are not. They are making no new karma thereby, just unwinding the old. Think of Swami Abhedananda. Such a great yogi, an illumined soul and all that, yet he *knew* that jealousy was the bane of his life — it nearly took him out of the order — and he never did entirely overcome it!

Question: Can isvarakotis, then, get involved in worldly life?

Swami: There is the case of Purna [one of the remarkable young men who came to Sri Ramakrishna. His family forced him to marry and raise a family; the Master counted him among his isvarakotis]. But don't ask me; I'm not an isvarakoti. Thakur showed us that there is a state higher even than nirvikalpa — that which has all along been thought to be the highest — and Maharaj said that spiritual life *begins* with nirvikalpa.

Question: And yet none of us can hope to have nirvikalpa in this life, not being isvarakotis!

Swami: Ah, but you also can *become* isvarakotis; you can go to that realm.

After a time he added: "Prarabdha karma is a term which is used more for things like marriage, where there is an element of choice involved. Especially is it true that the illumined souls can choose or avoid a thing like marriage, to a large extent. They are not bound by such acts."

Odd, our little fledgling minds popping up with questions like these, remote from their immediate needs; lovely, his unpompous patience, to enter into the spirit of it all. It may have pleased him, too, just to know that he had succeeded in engaging these young minds in such intricate spiritual questions. One evening a novice asked, "Pleasure, they say, is attended by pain; does that mean *vice versa* also?"

Swami: "No! Pain is just pain. *And* pleasure becomes pain. The sense of relief when pain ends cannot be called pleasure. We are speaking of worldly experiences now, not spiritual ones." Somebody wanted to know how can we "yearn" for that which is quite beyond our imagination, i.e., God? His reply was subtle:

"It is not exactly beyond our imagination. We have some idea of That by seeing what we *don't* want: these things. Dispassion gives us the knowledge of God in a negative way, though we may not be able to imagine him positively. We can get an idea of what liberation would mean by examining our bondages." As one can see, these sessions were apertures for poking through to some of the finer points of the teachings. The peculiar condition of Sri Ramakrishna called *bhavamukha* (a state of spiritual awareness between the relative and absolute) was brought up on one occasion. Sri Ramakrishna said that when he had wanted to merge in the Absolute, Divine Mother told him to stay in this condition.

"It was a condition between savikalpa and nirvikalpa, you

can say. He was the observer of both these kinds of samadhi. Put another way, he *was* God (Personal) and he *was* Brahman — so the both of these together is just what he was; naturally his mind could alternate between them. He had savikalpa on his left hand and nirvikalpa on his right, so to speak, whereas others, jivas, come from samadhi down to 'normal consciousness,' he came to this bhavamukha instead, being both Iswara and Brahman."

Swami had beautiful hands. The fingers were long and extremely graceful and somehow seemed to dangle from the palm. He was double-jointed and would amuse us by bending his fingers back with loud cracks. With the same gracefulness with which he performed the *puja* (formal worship) he would do such mundane acts as the smoking a cigarette. Under doctors' advice he later gave up smoking.

Catty remarks would inevitably come out in these family gatherings, but Swami never whitewashed anything. If other people's foibles were pointed out to him, more often than not he would bend his head a little to one side (an Indian affirmative) and laugh or chuckle it off. I learned to appreciate this way of his.

Formal teaching was given to the public and to us in the Sunday services at eleven o'clock and the two weekly evening classes. Since in my time Swami Prabhavananda always had an assistant, one of these classes was assigned to the latter and the swamis would alternate on Sundays, with Gerald Heard often taking a turn. He was paid for this, and had a following of his own which helped swell the attendance and contributions. On one morning I listened, duly impressed as Aldous Huxley took the pulpit. He was uncomfortable as a public speaker, but held one easily in his spell. Swami had a preference for one-word subjects: Peace; Joy; Wisdom; Renunciation; in any case, short.

"No matter what the title is," someone first summed it up, "it all comes out GOD," an observation echoed forever after. Like their titles, the lectures themselves were simple and ended on the hour. Of course I refer to the language and style. Nothing simple about Vedanta, one may say; yet here was the loftiest philosophy presented in easy and common terms. Like most of the Swamis he used stories and jokes with great aplomb. Almost always when he spoke there was a hushed atmosphere, it seemed, as if listeners were feeling more like meditating than anything else. Swami Prabhavananda was never one to plead political or social concerns, rarely even ethical ones. It was mysticism, the lives of the holy, what the scriptures said, the principles and their practical application in the individual life.

With the scripture classes he was never academic or unnecessarily erudite in Sanskrit, but rather he attempted to place each point in a setting the Western student could appreciate and identify with. He tried to see and frame an idea as he thought it would look in our eyes, and of course his long background in American life, particularly Californian, made this possible. Swami could also land a punch, using his abundant humor with devastating effect. Is sarcastic too strong a word? Let the reader find his own term to apply in the following incident.

In the public class Swami had given a thorough airing to his favorite theme, that the best and easiest way to realize God is to keep the divine thought going constantly in the mind. The question period was in progress. One lady ebulliently said, "But Swami, what if I am already thinking about God all the time? What do I do then?"

"Madam," came the cool, measured tones, "if you can think of God constantly you are either a fool or an illumined soul. And I know you are not an illumined soul." The air was electric. It was truly difficult for some to make anything of this quiet little man who could smilingly drop such depth-charges, and who harped on God as if he were someone daily passing in and out of the house. Someone was once heard to complain after a lecture, "Why does he talk about *God* so much? To me it sounds almost obscene."

Sometimes in attempts to explain how Vedanta has flourished in California we credit the coastal location or the physical and mental climates, or the cosmopolitan origins of the populace; more than these, surely, was the personal determination of Swami Prabhavananda and Swami Ashokananda, head of the Vedanta Society of Northern California, to put India behind them in a sense; to try to *feel* themselves Western and American, in order better to identify with us. They saw, as we said, through our eyes. They accepted the students as Westerners, rooted in American values, customs and culture, destined to remain West-

ern, and so encouraged them to feed their spiritual life from
these nutritive capillaries. Their own self-adaptation replaced,
through their surpassing humility, attempts to Indianize the students.

One of the better illustrations is in the way they dressed.
Both generally wore Western clothes. Swami Prabhavananda,
however, was the only one of our Indian swamis in the United
States who wore the Indian sannyasin's robes for the sacred functions — discourses as well as meditation and puja. For 30 years,
while all the other heads of centers used the long cloak adopted
by Swami Vivekananda, Swami — dubbing it "the bathrobe" —
rejected it for the original *dhoti* and *chaddar* and requested his
assistants to do the same.

On most other occasions his clothes were quite informal.
He preferred sweaters to jackets and wore casual slacks (there
was a washable light blue pair he wore for years). When I think
of him at Trabuco I always picture him that way, with his enor-
mously broad-brimmed sun hat in summer, a cap in winter. He
always looked ready to pitch in and help us with the manual
work at any moment, and sometimes he did.

His unabashed patriotism I found charming. It was not
of the "My government, right or wrong" type, but a childlike
pride in being a citizen — an American in name as well as in
spirit. Since he had arrived in this country before the new immi-
gration restrictions of 1924, he eagerly took the opportunity to
apply for citizenship and became the only citizen among our
Indian swamis. In the early days he often recounted with glee
how he had studied the manual and taken the oath, having passed
the test handily. Did he ever vote? Indeed he did. He favored
our using the English language for chants and songs, retaining
however, the traditional Sanskrit vesper service used throughout
the world. Even for these hymns he wanted translations made.
He made no particular effort to encourage the study of Sanskrit.
We had, he thought, more important things to do.

Living around Swami one always felt that every moment
must somehow be employed in the direct pursuit of the one goal
of life, to realize God here and now; Maharaj had promised this
was possible and not all that difficult; did we doubt him? Did we
really want to make scholarly and egoistic detours? Already I

had a habit of Sanskrit study and so could not so much appreciate the fact that the monastics were not learning it. On the other hand, this bent of mine Swami never discouraged or hindered.

One might suppose that, with his penchant for the use of English in liturgy, he would have made a translation of the daily puja ritual. Perhaps because he had a most reverential attitude toward it — not teaching it, for instance, to non-initiates and conducting it in silence — he may have thought it too sacrosanct for a public translation. Rather, he made an outline, part explanation, part translation, for the use of those being trained in it. He chanted in Sanskrit every morning in the shrine room at the close of meditation, choosing from some dozen brief stanzas. I do not know to this day how musical they were, for to my ear the pitch seemed to wander when he sang alone; but they were something to look forward to.

If Swami Prabhavananda seemed unusually proud of the Hollywood center and inclined to be articulate in asserting its merits, one should realize that this was nothing uncommon in the pioneer swamis during these first years while their work became established. It was a way of inspiring people new to Vedanta whose underpinnings were shaky through doubt and the alien quality of Oriental things. Like others he boosted his own, and Swami Prabhavananda, being an "original," had to fend off the jibes not only of the uninformed public but of well-meaning brother monks as well.

Then there was the Northern California *vs.* Southern California rivalry. Like the two regions' football teams, universities, politics, climate and water rights, Vedanta had to share in the feints and fortunes of a longstanding geographical partisanship. The bees had to be kept in and around the hive, prevented from losing their way too far afield. Devotees at every center were encouraged to think of "their" swami as the best and his ways of teaching and training superior. Spiritually this was life-preserving, one supposed, but one could also suppose it would one day have to be outgrown. If they were at opposite poles on some matters of method and emphasis, there was one issue which brought Ashokananda and Prabhavananda onto common ground: the lack of understanding at Belur Math of the special requirements of the Western work — about the women, most of all, and the status of the convent. For at this time, a parallel order for women had not yet become a reality in India.

Swami wrote to me from Santa Barbara in 1967, "The Swamis, even those who are in authority, have no idea of our work in the West. So the present authorities try to create trouble for us. Prabhu Maharaj (Swami Vireswarananda), Sujji Maharaj (Swami Nirvanananda) and the older ones are different. For the past year both Yogesh Maharaj (Swami Ashokananda) and I had to pass through many heartaches because of the ignorance of some of the authorities. At long last things have been straightened out."

He would remind us of his earlier adventures in spreading the word in Oregon, Washington, San Diego, etc., and imply the debt that those arriving later owed to him. Hollywood now had the largest Vedanta congregation in the country. Convents had been established in Los Angeles and Santa Barbara. There were monks at the home base as well as at Trabuco Canyon. Choice properties had been handed over to him at enviable locations, and he had utilized them with efficiency and flair. Young American women and men had been inspired to renounce, and to aspire to be lifelong embodiments of the Ramakrishna ideal. Why not be proud? Swami wrote to me later, in 1967, that the attendance had been 357 on a certain Sunday; the following year he wrote similarly, "370 came last Sunday." Did he really keep count? Of course! What follows is extracted from a 1969 letter I received in London, and this is what he lived to see:

"We had the puja [of Sri Durga] in Santa Barbara. Three hundred devotees were present and partook of prasad. Let me know how the puja there [in London] was performed by you. I am sure you must have done well. To do puja well, all we need is devotion. Mother [Sri Durga] does not care for formalities. She looks at the heart of the devotees."

Even in those days Ramakrishna Vedanta did not have the India-oriented field to itself. Paramahamsa Yogananda with his Self-Realization Fellowship settled in the same city, eventually offering monastic life for both women and men. Swami Paramananda's Ananda Ashrama in La Crescenta, spiritually closer than Yogananda's organization and not much farther away spatially, thrived — attracting mostly women. Naturally there

was a certain amount of window-shopping among the spiritu-
ally-minded, who might visit the Vedanta Society one week and
SRF the next, until they got themselves sorted out. So far as Swami
Prabhavananda was concerned, the sooner the better — and once
your brand had been chosen, see that you stayed in your own
corral. He had known Yogananda from college days in India,
and was not going to be swayed by the opinions and effusions of
the local people.

Conscientious about the importance of maintenance,
Swami Prabhavananda saw to it that the Society's building and
properties were well kept. He was not enamored of junk piles or
shoddy workmanship or of quarters kept unappealing in the
name of poverty. Poverty, for him, did not mean dirt or scaveng-
ing. He would not allow the monastic members to wear clothes
cast off by non-monastics. Certain orthodoxies of this type only
added color to one of the more maverick and independent of
swami-personalities. Although his appreciation and judgment
of beauty were keen, he knew his own boundaries in matters artistic and aesthetic, and would seldom force anyone's hand in
these directions. It was something a number of us much appreciated.

Artists of all kinds were around him as students or friends.
There was the seascape painter and the movie set designer. One
week famous writers would be huddled at his feet, the next a
singer and composer, working on an oratorio for a puja. Crafts-
men, dancers, a sculptor or two; then the chief costume designer
at MGM. Amateurs, too, were welcome to try. Did someone han-
ker to refinish all the furniture at Trabuco? Another to rearrange
the rooms in Brahmananda Cottage? "All right, if you can manage it..." Most of the lights were green for what one wished to
undertake; even some outlandish proposals swept through.

Swami gave more praise than criticism, which is not to
say that he was a "softy;" he had his limits too. Before my time,
one of the early candidates, seeking more solitude, had pulled
together some gunnysacks, cartons and whatnot, to construct a
"meditation hut." This might not have drawn much attention, as
it was placed high up on a part of the Brahmananda Cottage,
next to the temple. But one day Swami came on his stroll to the
back of the temple where the ground is higher. Short as he was,

it put him high enough to see what had transpired on the roof. He found someone and asked, "What is *that*?" Of course he was told. "Doesn't anyone ever think of consulting *me*?" Swami exclaimed.

To me, brought up in a much more formal monastic environment, it seemed that people scarcely did consult him. We had a lot of rope, no question about it, and some of us hanged ourselves with it. The ashrama's atmosphere was casual and open. Swami did not attempt a conversion of one's ingrained Western habits — using both hands at the dining table, for instance — and when the training meted out by some other teachers in this regard was quizzically mentioned to him, he said with one of his notorious grimaces, "Yah! Monkey-on-a-stick monks! Stand up, sit down."

What mattered to Swami Prabhavananda was where one's mind was. For some months I lived at the Hollywood center. On a sunny afternoon I was mowing the back lawn while he paced the stone walk in front of his room. He surprised me by coming up close behind, then looking into my eyes and asking, "Are you doing japa?" I think it happened to everyone.

There seemed always to be a number of eccentrics wandering about. Not only wandering; some of us were even fixtures. Swami had his own understanding of mental aberration, to which he gave voice one day. "I believe — and for this I have no book learning nor theories, it is just what I have concluded — that mental illness or lunacy is organic; it is due to a derangement of the *brain*, not the mind. All our minds are more or less insane in our present state. But the so-called normal person puts a dam before the many crazy ideas and acts suggesting themselves in the mind. The insane person has lost that check, that discrimination of the real from the imaginary, due to some malfunction of the brain. The schizophrenic *doesn't* hear voices or see visions; he *thinks* he hears voices and sees visions."

This accommodation on his part to the non-normal; the freedom between the sexes; the fact that entrants were not required to pitch in their personal funds; the entry, exit and reentry into the family three times over of certain candidates all can be digested only if taken in, measure for measure, with the condiment of Swami's own nature. For him, freedom being the goal, freedom was also the means. Any discipline that did not spring from the bosom of a soul bowed at the feet of the Lord through irresistible attraction was not worth much in the long run. Often we compared and discussed the relative merits of various systems of spiritual training. It always ended in the same way: "I have just *one rule* in the monastery or convent," he would declaim. "Go to the shrine room three times a day and try to practice meditating on the Lord. That is all I insist on."

II. VISTA, SOMBRERO, SIESTA, FIESTA

Terra cotta everywhere. Long corridors of brick, matching tiles overhead. What better complement could there be to the ochre of the sannyasin's robes, dipped in the red earth? Fire — it was the color of fire, symbolic of the transience of earthly things; fire, in which the monk's body would finally shred and crumble on the pyre. This was the Ramakrishna Monastery in Trabuco Canyon, 66 miles south of Los Angeles, straddling a foothill of the Santa Ana mountains. On a clear day, as we told every cloudy day's visitor, you could see the Pacific Ocean, lying 17 miles to the west, over the valleys and lower hills in superb display.

Built like a monastery, true; yet it was not built *as* one, exactly. Gerald Heard and his friends had garnered the funds to create this handsome pile of brick and tile in the Italian fashion. It sprawled from the water reservoir at the top of a long slope to the dormitory at its bottom, the whole structure exposed to a magnificent overlook of sky, cloud, valley and farm, distant roads and a spot of sea. The old engraved bell, nearly two feet in diameter in a modest tower and the hexagonal chapel, original and controversial, as well as the oversize bricks, were features of true distinctiveness. Felix Greene, famed later as a reporter in China, had been the construction manager, finishing it in 1942. When I visited, three years later, more than twenty women and men were in residence, either full or part-time, attracted by one or more of its three avowed *raisons d'etre*: the study and practice of mysticism, high-level experimentation in ESP, rest and recuperation for tired religious workers.

Heard stopped living there in 1947, and after a period during which a Board had run the place in the interest of child

education and incurred debts, Gerald wished it to be turned over
to the Vedanta Society of Southern California. The latter took
possession on the assumption of the debts. It was subsequently
dedicated and renamed. By this time I was living at the Vedanta
monastery in San Francisco; Swami Ashokananda, our abbot, who
had been invited to see the new acquisition, returned with a glowing description: "He has not only got a brand new monastery,"
he sighed, "it is furnished down to the last dot on the 'i' and
cross on the 't'!" We marveled. How was it possible, Swami? "That
is his karma. For that swami, things just drop from the heavens,
so to speak."

Several men from the Hollywood center occupied the
quarters and begin to work. I arrived from the north a few months
later, in October. There were gardens to be rescued and grounds
to clear, grass to be planted, fruit from the trees to be picked and
put up. Add to this the daily monastery routine of worship, chanting, meditation in three periods; there was the weekly shopping
trip of more than 20 miles to Santa Ana; a washout entrance
road to maintain. In the days of the College, Gerald used to say,
"We've found that when there are four of us here it's purgatory;
when only three, it's downright hell." No wonder, then, our wide-
eyed watching of the phenomena taking place at Gethsemani
and the emergence of Merton. Well, they were having the publicity. We were not, and I'm thankful now, for that.

Swami was in India. During those early months we looked
for guidance to Swami Aseshananda, who had known Holy
Mother and was experienced with young men in India and who
spent much time with us. Although he had to encompass the
work at the three places, Santa Barbara, Hollywood and Trabuco
by turns, he made his "home" with us. It was he who taught the
morning class, answered our commonplace questions, shared his
experience in the order and on whom our numerous crises had
at last to fall.

Swami Prabhavananda, when he had returned and settled
into a new routine, made his usual visit to Trabuco once every
two weeks, for three days at a time. Rarely would he stay longer.
He liked to sit in the courtyard near the arched entrance gate,
looking past the trumpet vines out into the Great View. Or he
would walk to the work sites to see how we were doing. He had a

distinctive walk, clasping his hands behind his back and pacing with his short legs back and forth, which made him sway a bit, down the brick corridor or out along the paths. Sometimes he might appear very serious, but one discovered this mood could be altered by someone's joke — or need — into a charming smile and comment. One of the early things we had to do was to exorcise a ghost. Builders of the College had left intact as guest quarters the wooden dwelling of the family originally settled on the property. This four-room cottage, as it was known, covered with wisteria blooms in spring, had still a certain charm; but one guest who slept there saw peculiar things at nightfall and was awakened by a vivid dream in which he was told, "Don't you know this place is haunted?" Swami arranged for the "Ram Nam" to be sung in the cottage for several nights to rid it of the unsavory associations.

It was clear that the heart of his living at Trabuco was the shrine room, and that is what he expected of us as well. There would always be work. Who does not feel the pull of assorted activities? As Jesus said, "The poor you have always with you;" Swami knew that our nature would make us work. External efficiencies were not what he was all about. He was faithful to his meditation in the shrine here as in Hollywood, and more so, one can say, as we got up earlier in the morning.

His eyes were moist much of the time. One could come upon him as he sat alone and find his cheeks wet with fresh tears; what mood, what memory had touched the tinder of his mind to that ecstatic spark, the Lord alone knew. "I feel great joy," he told us one day, "when I see you boys trying to meditate on the Lord! I count *this* as my success. This is all I care about in my work — not the buildings and works, but the lives of you children; whether you are growing in devotion to God." Sometimes our minds play that game of categories, trying to spell out the *margas* or patterns of particular swamis. "Swami Prabhavananda," I used to tell myself, "combines bhakti yoga and *raja yoga* (the path of formal meditation)," and it may not have been a bad generalization. But more than once he told us this: "Just keep your minds in the Lord, like the tick-tock of a clock; and pay no attention to 'bhakti yoga,' 'karma yoga' and the like." And on another occasion, with all his rich solemnity: "After reading everything, following all sorts of practices, etc., you come to just one conclusion: that the essence of religion is just to remember the Lord constantly."

Swami's knowledge of Christianity was exceeded only by his sympathy for it or empathy with it. This was one of the potent factors, throughout the years, in his obtaining and retaining the attraction of his Western listeners. It contributed much to the success of Vedanta in Southern California. On a day in 1951 he came to the lunch table at the monastery and announced that a sentence had come to him while prostrating at the end of noon meditation. It was, "The pure religion of love as taught by Christ to his disciples, perhaps more in silence than through words, has become obscured by too many impossible theological dogmas and doctrines of the church."

Once, as we came, one by one, back to our rooms from early morning meditation he passed me in the courtyard and said (seeing perhaps a shadow of gloom or glumness across my face) "Cheer up! You are not a sinner!"

If one compares him with other swamis we have known, his choices and preferences were fairly predictable. Yet there were surprises. I doubt that anyone could have known, when in the first year at Trabuco a set designer trying out the monastic life offered to "re-do" the shrine in a modern mode, that Swami would specify, while assenting, that it should hold but one picture, a large photograph of Sri Ramakrishna. Surprised, too, were those who thought it would have been that of his guru, Swami Brahmananda, when they saw the Hoffman bronze bust of Vivekananda installed in the center courtyard.

It was fun to watch our two swamis together. There wasn't a great difference in their ages or in their backgrounds. Much of the humor was in Bengali, the language common to the swamis, when they would rather not be overheard. They made sport of playing "Father" against "Mother," i.e., Sri Ramakrishna vs. Sri Sarada Devi. Swami Prabhavananda, not a disciple of Holy Mother, would begin by trotting out various statements about Mother being greater than Father: She is the doorkeeper, Her grace is necessary; since she was the Divine Mother on earth, she was Ramakrishna's *Ishta* and so on. Swami Aseshananda, Sarada Devi's own disciple, would demur. No, no; how can that ever be?

The Master was the incarnation; he always stands paramount; who could surpass him? And so it would go on, to the amusement of all. I thought Swami Aseshananda did a good job of playing second fiddle in a tight harmony. As later assistants discovered, Swami Prabhavananda's was not an easy act to accompany.

When Swami returned from a trip to India, many of the family accompanied Swami Aseshananda to the airport to greet him. It was a memorable scene. Here was the elder coming home to his flock after months overseas, and here was the caretaker who had faithfully looked after them in his absence; none of the emotional implication was lost for either; the tears flowed down Swami's cheeks as he embraced his assistant. For the record, it was in 1954, not long before the younger swami was sent off to Portland, that I was alone with Swami one day when he said to me, "I couldn't have asked for a better assistant than Swami Aseshananda; I've seen so many swamis!" The assignment had not been the his own choice, but arranged through convenience. Sometimes, like the rest of us, he would get annoyed by some of "Swami A's" eccentricities. At Trabuco they had one difference of opinion which in retrospect seems instructive. Swami Aseshananda had elected to teach us the *Brahma Sutras* in our daily class; Swami discouraged him, but the other was keen on it and commenced the class. After a few sittings covering exactly four verses, it was over, abandoned in a humorous confrontation between teacher and students over the principle of *sruti-pramana*, according to which the author claims, in effect, that the Vedas are true because the Vedas say so.

Evening, at Trabuco Monastery, with Swami in residence — was it the absence of the feminine set that made this scene such a contrast to those in Hollywood? We met in the library and sat in chairs. We began with a formal reading, usually from the *Gospel* or Swamiji's works, after which Swami Prabhavananda would be ready to answer any questions. Sometimes questions arose, often not, and the hour might pass almost in silence. Silence in his presence was pregnant, as already mentioned. Still, it was a vastly different atmosphere from the center's. It was here that he could give us the full blast of renunciation.

"*Nude* we must go to God; absolutely nude, devoid of

possessions, wealth, pride, learning and everything." We took
turns reading, and the fatigue of the day's labor could make itself felt. Some were just sleepy by nature. One night a boy was
reading to us from Vivekananda's *Complete Works*. He had a southern drawl to begin with, and as the pages went on his words
came forth more and more slowly, till Swami suddenly interrupted, "You know," he said, "Swami Turiyananda once remarked,
'Reading Swamiji, the dead man becomes alive!' But here you
are, you are reading Swamiji and you, a live man, are falling
asleep."

An odd thing we used to notice at these evening readings
in the library: Visitors would come, men who would spend a night,
a weekend, a week. In their hearts was often a burning question
or problem. The subject might come up, in a guarded way, at
our work or at the table, and if there was no swami present, the
guest might feel the absence of any experienced counsel. At night
the reading would begin and before long that very subject would
come up and be dealt with therein, offering just the remedy for
the illness.

At one point, things picked up a bit when a real come-
dian arrived as a probationer, someone who could hilariously
misunderstand almost anything, mispronounce Sanskrit and
generally lighten the tense or cloudy air. Some of his clowning
would make the tears flow from Swami Prabhavananda's eyes,
and though he was fond of him, the brahmachari inadvertently
embarrassed Swami royally on a certain occasion. Swamis
Madhavananda (longtime general secretary of the order) and
Nirvanananda (soon to be vice-president of the order) had come
from India as the center's guests for several weeks. The dedication of the Santa Barbara temple was about to be held and they
would preside at the inauguration. This particular day was their
official visit to the monastery and of course there had to be a
grand tour. Swami led it off, walking the older swamis down the
courtyard, into the shrine room and on down to the living quarters we called the dormitory. "Would you like to see one of the
brahmacharis' rooms?" he asked the dignitaries and opened a
door. Consternation! It happened to be the joker's room, the
least tidy of all.

Three of us lived there who had arrived early and somehow survived longer and who "ran" the work; we were known to ourselves and a few others as "the unholy three." All sorts of problems had to be tackled, in spite of the place's supposedly being finished down to the crosses on the t's and dots on the i's. Water was scarce and treated like honey. Orchard and gardens had nearly disappeared in overgrowth. The soil was saturated with boron — a deterrent to plant growth. Fierce winds called Santanas or Santa Anas would blow up from nowhere to fell favorite plants and trees. The chickens would "catch cold" and drop by dozens, or the price of feed would climb again. Madame Cow was affected by the renunciatory mood around her and was forever having to be artificially inseminated. Acres of wild grasses had to be cut, enormous rooms and verandas had to be swept. One brother did the gardening of ornamentals, the landscaping and the guru service. As he came more often in contact with Swami he reaped the double effects thereof — more arguments and the occasional ire, more blessing and affection too. Another, a man of all trades, raised the chickens — first a dozen scattered around the yard, later the full-time job of 700 laying hens.

My work was cooking and baking, orchard and vegetables and music. We all took turns at the daily worship and did some cooking. Boys would come in all enthusiasm, all agog with "yoga," get yoked to one of these routines, sing sweetly their parts in the chorus, show all sorts of talent, give us the benefit of their developing personalities and then disappear into the night. Through it all Swami would keep his serene detachment, setting an example to us all as he walked, watched, asked questions and made suggestions. His ideas were often practical. He had favorite vegetables he wanted me to grow: the Indian *patal* or bitter melon, okra and artichoke. A few words from him, or one of his benign and melting smiles, could make one's day. I treasure the day one summer when the quarter-acre fenced for vegetables was packed with lush, varied foliage, row upon row of comestibles waiting to be picked. He threw open the wide gate and came in to watch my watering. "All this is the expression of your ecstasy," he said, face beaming.

If one broke the pace to go and sit down beside him on the loggia, Swami would be pleased and welcoming. These were the opportunities for airing one's problems: conflicts with others over work, doubts about one's fitness for the life, obstacles found in meditation, claims from one's relatives, all encroaching on one's peace of mind. Few of these early recruits had Catholic antecedents with a monastic tradition; how would their families comprehend what they were attempting? Swami was more an ear than an oracle, listening seriously, quietly absorbing the question, responding with a few sentences of caution or consolation, perhaps an anecdote about Maharaj, or an experience of his own. He might even simply brush you off; more than once I felt myself talking to a blank wall.

On the other hand, I was spoken to on one occasion by a brother in such cutting words that I drove all the way into Hollywood, my mind on fire, just to sit down at his feet and unburden myself. There was nothing external I could have expected him to do about the matter, so why go through all that? Just to quench that fire in the coolness of his voice and countenance, and because what he said to me that day has rung in my ears down the years. "Oh, I am sorry," he whispered. "Let me tell you something: Never pay attention to what people say to you like that." The visit was over. I had my lunch and drove back to the canyon. But the counsel had sunk in to stay.

One day while walking the long brick corridor he met one who asked, "Swami, we are told to approach our brother monks with love in our hearts in all our dealings. When we try to do so, and meet with a rebuff, that love dries up so fast. What to do?"

"I pray for that person then and there," he answered. Similarly, he told a disciple, "You can never control people from here; only from here" — pointing first to his head, then to his heart.

It was not all manual labor and the "shrine grind" at Trabuco. In addition to our joker, there stayed for a couple of years a lively black lad who had been a dancer. He kept things hopping with his accent and his ever-ready laughter. When the membership reached seven, and one of the newer men got his fill of preparing supper with one or two special diets involved, he came out with this: "I see, now, what monastic life is. It's like being married to six husbands at once."

There was the annual Fourth of July festival held as a

kind of open house for the public, once the bust of Swamiji had been installed. This was cast in bronze, in the original mold of the first, created in New York by Malvina Hoffman who claimed the fame of having sat on Vivekananda's knee as a child. Swami Prabhavananda had liked the sculpture and ordered a copy. Those responsible for landscape had designed as setting for the statue a lily pool and surrounding plants. The dedication in 1951 brought the first crowd of nearly two hundred, devotees and the curious, to hear the speeches of the swamis, Christopher Isherwood and playwright John van Druten, listen to the choral piece written and sung by our composer and chorus and enjoy a feast outdoors.

I find people are shocked when they learn that Swami took the family out to movies. At Trabuco it was a half-hour's drive to Laguna Beach and about once a month we would pile into a car or two and be off. Back around 11:30 p.m. if it was double feature. The influence of "the industry," the motion-picture business, was all-pervasive for Southern Californians in the heyday of Hollywood. Seeing the shows was like the Brahmins of Bengal eating fish or the French clergy drinking wine. The local news spewed out a daily diet of the doings of the great studios, actors and directors. Swami Prabhavananda counted among his friends, students, and visitors, some of the big names in several categories. Garbo had made a celebrated visit, Tyrone Power another. Movies were the livelihood of many of the devotees and contributors, and on those funds we subsisted. They were our acquaintances and associates; the Hollywood milieu was a fact of life. Swami appreciated films, but he would not go without taking all who wished to go — and even some who didn't. There was a bit of pressure put on it. He disliked pious pretensions of moral superiority, the priggishness in being different. Usually we would go when vespers were finished, but once for some special reason the movie trip had to be started very early.

"But what about vespers?" I expostulated.

Swami screwed up his face and said quietly, "Look, do you really think you will go to hell if you don't do the vespers for one day?"

In Hollywood the acquisition of a Volkswagen bus facilitated this recreation considerably. Swami once gave us a definition which revealed how much he had become a connoisseur: Real acting is when the acting itself, after being studied carefully, is hidden. Ham acting is when the studied acting shows. Readers may be reminded of Sri Ramakrishna's patronage of the theater, which developed from his acquaintance with playwright Girish Ghosh, and his reactions to the various dramas. "Westerns" were at their peak in those Trabuco days, and we never knew just what we were likely to see; they might be shallow, they could be profound. I remember asking Swami on the way home if he had liked one of these. He gave an enthusiastic affirmative.

"But, Swami, they were such *bad* men!"

"Ah, but they were very interesting," was his comment. As he had his interest in social and political issues and in the news of the day, so did he follow the film figures and productions in his own disinterested way. It was all there, but none of it ever disturbed his inwardness.

Swami had received the order's permission to administer the vows of brahmacharya to his monks after a minimum of five years of probation and when he regarded them fit for it. We were treated to the first performance in 1954, when two of the Trabuco brothers became "Chaitanyas."

Performance was indeed the word, for Swami Prabhavananda *was* dramatic, without even trying. Emotions swept across his face with the swiftness of wavelets on sea sand, and one rarely found him prosaic. Everything under his management had flair, and when it came time for American young men to enter the novitiate and cast their fate into the fire of renunciation, none of the significance was going to be lost. There was little precedent to bind him, either. In the library fireplace, with all due ceremony and as much of the aura of ancient India as could be commanded, the sacred fire was mapped and kindled. As three swamis' presence was required, Swami Pavitrananda had come from New York. I was immensely impressed by the whole historic affair, and when these two men had their heads shaven as prelude to the vows, I picked up some of the hair. For years I kept it in envelopes as a memento.

The following year there was a replay, this time for a Hollywood brother and myself. A detailed amusing account of this event has been given elsewhere (in *Prabuddha Bharata* of July 1981) and I would not attempt to add anything to it. For a while I had been telling Swami that I felt disinclined to take the vows so soon, lest I should not be able to keep them. He would encourage the idea of plunging in anyway and I would hang back. So I asked Swami Yatiswarananda about it. He wrote promptly. "I have seen in many cases, including my own, that vows sincerely taken with appropriate ceremony positively help to strengthen the will-power." With this guru-decreed approval I became reconciled to going through with it. The year that followed the momentous ceremony of investiture was a golden one for me. In the important matter of name-bestowal I felt gratified at Swami's choice and will forever thank him for it.

Next year, though, the tide turned. Like all illumined souls, he was not a person with whom one ought to have a serious argument. We saw this again and again and I should have known better. I disputed his judgment in a major matter involving monastery administration. Tempestuous winds roiled the calm seas of our relationship. Just then, a well-to-do devotee had given Swami the use of a beach house at Laguna. It was summer and he decided to stay there for a week or so of vacation. To cool me off he took me with him, bless his heart. But already it had become clear to him that he would be forced to break my attachment to Trabuco by moving me to Hollywood. I hope he had a vacation — knowing his intention, I was daily making the sea saltier with my tears.

Trabuco with all its grandeur and isolation never drew Swami Prabhavananda into itself in the way Santa Barbara did. We felt, during these years, that we were not able to give him what he liked to have around him. Was there the factor that this place had fallen to him late, when his youthful energies were spent and he had not had the struggle to build it up which brings identification? Or was it that we made it difficult for him to feel needed, busy as we were with far-flung enterprises, our minds not yet centered in deep inquiry? He did not hold a formal class at Trabuco: there was Swami Aseshananda for that, and for answering day-to-day questions. Perhaps all this worked to put some distance between us. Most of all, probably, as we shall see in the next chapter, was the intensity of his concern for the nuns.

As a counterforce to the draining pressure of the public work, relaxation was what Swami most needed. It was understandable; tending to be silent and indrawn much of the time, he experienced in the company of the nuns a flow of conversation, laughter and verbal play — offering a contrast he would not get in the seriousness and somnolence of the silent, spread-out monastery.

This is not to say that Swami's days at Trabuco were unfruitful, jejune or empty of loftiness. I am certain that in the wide views and spaces of the loggias and yards of Trabuco monastery and in the peculiar silence of its dim, round shrine room he had many a spiritual insight, and experiences never told. One such exalted mood came to him during the last few months I was there. He had come to the table for breakfast, which for some reason we were eating that morning in the long refectory instead of the kitchen. After saying the "Om Brahmarpanam," a blessing said before meals, and a moment of silence, he looked from one face to another and announced, "This morning I am seeing nothing but Brahman — I see John-Brahman, Phil-Brahman, Jim-Brahman..." The divine substance had taken over his consciousness, and individuals were different names and forms. For me, at least, those words were a revelation I carry with me to this day. With my heart in turmoil I made the move from Trabuco Canyon to bustling Hollywood, scarcely realizing it was the end of a chapter, brought to a close all too soon by a mind still immature and unyielding.

III. FATHER WITH THE DAUGHTERS OF THE MOTHER

If Swami Prabhavananda seems to have bent over backward in promulgating a monastic life for American women in Vedanta, why not? Who else had taken up such a cause? Swami Vivekananda himself had given holy orders to several women, and had outlined his plans and hopes in this regard. In India, political realities and societal conservatism had obstructed and delayed their fulfillment. Swami Abhedananda in his Western work had made a start. Swami Paramananda, and Swami Siddheswarananda in France, having ventured boldly to implement Swamiji's ideas, suffered abuse at the hands of their critics. It was left to Swami Prabhavananda to succeed in attracting young women to the life of renunciation in the patterns of Sri

Ramakrishna and the Holy Mother, inspiring them to lifelong dedication and, with Herculean struggle, establishing their place in the Ramakrishna movement. It was no small accomplishment. The swami was a feminist long before the term was coined and it became fashionable to be one. This chapter should be written not by me, but by them, his nuns. Let us hope one day it will be; meanwhile, I will report whatever I saw and understood.

The Santa Barbara property of Spencer Kellogg in the suburb of Montecito had been in use for several years as a cloister for Swami's recruits, the women and the men alternating in spending periods of time there. In 1947 it became the main province of the nuns, and the first vows were given. With the acquisition of Trabuco College, a new pattern emerged. Just as most of the convent members were living permanently at Santa Barbara, most of the would-be monks now lived at Trabuco. A smaller selection of each, their talents or requirements suited to the life of the center, remained in Hollywood.

Swami had had an ideal relationship with Sister Lalita. I sometimes think it set the example in his mind for what he would like to see all of us realize or experience. I saw Sister on one brief visit I made just before her passing away. She was impressively indrawn and silent, just like Swami. They had lived together for years, she as his hostess, support, domestic adviser, friend and student. He told us, "Sister and I lived as close as brother and sister all those years and never once did we have an argument." It set a standard a bit too high to be realized daily in our life in Hollywood!

At mealtime in Hollywood we sat at the long table which nearly filled the room, women down one side, men the other, with Swami's place carefully reserved at the head. Everything would depend on the swami's mood: If he was serious all was silence; if lighthearted, great repartee could ripple up and down and back and forth. It was more difficult when he was out-of-station. There could be tension. I had expected to be bothered by the mixing of sexes in close quarters. But through the grace of God and the swami I not only found no difficulty in it, I came to understand and appreciate it. It was clear that he hoped to engender in us all a true spiritual freedom buoyed up by holy company, an in-group which would supply physical food in common and spiritual food for our souls, purified so far as possible of sex-and-gender consciousness. No one can say that it did not at least partially succeed.

Overcoming opposition, he obtained permission from headquarters in India to give both the brahmacharya (novitiate) vows and the sannyasa or final vows to the nuns in ceremonies performed in California, and accordingly these were given at regular and appropriate intervals. This is still the custom today, while for the monks sannyasa must be held in India. This means that not only are the brahmacharinis and *pravrajikas* (as the sannyasinis are called) members of the Ramakrishna Order, but a few who came to Swami long ago, answering his call to renounce, are among the most senior of the Western members. On his trips to India he took nuns with him. I recall one incident he reported to us on his return. When they had wished to enter a certain temple in South India, a *panda* (guardian-priest), seeing the Western faces, had stopped them. He asked Swami Prabhavananda his caste.

"Are you a Hindu?" Swami inquired of the priest.

"What do you mean," said the other, "asking *me* a question like that?"

"Well, no Hindu ever asks a monk his caste." And with that they all went into the temple.

The feminine contingent in the Hollywood center was not restricted exclusively to the professed. Swami Prabhavananda also opened his heart and home to a few others whom he believed belonged there or who could profit from the opportunity. Such, in my years, was Ujjvala, Ida Ansell — the little lame one Swami Vivekananda had known as Baby; the aging mother of one of the senior nuns was another. Ujjvala was almost sacred to some of us as a last link with the age of Swamiji. Those who had known him were becoming scarce, and here was one who was responsible for giving us the notes of some of his very best lectures. Lively, game, alert, intelligent and sometimes pathetic, Ujjvala added much to the life of the center. Her story has been related elsewhere by those who saw her much more than I did. Now and then I would coax her to a quiet corner and ask her about those historic days.

The men at Trabuco would travel to the Sarada Convent,

not only on special occasions, such as the Durga Puja, but at quieter times also. We had there the privilege of seeing Swami Prabhavananda at his most relaxed. He felt there the sort of freedom, one imagines, that Holy Mother knew in Jayrambati, her native village, leaving behind the strictures of society and demands of the devotees. Santa Barbara was a different world for him. In the first years he enjoyed the company of a beautiful Great Dane, Rama, who was his pal. One afternoon, while all were sitting in the convent living room, the dog on the floor, a little bird flew in an open window. As it beat about for exit, Rama, alerted with a start, stretched herself toward it with wide-open jaws. The poor bird, seeing its danger, flew frantically from ceiling to floor, and suddenly hurled itself right into the dog's open mouth. Rama was so surprised she had no time to react, and birdie was out before the jaws closed. Swami at once deduced the moral: We, too, plunge often blindly, headlong into the trap, our very death; such is the way of maya. But then there is grace.

There were beds and beds of flowers, profuse and gorgeous, as well as those woven in among the rocky paths cut steeply into the hillside which gave Swami exercise and distant vistas out to the sea. The food — well, the women had learned to utilize their ample talents in preparing Bengali dishes close to those Swami had known in his own land. There was not, however, any weakening of the traditional monastic ideal. Surrounded as they were by what would seem to be all the good things of this world, the nuns might be reminded by the teacher that Holy Mother had once taught a rather peculiar and difficult prayer: "Ask to be desireless." Swami once elucidated this with the following comment: "Liberation is really beyond our conception. Buddha described it the most logically by negative terms — the complete cessation of suffering and misery. 'Desirelessness' is really not a correct word; *freedom from craving* is a better expression, because we may have desire to continue spiritual practices, etc., and these do not prevent liberation. Are they to be done away with?" Before the nuns was set constantly the ideal life of Holy Mother and the fidelity and devotion of the other women disciples of the Master. Swami was always delighted if one felt inclined to do the formal worship and many of the women performed it daily, either in their turn at the shrine or in the privacy of their own rooms. Santa Barbara had an atmosphere heavy with the perfume of devotion and worship..

A Vedanta nunnery being something new in the order, experiments had to be made. It seemed they were forever devising and designing a new habit. Various styles and colors were tried. At one point Swami may have thought it was becoming obsessive; his comment was terse and pointed: "Color your mind with gerrua *inside*. That's what counts."

There were intense disappointments for Swami, both in the monastery and in the convent. Some with whom he had had years of association, or of whom he was particularly fond, drifted away in the course of life's exigencies. We could only guess what he must be silently going through on these occasions. Again it was the women, in whom he had such high hopes and who had needed all the support he could give, over whom he agonized more. These are personal stories and have no place here, but looking back one can only wonder at the heartache they must have stirred in him and at how he withstood it in cheerful serenity.

Swami kept a watchful eye over the nuns and monks when they were together in his presence. So long as he lived, something mysterious was at work making what he envisaged jell. By and large he was successful in establishing the mood in which high thought and detachment hold sway and unseemly tendencies are overcome. Even today I feel that family bond among us. Perhaps in his powerful thought-force wrong ideas would not arise. So far as I ever saw, his dealings with everyone were unambiguous and exemplary — a lesson to us all, a ballet choreographed and executed to perfection.

IV. DANCING TO GONG AND SYMBOL

To me, with a Quaker background, Vedanta in Hollywood seemed a world awash with worship. In the San Francisco center we had learned the theory of Indian ritual as performed in the order and, by general participation, learned also to appreciate the atmosphere of devotion and inwardness it can generate. But it was Swami Prabhavananda who employed worship as a primary function in his work and who by example and instruction led us to attempt it and to understand its deeper meanings. He made me, I confess, a ritualist.

He, too, had been skeptical as a young monk when Swami Brahmananda had told him, "Be ritualistic." Let the reader not misunderstand; this did not and does not mean being orthodox or punctilious in daily conduct or dictatorial about ritual details. There was an air of freedom, a joy borne of spontaneity in the way Swami did the worship and taught others to do it. He made clear that the expression of one's own inner feeling was what was wanted, not slavish adherence to rulebook gesture or sequence.

The prescribed daily worship of Sri Ramakrishna is carried out in a number of our centers in the West, each adapting it to its own requirements and convenience as to length, the hour of performance, elaborateness, items to be offered. In Southern California it was begun around noon, consumed about an hour and a quarter and closely approximated the ceremony as offered at Belur Math in India. It was known as the *dasopacarana*, the 10-item worship. More elaborate were the ceremonies, such as the 16-item worship, performed on special occasions. These included the annual birthday celebrations of the "Big Four" (the Master, the Mother, Swamiji and Maharaj). Durga Puja, Kali Puja, Sivaratri and *homa* (fire ceremony, a relic of ancient Vedic ritual, in which fire is regarded as the deity and receives the offerings) each had its own detailed format. I was present in the living room when — it must have been as late as 1956 — a devotee thought to ask Swami why the traditional birthday of Sri Krishna was not observed and celebrated here. It struck me as curious that this point seemed never to have arisen before. For a moment he appeared to be at a loss, then replied, "I guess it's because *I* am here." Nothing more, and it was to my knowledge, one of those utterances which were never explained.

When Swami presided at the daily worship he would execute the requirements without losing his mood of absorption. I believe tears rarely came during his worship. If you were present it seemed the most natural thing in the world just to close your eyes and allow yourself to be caught up in — what? — an indescribable elevation, a bright fog of abstractedness, for which the mystics have scoured their vocabularies. Only those know who have experienced it. But then, to become in this way made one lose sight of that element of theater and elegance which Swami's natural grace imparted to the whole procedure — and so you peeped out, now and then, just to be sure you were still on the floor, and to watch the Swami's unselfconscious ballet of God-absorbed devotion.

As others learned to make the offerings and the swami grew older, this scene became less frequent, but we were thus afforded an opportunity to experience what he had always said: The ceremony has its own power. Yes, the *pujari* (the person performing the puja) makes a difference, and to some it will come more naturally than to others, but the puja or *seva* (some prefer to call the daily function *seva,* service) is not a human performance. Where He, the Lord, is sought and implored, where one sincerely offers the least of things to Him, even without feeling devotion but merely asking for it, He will manifest Himself; He is bound to. And so, with or without Swami the work of this form of bhakti was accomplished for all. Swami would train the brahmacharinis by putting them in the role of pujari for many of the special pujas, while he became the *tantra-dharaka,* the "prompter".

Kali Puja and Siva Ratri in Hollywood and Durga Puja in Santa Barbara were real dramas, the former starting in the evening and running on till four or five in the morning. To see an auditorium full of Western devotees, making the best peace they could with the squatting posture, spending the night silently meditating and attending to the exotic motions of a Sanskrit ritual, is to comprehend the conviction of its value infused in them by Swami Prabhavananda. Then, when it was finished, he would be the freshest of us all, and this went on for years.

Reference has been made earlier to the fact that the worship was usually done in silence, punctuated solely by the ringing of the hand-bell at prescribed points. So it had been in Northern California, and I therefore supposed that this was the standard practice. When later I experienced in India and other places the noise and distraction which sometimes accompany these public rituals, I realized that the swamis in the West had favored us with a setting and a context for the sacred worship which made of it a different genus, more an act of corporate meditation and devotion than the carrying out of a rite, or an exercise to be explained.

Swami Prabhavananda did explain it, in detail, not publicly but in classes for the monastics who were learning it. As a sidelight to discussing the Kali Puja he once made reference to the following:

The Rani Rasmani [founder and proprietor of the Dakshineswar temples where Ramakrishna lived] constantly referred to herself as "the servant of Kali," etc. But this does not mean necessarily that Kali was her "*ishta*." In India it is common for devotees to express devotion to one aspect of the Deity outwardly and cherish another aspect in his or her heart. This is because he or she may feel that the Chosen Ideal is too sacred, too precious to reveal to others. But the said devotee regards all other forms as aspects of the one Deity. This also prevents sectarianism.

"In the homa ceremony," a novice questioned, "should one offer also one's meditation, japa and their fruits?"

"No, no," Swami replied, "those are already offered."

The kitchen was no less the shrine room than the one in the temple, and since the noon meal was prepared in such a way that it would form part of the daily offering, the food had always to be cooked with great care and taste. One good reason for this was the experience Swami had had as a brahmachari many years before in Madras. There it was the custom to leave the shrine as soon as the food was offered, and wait outside. One of the delicacies offered the Lord in the hot season was cucumber sticks. As the swami was seated outside doing japa he thought he heard a voice ask, "Where is the salt for the cucumber?" He thought the heat must have made him doze off and dream. But when he went back in to pick up the food he looked at the tray and found that sure enough, the salt was missing.

Comments on the puja which Swami offered us in a monastery class in 1950 were taken down in my notebook. As they may not be of the same interest to all readers they are placed in Appendix B.

V. SATURATED IN MAHARAJ

We read in the memoirs of Sri Ramakrishna's disciples references to a strong resemblance of Rakhal, Swami Brahmananda, to the Master. Although a physical similarity seems to be intended, I could never understand it, thinking that they did not look at all alike. After years of watching Swami Prabhavananda and hearing him speak of his master, some idea of what must be meant has come to me.

If it is true that our present body is the result of our many thoughts and habits from past lives, then when in this life one begins to dwell deeply and constantly in thought on a given model, it follows that one can grow into a kind of resemblance of that prototype. Swami was not physically much like Maharaj; yet his attunement and assimilation into the being of Maharaj was definitely more than merely mental. He was steeped in the thought of his guru, obsessed with him, possessed of him, merged in him — and everyone knew it. He had become his shadow.

Swami did not imitate Maharaj, as many idolizers do their model, nor was he in any sense a "clone." Whatever it was, this unity or harmony or synergetic relationship was not on the surface. The identification was in what in Sanskrit is called the *bhava*, mood, tone, affect — an outlook on, or approach to, life, to others, to disciples, to sense objects — in short, to the world. Probably it should be called the oneness of their realization.

In Swami Prabhavananda's eyes and face one very often saw the combination of deep inward joy and the shedding of light from that joy, like a beam, on everything encountered, which one sees in most of the photographs of Swami Brahmananda. It is apparent, too, in photographs of Prabhavananda. I have written of Swami's face and the mobility of his features, the ease with which they modeled a mood and how rapidly they could change. His eyes were of a type seen in a number of Bengalis, with their complex racial origins; almost almond eyes, Far Eastern in the outer corner fold of the upper eyelid. It must have heightened the air of inscrutability already conveyed by his inwardness and his silence. As he aged, the wrinkles came and the hair grayed, but it had little effect on his beauty.

Swami's lectures and classes, letters, conversations and instructions were filled with expressions such as, "Maharaj used to say...," "You know, Maharaj used to...," "I will refer it to Maharaj," as in the letter he wrote to me in 1970: "About another assistant to give me a little relief — I have completely surrendered myself to the will of the Lord. Do not depend upon *any man*. It is the Lord's work and He will see to it. As long as any breath is left in me, I shall try only to be the instrument or rather the witness to His work. Maharaj taught me 'The Lord does his own preaching. Be the witness.' I try to be that. And I am myself surprised to witness how He is preaching His word. 'His will be done' — let not any least trace of ego (I am the teacher) be left in us. Thus only we can make our lives blessed."

When he was about to go off to India a "daughter" asked him how he could think of leaving all of us to our own resources; after all, what if someone got into a crisis, like ...going into samadhi! Swami laughed and looked around the room at our faces and said, "Well, if you get into samadhi you won't need me anyway! Why, I have thrown you all at the feet of Sri Maharaj! He will look after everything." He called Swami Brahmananda a "fountain of love" and an "ocean of mercy."

A choice story concerns the era, in the early '30s probably, when Swami had decided to learn to drive a car. He did learn, and drove for quite some time. But he confessed that once while he was driving somewhere alone on a slippery unpaved road, the car ran off the road and the brakes proved useless. So he folded his legs under him on the seat, crying, "All right, Maharaj: you take over!" After careening awhile along the shoulder of the road, the automobile came to rest just as it approached a tree. Many of us felt that Maharaj had indeed taken over his whole body, thought and will, long ago. I never cared to record his many utterances and stories about his teacher. Who would? You were spellbound in the mood generated by his recounting them. One story made it into my notebook:

Swami Brahmananda, as we know, always advised, "Speak the truth, but never a harsh truth." He was so conscientious about this himself, Swami said, that even in seemingly inconsequential matters he would try never to deviate from truth. Once a person passing through his room on an errand happened to ask him, "Has the milkman brought the milk yet, Maharaj?" "Yes," replied the swami, and then added, "So I have heard."

Maharaj could be naughty, too, and play practical jokes, some of which are now famous. Swami would confide to the monks now and then some of his naughtier tricks, and like so much about Maharaj, they were subtle.

Swami Prabhavananda never let up his challenge to one and all to think constantly of the Lord. How does one do this without going crazy? As Christopher Isherwood has well explained in his introduction to *Religion in Practice*, a published collection of Swami's discourses, this becomes possible, even easy, when we have had contact with a life in which God is obviously embodied. For Swami, so identified was his guru with God that when he thought of the former, which was the natural and insistent bent of his mind, remembrance of God was accomplished.

"Every time you think of the Lord," he told us, "he knows about it and so do his saints. Every time you think of him he nods at you — but he does not always let you know that he is nodding at you, otherwise you'd go crazy — like a beggar who inherits a hundred thousand dollars."

Each of us has his or her own heroes. I used to feel embarrassed when comparisons between the swamis Vivekananda and Brahmananda were brought up in Swami Prabhavananda's presence, and thought it was unfortunate. It was like baiting someone, albeit unconsciously. Swami had not seen Swamiji. Not only had he seen Maharaj, he had lived with him, soaked up his teachings and his enthusiasms, built his life around him, made him his all-in-all. What could he be expected to say? Occasionally one heard that Swami Prabhavananda did not acknowledge Swamiji as the chief disciple of the Master, having accorded that place of honor to Maharaj instead. But both in his speaking and his writing Swami was careful to make the distinction between "disciple" and "child"; that Maharaj was Sri Ramakrishna's own spiritual child had been owned in all the accounts — the Master's vision of Rakhal, his utterances about the boy, the love and reverence in which Maharaj was held by the other disciples all attested to it. Swami told us during our group reading in the library of the *Lila-Prasanga, The Great Master*, that Swami Saradananda, the author, had desisted from giving the material he had at first intended to write on Swami Brahmananda, because the latter was living at the time the book needed to be published; otherwise the proportion of report given of the two would have been different.

Swami referred to Naren, to Swamiji, as the apostle, the message-bearer, the great "active" whose mission it was to bring

Ramakrishna's thought and life to the rest of the world. So far as this role on the world scene was concerned, no one could be compared to Swamiji. Swami was a thorough student and interpreter of Swamiji's works. But when the photos had been framed for the shrine in Hollywood and the library at Trabuco, he had placed the two brother disciples side by side as equals. He felt that India had lionized Vivekananda because of his success in the West and the implications his mission had for the political history of the country. Therefore in India the authorities had everywhere enshrined the "Big Three" for public veneration, and others coming west had followed suit. For Swami, those were not necessarily the greatest *spiritual* attributes. While all that external activity was going on, necessary as it might be, great power — power for life-changing, for uplifting the atmosphere and thought current of those round about — was dwelling and developing in Maharaj, all hidden from public notice. He would cite the incidents of Swamiji's touching the latter's feet after returning from abroad and his remarking to Saratchandra Chakravarti about Maharaj's spiritual elevation and power. So Swami would equate them, the twin stars of equal brilliance, offspring of the Father and the Mother.

Swami was aware that this view had its detractors. When this was brought to his attention, it would move him to command silence with a classic one-liner: "Anyone who makes a distinction between Swamiji and Maharaj has not understood *either* Maharaj *or* Swamiji." After the Vivekananda sculpture was installed at the heart of the monastery at Trabuco, he turned to me and said, "Well, at least they can't say I put up Maharaj!" It was a point of view, all of a piece with his own spiritual existence. One might argue with it. One never wanted to argue it with him.

Quite naturally he felt closest to the other disciples of Swami Brahmananda in America. It was they whom we saw as frequent visitors. To see and hear these children of Maharaj, grown men and serious swamis, playing and laughing together was a treat for us — and it helped us to understand the divine joy in which, as spiritual beings, they were born. Someone in India, I have forgotten now who, told me that Swami Prabhavananda was Maharaj's favorite child; it accounts for much. With these observations I should like to couple what Swami wrote me in

1958 when I had returned to Northern California:

"I am glad to learn that you are getting better acquainted with Swami Shraddhananda (then assistant minister of the Vedanta Society of Northern California, recently arrived). You will be greatly benefited by close association with him. Remember, whatever outer coating the swamis may put on, inside they are all bhaktas. It reminds me what Swami Turiyananda once said. A young disciple had remarked, 'Swami, I wish I could read your mind.' And the Swami replied, 'You may read many thoughts that may be there, but if you go deeper, there is no other thought but *Ramakrishna*.' And thus must we all mold our lives, so that deep inside there may not be any thought other than that of Ramakrishna."

Yet among all the swamis whose association I have been privileged to have, it was Swami Prabhavananda who most emphasized the supremacy of the guru in spiritual life. At one of the sessions at his feet, someone had asked: "Sri Ramakrishna says, 'Always test your guru thoroughly' — but there is the old saying, 'Though my guru visits the tavern, still he is my all-in-all.' Is there not a contradiction here?"

"The first," Swami had replied, "applies *before* you accept him; the second, *after*." So it had been with him. He told us that his own younger brother, though not a monk, had received the grace of Maharaj to the extent of experiencing samadhi.

It was, I believe, when we were seated one evening in the living room of the Green House after class and Swami was in one of those affectionate and confiding moods, that he shared the following treasure from his experience. Some may find it puzzling or shocking; I was not surprised because I'd been led to suspect it already. "Do you know," he asked, "who is manifest very much? Three: Mother, Swamiji and Maharaj. Thakur? I don't know! But these three are very much manifest wherever anyone takes the name of Sri Ramakrishna." I wondered if it was not like Christians who "knock on the doors" of the saints and apply through them.

Then there was the day, it may be in 1955 or so, when some of us were transfixed with awe as he told us: "Through His grace, the world of Thakur, Mother, Swamiji and Maharaj has become more real to me than this one."

VI. SPARE-TIME HOBBY

Millions met Swami Prabhavananda in his books. It might have been more accurate to have begun this account in that way, for even if we come to know a writer in person, we form a mental set about him when we read him first. In the Philadelphia center on my first visit, lacking the money to buy *The Gospel of Sri Ramakrishna*, with which I was acquainted, I had purchased *The Eternal Companion*, about which I knew nothing. The book became a kind of second Bible for me and surely it has been so for many others. In his presentation of the life and teachings of Maharaj, Swami has subtly, almost seductively, enticed the skeptic or agnostic to admire this portrait of contemplation and to entertain the possibility of relating oneself to God, the Person. That very first declaration of Swami Brahmananda, that *God is*, was what caught Gerald Heard and changed everything for him.

As I made my way west I carried with me as well the other small volume, which had recently come out, the *Bhagavad-Gita* translation, first fruit of Prabhavananda's collaboration with Isherwood. When Swami Vishwananda of the Chicago center (the second swami I called on) saw it in my hand he praised it highly. "I am so glad they have done this," said he. "You have done well to buy it. You see, they have tried to reproduce something of the original style — a measure of prose and a measure of poetry, like the two meters of the Sanskrit."

It is not my intention to try to cover or review Swami Prabhavananda's phenomenal literary output. That is not within my competency, nor was I witness to much of its making. Of all his original volumes, collaborations, translations, magazine articles and editing, very little, I believe, was done at Trabuco. Nor did he discuss it with us, except now and then. I remember that the table talk for a couple of meals in his presence consisted of our knocking around the question of the best title for the Yoga Sutras translation he and Chris were about to complete. *How to Know God* was what Chris finally wished to settle upon. Some of us thought that a mistake. But who were we?

Swami's capacity to push on with the literary work must have been immense. In 1968, when he was 75 years of age, he wrote to me, "For some weeks I was too busy in Hollywood. Ev-

ery moment of my time was taken up reading proofs of a new
book — a collection of some of my lectures, titled *Religion in
Practice*. Chris has written a beautiful introduction to the book.
Allen and Unwin will be publishing from England and Vedanta
Press from here. The publication date is June 6th." Four years
earlier in another letter he had said, "No, there can be no real
retirement for any of the older Swamis, until they either become
invalid or die. The older you are, the greater the demand. Such
is the lot of the Swami."

Those who take even a sample of the fruit of this prodigious labor must be struck by the simplicity of the swami's style,
the total absence of academic pretension and literary conceits.
His English, even without a collaborating "polisher," was excellent for its purposes. It was not a studied technique; he spoke
and thought in the same way. The reading of one book or two
may thus mislead one into supposing that he had only an aver-
age education and was not deep or wide in his scholarship. A
perusal of the Biblical supports of his *Sermon on the Mount* or the
homework buried in *The Spiritual Heritage of India* quickly dis-
solves such a notion. It was the same with Swami Vivekananda,
who was a devourer of encyclopedias but whose style is even now
too simple and academically unsophisticated for the literary world
to be bothered with

Swami Prabhavananda never paraded his scholarship. In all
my notes I have been hard put to dredge up one which even
hints at his considerable erudition. But here it is: "Yes, Hegel
arrived at a logical proof of the Absolute. But how do we know
that the conception of the Absolute tallies with the fact of the
Absolute? And one *can* realize the Absolute as a fact — but there,
no logical formulation of it can be made. If one were, it would
not be Absolute." It almost makes one feel it was the swami who
was really getting the point of existentialism. *The Spiritual Heritage of India* came to be used as a textbook in the '60s and '70s for
courses in comparative religion at numerous colleges and universities, especially in the Midwest.

With regard to the translations from Sanskrit, these can
be no exception to the observation that any translator is an interpreter. Unambiguous one-to-one equivalents exist between
scarcely any languages so distantly related. By choosing from a

set of near-synonyms those which most nearly express his own understanding, the translator inevitably re-colors and redefines the original thought. "Very faithful and almost literal" is the way in which Swami Prabhavananda's translations were described by one Sanskrit scholar. I think the description too strong, but be that as it may, he was both consciously and unconsciously aware of Western taste and expectations and knew very well how to fulfill these through the language employed. He understood which *samskaras* of the Western mind and culture would be evoked, which harp strings of the American memory touched, as he wrote — and all his literary work has this cast to it. It is best seen perhaps in *The Wisdom of God*, in which Swami Prabhavananda has, without anyone looking over his shoulder, produced a version of the *Srimad Bhagavatam* cut and trimmed and tailored to his own specifications and tastes. It is a beautiful and spiritually inspiring work, but a different entity from the original.

Whenever a new book would be published, each of us in the monastic family would be presented with a copy paid for by our senior American swami and inscribed by the author, our abbot. Sometimes this was our first glimpse of the material, but many of these works appeared serially in the pages of *Vedanta and the West*, the center's bimonthly journal. Was any other "little" magazine ever loved as much by its readership? And was there ever greater disappointment that when, unbelievably, Swami terminated its publication? We used to greet each issue's delivery with an unabashed anticipatory excitement, pronouncing upon the color of the jacket and the number of articles. Numerous shorter ones was the favored format. It was pocket-size and the devotees could carry it off to work, bus or plane. In this brilliant little periodical could be found, for many years, the Vedantic musings of Heard, Huxley, van Druten, Isherwood, John Yale, Dorothy Mercer and Nancy Mayorga — as well as gleanings from the disciples of the Master and speeches and writings by Swami Prabhavananda himself and other swamis of the order. This corpus of material, comprising 32 years of publication, is a mine of spiritual gold and a treasure of recondite information.

Some of us, too, would write for *Vedanta and the West*, as requested by the editors, and there was naturally a special anticipation in the heart when what could easily be one's sole adventure into print was about to appear. But when most of the really good writers, who had addressed themselves to Vedantic themes not only in our publications, but to the world at large as well (witness *The Perennial Philosophy*) had passed on, having made their contributions to the burgeoning interest in mysticism and the East, of the '50s and '60s, times changed. Swami's paramount feeling seems to have been that the journal had played its role.

Swami Prabhavananda's literary accomplishment extends to more than what appears on first examination. In addition to the titles which bear his name as author, there are the two compilations of essays, *Vedanta for the Western World* and *Vedanta for*

Entrance to Ramakrishna Monastery, Trabuco Canyon, California

Modern Man, in the selection and editing of which his hand was present. There is also his indubitable influence in Isherwood's biography, *Ramakrishna and His Disciples*, not to mention *My Guru and His Disciple* and other writings, and in a less direct way in many of the writings of Heard, Huxley and John Yale. He wrote to me in 1958 that Chris was reading aloud to them the first chapter of the life of Ramakrishna he was writing:

"It is excellent. A very dramatic beginning. It grips you immediately. He asked for criticisms from the audience, but all remained silent, spellbound. The only remark was, we wish we could hear the whole life read."

I was not witness, to any extent, to Swami's relations with Gerald and Aldous. The closeness of the former's identification with the Vedanta center was lessening when I arrived and he was withdrawing from Trabuco. For a couple of years, until his untimely death, John van Druten gave us the pleasure of his company now and then. He was open, rather like a child in Swami's presence, one of those "great men" around whom one never felt uncomfortable. His dedicatory speech on the first July 4th at Trabuco was impressive and appreciated. As we sat in the library during this visit — with the two swamis, van Druten and Isherwood present — the question of whether it is possible to write a *successful* spiritual drama was explored. I wish I had taken notes. I recall that van Druten seriously doubted it; his play "The Moon and Sixpence," his own attempt recently staged, had folded.

Christopher's whole story, in spite of his own successive literary exercises in revealing it, is yet to be told. Though he was with us all innumerable times at the center, his visits to Trabuco were few and not of long duration. Of course I treasure those for the opportunity they gave of knowing him well and for catching the sparks from the brilliance of his wit and intellect. I thought of Chris as a good friend and believe he considered me his. He was a delight, and for Swami Prabhavananda a magic formula. We would say today that their "chemistry" was right. It was Chris's conviction that with all the acceptance on Swami's part of this disciple and his controversial nature, a thorough understanding — a complete placing of himself in Chris's point of view — was probably impossible. Whether he was correct, who knows? Not

that this relationship did not cost Swami something. He, however, never shunned anyone anyway, never avoided people, was
never reluctant to be seen in anybody's company.

So stupendous is the contribution of the work and service of Isherwood to Vedanta that whatever detracting aspersion
be cast, whatever handicaps, in the judgment of the world, he
may represent, will have one day to be swallowed up in a sub-
suming acceptance/forgiveness. This will be history's assessment,
I am sure. A letter Swami wrote to me in November of 1963
should dispel any supposition that Isherwood's Vedanta writing
helped to fill his own pocket: "Christopher, Krishnananda [se-
nior American monk of the center], and I will be leaving for
India on Dec. 18th and will arrive in Calcutta on the 21st. Swamiji
Centenary Committee have been urging Chris and me to come
during the Parliament of Religions to be held in Calcutta from
Dec. 30 to Jan. 5. Chris will preside one day and I will have to
preside another day.

"They were even willing to pay for our expenses. I refused to accept, but Chris had to accept because he has no money.
This year he devoted himself completely to finishing writing the
Life of the Master. He did not have time to earn any money for
himself. He is now revising the book and the ms. will be ready
before we leave for India... The publishers in America and England will give substantial advance royalty as soon as they receive the ms. But of course Chris would not accept it — the
Vedanta Society will receive the royalties."

Is it possible to be totally "objective" regarding the nature of one's own drift and leanings? It seems doubtful. While
editing the London magazine *Vedanta for East and West* which, by
the way, had been started with Swami's magazine as an evident
model, I received from Hollywood his letter of complaint about
unorthodoxy, from which this extract: "In your last issue I felt
disappointed to see another article, written by some professor
who suggests *modernizing* Vedanta. And all his ideas seem to me
nonsensical. I would have refused to publish such an ignorant
article. Don't mind my criticism. The scholars (so-called) live in
theories — never apply the truths of Vedanta. Ready to give advice. God bless them." Was he unaware of the extent of his own
bending — perhaps in other directions, but in some sense

modernizing — of Vedanta?

VII. AND SELECTED SHORT SUBJECTS

Reference has been made to a "vacation" at Laguna Beach in which I was included. A very different and much happier one took place in a Southern California resort, Idyllwild, in the San Bernardino Mountains. Swami Prabhavananda went off for a week's rest taking his faithful charioteer (Swami Krishnananda) and me. Two motel accommodations were reserved, a single one for Swami, a larger one across the road with kitchen, for us. In the latter the meals were prepared and eaten. Swami seemed to like my cooking. In the forest calm and seclusion (it was not the peak of tourist season) he was able to walk, catch the fragrance of the pine needles and the sparkle of the lake and view the mountains, go through the newspaper and chat or keep silent as befitted his mood. I wandered off on explorations by myself. We also attended the local movie. At meditation in the morning I would sometimes squat on the front porch of our cabin; on other days I would go over to his porch just to feel nearer to him as he meditated inside. It was a time of monastic fellowship, rapport and blessedness. On one of the first visits he made to the monastery in 1950, Swami had been in a similar playful mood and commented to me, "You are in the right place. You know, you can have more fun with 'Uncle Guru' than with the guru himself, we say in India." (He and Swami Yatiswarananda were brother disciples.) Like going on holiday to Uncle's house, I thought.

The playful Prabhavananda was frequently very much in evidence. Someone, a new arrival, had been expecting somberness and sobriety, silence and suppression as the prevailing atmosphere of monastic life and in surprise brought this to Swami's attention. "Oh," he said, "those things will all come afterward. Don't you remember what Jesus said about the bridegroom being with them?" It was an era when young people still knew what Jesus said!

Christopher's presence often served as the catalyst for this chemistry of play. How Swami enjoyed his wit, his spoofing, his slightly acid comments! There was an annual event, a party held on Fathers' Day in June. Often there was amateur and professional talent and the bellowing-out of old songs in chorus.

Chris would be there and would be asked to sing "his song."
Chris's song was a parody he had concocted to the old tune of
"Bye-bye, Blackbird." "Krishna, jai, jai!" went the refrain.
Ramakrishna, Naren, Keshab Sen, Girish Ghosh, "M." and the
Queen of England are all entwined in those doggerel verses, now
indelibly stamped in the minds and hearts of those exposed to
that classic spoof. It invariably reduced our swami to tears. His
laughter was silent but entire: face streaming and limbs shaking.
It was predictably the same from year to year. As I look back now
it is remarkable how many kinds of things provoked him to smiles
and laughter — and how easily.

It was surely the moment of his utmost candor: "My mission in life," he confessed to a few of us at Trabuco, "is to spread
ananda — joy."

Would one call him truly sophisticated? I would not, as I
think of that word. But he *appeared* to be so — and for Hollywood that was the point. Sometimes he was unintentionally funny,
as when missing an American idiom by a word or two. It delighted us immensely when, in his room one evening, he addressed a brahmachari with a real attempt at seriousness, "If you
don't behave, I'll give you a good kick on the pant!" And again,
at the mention of some troublesome devotee, "She rubs me on
the wrong end." Catching on, he would join in the general hilar-
ity.

In the path of devotion very much is made of the power
and function of the guru and of the disciple's need to be in close
touch with him or her. There, one's personal relationship — its
smoothness, its intensity of feeling and intimacy — is of paramount importance. As he emphasized bhakti, Swami was extraor-
dinarily conscious of his role in this respect. That he *was* personal in his relationships, who would deny? He demanded alle-
giance and expected loyalty. To those who gave it he could be
amazingly warm; yet others seemed just as faithful or devoted
but their greater distance from him was evident. Some he just
never warmed up to. How can we pretend to know the reasons?
I recall a disciple against whom he fretted and fumed. He was
really angry! When I opened my mouth on that person's behalf,
troubling to call his attention to certain sterling qualities, Swami's
voice was dry with the heat of his wrath: "If a few drops of cow's

urine are mixed with the milk, how will that milk taste?" On the other hand, when a new disciple remarked, intending to be jocular, "Swami, I thought there was nothing I could give you; but now I understand: I can give you my karma!"

Swami, smiling: "Yes; who takes whose karma?"

My own experience, however, is one of angelic forgiveness. I gave him unbearable trouble. Disappointed and sore-at-heart, Swami nevertheless sustained his untarnishable faith in the underlying me; his optimistic surety that all would come out right in the end. Years later I was keeping him informed by correspondence of my attempts to adjust to life in India. His love and concern for me and my future well-being are clear here in one of his replies: "I understand Narendrapur [the large educational complex operated by the order south of Calcutta where I was stationed] is the right place for Westerners, healthwise and foodwise. Why do you say it all seems secular? Don't you want to teach the boys?

"There are the other Swamis and Brahmacharis there. Associate with them, and keep up your meditation hours regularly. I hope you will be able to get yourself adjusted. If you find insurmountable difficulties, let me know. Do you have any preference to live anywhere else? Do you have any preference for any kind of service, other than teaching school?

"Please write to me and let me know. Or, you may see Prabhu Maharaj [Swami Vireshwarananda, president of the order] and open your heart to him. You have friends there. Thakur and His Family are your own, your own relatives and friends. You are not amongst strangers nor are you a tourist and a visitor. You belong to the Family of our Lord."

He also shared his private views, as in the letter about his difficulties with the swamis in India, quoted in the first chapter. In spite of the storm which had passed over our relationship, his support for my cause seems to have been automatic: "You should know that I recommended you for *brahmacharya* and *sannyas*. However, what I wrote about sannyas stands as I said. Color your heart and mind in *gerrua* — the emblem of dispassion and egolessness. I am sure President Maharaj will do the best and right thing for you. Surrender yourself to the Lord and Mother and you have nothing to worry about."

My suspicion is that we comprehend very little indeed how deep and numerous were the shocks his heart and mind sustained through the years of guiding and nurturing such a diverse and meandering flock as his. When anyone would "leave" him, he would often drop little one-line private predictions about the apostate's future. The percentage of accuracy of these was high.

During this period of his life Swami Prabhavananda was seldom ill. Obviously he could not have carried on all this activity of center, convent, monastery, correspondence, interviews and creative writing without a strong constitution and the grace of sound health. It was novel for me, because Swami Ashokananda had been ill a great deal of the time; we wondered how he accomplished his works in the face of that handicap. *Will* was once defined for us by Swami Prabhavananda as "a compound of mind and ego." On those few occasions when the Hollywood Swami was seen to be ill, we might notice a peculiar uncanny state in him. He frankly said that it was only when he was sick that he was psychic. Others may view it differently, but I think it fair to say that at other times Swami was not a manifester of the subtle powers. "I have seen quite a few illumined souls," he mentioned once. "The one thing I find outstanding in them all is their *common sense*." Asked sometimes by new arrivals if he read our minds, he would say, "If I read your minds all the time I would go crazy in five minutes." It doesn't mean he couldn't.

Swami Vivekananda once described those who carry out the Lord's public work as being of two types: Some work vertically, as it were, by sitting in one spot and putting their whole energy into the immediate surroundings, while others are horizontalists, moving like the bee over wide areas to carry the pollen from place to place. Swami was one of the former. Once he had settled in Southern California he traveled little beyond his "territory." As his name became well known and Vedanta spread, calls came from all over, and to some of these he responded. As a letter of his of 1968 informed me, "On the fifth of March I fly to Louisville and there someone will meet me to drive me to Hanover College in the State of Indiana. I am scheduled to speak there for two days and hold discussions. The college is paying all my expenses and will pay some honorarium. Krishna will accompany me, and I am back here on March eighth." It was a consequence of the increasing employment of *The Spiritual Heritage of India* as a college text.

Let us close this account with a few incidents related by Swami about the Master and his disciples. For the most part they have appeared in print elsewhere, but he was near to the sources; his words will have an authentic ring:

> When Sri Ramakrishna was kicked by the jealous priest who wished to extract his "secret of magic power over Mathur Babu" [proprietor of the temple, a man who took special care of Sri Ramakrishna], he said of it later something even higher than Christ's "Father, forgive them, for they know not what they do."... He said: "It was my fault, that I could not make him understand" (i.e., that he had no magic formula).
>
> At one time Swami Shivananda [disciple of the Master, and later third president of the order] wanted Swami Premananda [another disciple, manager of the Belur Math monastery] to make some changes in the way he was running Belur Math. It had to do with the way of receiving devotees. Baburam Maharaj [Swami Premananda] gave in to him. But as Mahapurush Maharaj [Swami Shivananda] went to meditate at noon, Sri Ramakrishna appeared to him in an angry and threatening form. He lost no time in going back to Swami Premananda, saying, "No, you run the Math as you wish, please."
>
> Jawaharlal Nehru's wife was a disciple of Swami Shivananda. The poor fellow had to come to Belur Math and sit on a bench while she had long talks with Mahapurush Maharaj, meditated in the shrine room, etc.
>
> A young monk once told Swami Shivananda of his strong desire to study the Upanishads intensively. Mahapurush Maharaj replied, "Why do you want to study the Upanishads? Study our lives: *They* are the Upanishads." If you love one of these great illumined souls (such as the Disciples) the meaning of his life will be revealed to you — this is my firm belief. The inner Upanishad will unfold. That love itself, if strong, is enough.
>
> Struggle, struggle, struggle! You have to *swim* across the ocean of worldliness.
>
> Remember that all help, whether it comes from inside or out-

side, comes from *God*.

Swami Vijnanananda [disciple of the Master] had been the
Jambuvan of the *Ramayana*. Jambuvan was second only to
Hanuman in devotion to Rama. He got the boon of keeping his
body until Sri Krishna appeared on earth, then recognized him as
Rama. Thus when Sri Ramakrishna saw Swami Vijnanananda he
knew he had wrestled with him before, and lost, so asked him to
wrestle again.

(About Swami Subodhananda, a disciple of the Master): When
he came to Sri Ramakrishna the Master asked him, "Are you not a
grandson of Shankar Ghosh?"

"Yes," said the boy, "but how did you know? This is my first
visit here."

"I saw, 30 years before you were born, that you would be
born in that family," answered the Master. (This, Swami heard
from Subodhananda himself; it is not in the books, he said. "One
time Swami Subodhananda was massaging the Master's head. As
he finished, he parted the hair with his hands, then held a mirror
up for the Master to look into. 'Oh, you are making me a Babu!'
exclaimed the Master, laughing.)

Once Khoka Maharaj (Swami Subodhananda) had a high fever and lay in sickbed. But while meditating he had a vision: The
Master came and sat beside him and spoke as follows: "Well,
shall I send some rich people to you, with proper medicines and
care for your recovery and all that?" The Swami replied, "No, let
me keep my fever.'" "What? Why is that? "So that you will come
and sit by me like this."

And here is a little-known episode about swamis in
America:

When Swami Vishwananda arrived in Chicago to take over the
work, he had a dream — a vision, rather. Swami Gnaneswarananda
(his predecessor) appeared to him, and patting Vishwananda's fat
stomach, said, "So, Brother, you have come to take over. Good,
good!" Then Gnaneswarananda turned into a little boy dressed in
gerrua, and at a distance appeared Sri Ramakrishna and Holy
Mother, luminous on a kind of altar. A path of light connected the
little boy to them. He then ran along this path and merged into

the figures on the altar.

One of Swami's most beautiful letters to me must be included: "I am glad to learn that you are happy there and keep yourself busy. That is very good. But do not neglect to meditate regularly.

"Yes, I went to Sacramento [written in 1969], San Francisco and Berkeley. I liked the Sacramento center very much. It has been done with a well-thought-out plan. Swami Shraddhananda has created a wonderful atmosphere there. I enjoyed my visit there.

"...I firmly believe all these Western Swamis should be called back to India and should practice *tapas* for some time. They don't understand what it means to be a Swami. They only want respect and power and authority, forgetting the ideal. To become a Swami is to become a *no-body* - that is the ideal. I want you to remember that. 'Be humbler than a blade of grass.' Give my love to Ghanananda [Head of the Ramakrishna Vedanta Centre, London]."

I am not certain how deep in him ran the stringency of this opinion and the mood it came from; he never carried out such a policy with his own Western swamis, at any rate. It was surely a reflection of the situation which had developed around a particular individual.

For Swami Prabhavananda it was now getting late. In London at the beginning of 1974 I had a letter from Swami Shraddhananda in Sacramento with this news: "I went to Hollywood for three days in the beginning of the year. Swami Prabhavananda looks very frail. He had just completed his 80th year, but his heart is as warm as ever and his mind too is very clear. He was very happy to see me." This helped me to resolve that I must try to meet him as soon as possible on my return to America. It was the spring of 1975 before I could do that. He had reached his 82nd year and beyond when, on a trip to the West Coast, I visited the center in Hollywood after many years. It was vastly changed. Where open lawn had grown, and a neighboring house with its backyard had been, there now stood a sprawling new monastic quarter joined as one structure to the Swami's room and fenced off from public access. I was informed that no personal interviews could be given, such was Swami Prabhavananda's physical condition. With a bit of begging in the right quarter and pleading the distance I had traveled, I got into the room. Swami had read my letter and he greeted me with warmth and his blessing as of old, but it was clear that he was no longer enthusiastic about anything here; he was waiting for "Indra's chariot" (like Elijah in the Bible, ready to "carry one on high"). His face was lined, stiff, his voice lackluster. I stayed but a few minutes, for polite inquiries and to ask a personal question and hear his reply. Then it was announced that Swami would now take his daily walk. Ritual again, here at the end of life, just as there had been all through. He was guided out of his room and down the steps and then with a cane walked unaided, scarcely looking to right or left, outside the fence to receive the salutations of the household and devotees of the community and indicate in the briefest gestures his blessings, and then back in, to circle the inner courtyard. Darshan (in the sense of granting audience, so to speak — an opportunity for the devotees to pay respects) was over for today. Only a few months later, physical darshan was beyond possibility. We who knew him carry another darshan within us. His is the face none of us will be able to forget — ever.

Swami Ashokananda

A BUDDHA AT THE GOLDEN GATE

SWAMI ASHOKANANDA

I. PLUNGING IN

1945. The train took me westward, leaving Philadelphia
and Swami Yatiswarananda far behind. But not in my thoughts.
My small list of "monastic possibilities" held promise and fasci-
nation, new worlds to be discovered. After brief visits to the family and the Vedanta Society in Hollywood and to Trabuco College, still in pursuit of some imagined and illusive ideal, I reached
in late March the Bay Area, which had been home in my college
days before the war. My destination was the San Francisco Vedanta
Monastery.

Little was known about it. In contrast to the Southern
California center, widely exposed to the open skies of publicity
and celebrity, the Northern center seemed appropriately
shrouded in fog. No one had been able to tell me much about
the monastery or its head, Swami Ashokananda. "He's a very
nice man," Gerald Heard had said unhelpfully, when I'd told
him my plans. But this may have been because they had had
such a brief acquaintance. In Philadelphia the swami had mentioned both southern and northern monasteries, also without
details. Lodging with a sister in Berkeley, I investigated. The

waters had to be tested with tentative toes.

It was still a streetcar, then, that took one along Union Street in the Marina District of San Francisco. It dropped me at the corner of Webster and in full view of what I was seeking: across, and down one block, the headquarters of the Vedanta Society of Northern California, known now as the Old Temple. And what a sight it was! "Is *this*," I thought, "to be my monastic home for the rest of my life? How odd!" Yet there was even then a dignity about the place, something indefinable which showed through the unmatched towers and turrets and Victorian gingerbread; which shone through the lath fences and frames, the pillars and quaint dormer windows. In that first untutored impression the feeling came through that here aristocracy was housed — an influence that was not to be trifled with.

The street front presented two doors and I rang at the one marked Monastery, wondering just what it would mean to join one and what in the world I would do if my plea were accepted. A lean man a bit older than I appeared at the door, which revealed a long staircase to the floor above. Clearly he was pleased that I wished to meet the swami and to know about the monastery. I would have to go through the secretary to see Swami, he said; hers was the other door.

She was a beaming, welcoming woman who seated me in a reception room. Above me on one of the walls was an enlarged photograph of an extraordinary face. I could suppose it was a swami, but he was dressed in the clerical collar and black jacket of a Catholic or Episcopal priest. The eyes were luminous.

"Is this a picture of Swami Ashokananda?" I asked, as the secretary was leaving.

"No," she replied, "it's Swami Trigunatita, the first swami here, who started the work."

Presently Swami Ashokananda came in to greet me and I rose. He was of more-than-average height, well-built, with wavy hair about to turn gray, his skin quite dark in color and his eyes bright; he wore glasses and immaculate "sport clothes." There seemed to be just a suggestion of a permanent frown, but behind the eyes, even on that first day, I sensed a kind of mirth going on. I greeted him with a handshake and that seemed to be all he was expecting.

"I am a friend of Swami Yatiswarananda," I said, not disciple or student, for I did not then consider myself initiated. He was very cordial and asked me into his small office. Although he spoke slowly and with dignity, there was none of the embarrassment of silence here that there had been in Hollywood. Giving first a brief history of myself, I stepped out on the tipsy raft of monastic aspiration. He asked a number of pointed questions. The conversation is much clearer in my memory than if it had happened yesterday.

Swami: Are you a vegetarian?

I: Yes, Swami, I have been for a couple of years.

Swami: That's good. Our monastery is vegetarian. Do you practice continence?

I: Yes, sir.

Swami: In thought, word and deed. (He spoke seriously and very slowly with emphasis on each word. His eyes bored holes through me. I gulped, and he continued.)

Swami: Did you like Swami Yatiswarananda?

I: Yes, very much. But he had no place where he could keep me.

Swami: Did he give you any instructions, how to meditate or anything?

I: Oh, he just gave me some general instructions; there was nothing formal about it.

Swami: But how do you know you will like me?

I (embarrassed): Well, I think I know what a swami is — they are all qualified teachers.

Swami: You mean you think all swamis are alike?

I: Yes, something like that.

Swami (flatly): No. All swamis are not alike. Why did you not stay with Swami Prabhavananda in Hollywood?

I (taking all my courage in hand): Because the swami is a slave to his cigarettes!

Swami (starting to laugh): That does not matter. That is not a serious thing. Well, I am afraid you will find many faults in me.

I (now really dismayed): No, no, I don't mean to be critical. I only meant, if the swami cannot overcome this habit, it may not matter for him, but how can he be a teacher?

Swami: Yes. But you must know: Whatever fault you see in another, that fault is somewhere in you.

I: Yes, Swami, so I have read.

There were more questions. In sum, he told me that they did not know me well enough yet. Generally, before giving admission to the monastery a candidate was asked to come around to lectures and classes, etc., for at least a year. I should try to get a room nearby and a part-time job to sustain myself and gradually become acquainted. Moreover, there was at present no room in the monastery quarters for another. He would be holding a class in the Berkeley Temple on Thursday evening, and as I was living over there I could and should attend it.

On that Thursday morning I went to the temple in Berkeley, met the caretaker, a monastic novice, and was shown through the place. The exterior had been familiar enough to me when I used to pass it daily between the campus of the university and my lodgings on the south side, but this was my first sight of the interior. The inner doors of the foyer gave way to a large rectangular auditorium with a very high ceiling. At the rear, over the foyer, was a small balcony for musicians; the congregation faced a grained, hardwood shrine on the dais consisting of a fairly small golden Om surmounting two pictures, the photo of Sri Ramakrishna on one's right, and of Swami Vivekananda on one's left. There were also an altar-like table holding the great scriptures of the world and a lecturer's armchair and lectern. Handsome chandeliers hung from the high ceiling.

I returned in the evening. At a minute or two after eight o'clock Swami Ashokananda entered from a side door dressed in a long reddish-orange robe with a sash at the waist and fasteners all the way up to the neck. With a mellifluous Sanskrit chant he initiated the period of silent meditation. Expounding of the text followed. It took some minutes for my ear to penetrate the heavily accented English and pick up every word, but when I had done so I found the words to be exactly right. I was amazed at the way he tossed around the heaviest philosophical questions and solutions as if it were fun, like a juggler warming up for a performance.

The *Viveka-chudamani* of Shankara, was, I think, the class text; but on this particular evening the main reference, and the subject which captured me, was from another book, the *Drig-drisya-viveka*, in which all the objects of our experience are analyzed as presenting us with five factors. Three of these, Swami Ashokananda explained, giving their Sanskrit names, belong to the Reality; the other two, name and form, to our false understanding of those objects. It is our preoccupation with the names and forms which hides from us the Real, the divine components, of Being, Consciousness and Bliss.

I sat entranced, my mind opening and reflecting by turns, and when the peace chant had concluded the class, I walked out with full awareness that this was the man I had waited my 22 years to meet. "I have found him," I said. "His arguments cannot be refuted." I learned later that among the concepts and teaching of Vedanta, this was one of the swami's favorites, this recognition of the five factors. No wonder he had affected me so much.

Although my heart was not in it, I made a serious attempt to find a room near the San Francisco Temple and made inquiries about part-time work. There was more possibility of the latter than the former. These were war days and the city was crowded. There was no housing of my means in the area. Employment would not be possible without housing, and I had come to the end of my rope. If I could not enter Swami Ashokananda's monastery, that was devastating; if there was no opportunity here, I should have to move on and try in Ojai, of which I had heard. J. Krishnamurti was said to have a religious community in the Ojai Valley. "Do you know about Ojai?" I asked the Swami.

"Yes," he replied. There was a long moment of silence. "All right," he went on, "you come over here with your things, and we shall try to give you some temporary accommodation until you can find a room." With great relief I went and was shown a bed in the living room and told I might stay there for a week while I searched for a room outside. I tried to make my occupancy as inconspicuous as possible.

The search became desultory. Not only did it prove unfruitful, but more and more I felt I would never want to step out of the blessed atmosphere in which I now found myself. It was not that this mood was established at once — by no means. Even in that first week there were days when one felt caged, trapped like a wild animal, and I had to go out of the building and walk quickly around the block. At times my eyes were red and wet, the sense of confinement being more than I could bear.

After several days I had had no further contact with the swami. He lived on the floor above, did not eat with us, and came to our quarters rarely. These first days — nearly a week — were transformed when one morning he came into the living room. "How are you?" he asked, giving the question a tangible sense of concerned affection which, I was to learn, always clung to him. I told him of my recurrent and overwhelming feelings of oppression.

"You see," he commented, looking into my eyes with great sympathy, "you must realize that you are *not* this mind. You are beyond the mind and its caprices." A byword for a lifetime! We suffer only when we forget it and forget it we must not. He said very little more and went on downstairs to his office. The week passed and yet more days. Then came another encounter and he asked, "Well, are you feeling at home here?"

"Oh yes!" I was quick to answer, for things had changed for me. Then no more was said about renting a room or finding a job.

II. THE ABBOT

There were four other residents in Swami Ashokananda's monastery then, on the second floor of the Old Temple. Swami had worked repeatedly on E. C. Brown to retrieve him from the claims of life in the world. Mr. Brown, as he was always called, seemed ancient to us: He had been a disciple and recruit of Swami Trigunatita (head of this Society from 1904 to 1915) and so a member of the first monastery of the order established in the West, in the first decade of the century. The monastic recruits of that enterprising disciple of Sri Ramakrishna had lived a life of austerity and sacrifice difficult for any of us to imagine today. Rising very early, they practiced monastic routines of meditation, yoga and study at the beginning and end of their day of outside employment. One day Swami Ashokananda made a point of telling me, "Whatever you may hear, always remember that this monastery has had a continuous existence from those days. At least one monk has lived here, lived that life in the way that he taught."

We did not go upstairs unless called. Our senior novice was Al, who had constantly to go up and down for he "ran" the monastery as Swami's trusted aide. The hierarchy was built-in: power and authority at the top; the monastery, complete with shrine room, kitchen and dining, below; public hall, offices and devotees on the ground; utilities, workshop and garage in the basement.

"You have created a fortress here," Swami Yatiswarananda had remarked, appreciatively, when he first visited his brother monk.

Swami Ashokananda was appointed to the San Francisco center in 1931 as assistant to Swami Vividishananda. At an early dinner party he had met four of his subsequent inner circle, four who were to become role players in the drama of his 38 years at the center. Al was one, first to renounce and formally enter the monastery. He accompanied Swami in 1934 on the latter's sole visit to India, receiving there and then the novitiate vows — a fact which was not generally revealed for some years. Swami held the opinion that the less others knew about one's own spiritual life, the better off one was.

He used Al as the proverbial whipping boy. In the Indian (and in how many others?) monastic system, those who are close, intimate, are used to teach others who have not yet become so. It is certain that no one else around could have stood the scoldings and chidings heaped upon him, reverberating all the way downstairs and through the narrow hallway of the monastery. Burdened as he was with all the business affairs of monastery and Society, and subject to the monitoring of it all "on the third floor," this man had austerity sufficient to become a saint — and did so. To get complaints through this line of command was not easy, but now and then it happened; one day Swami had to come down and ask us, "Look, who makes all the rules here that I don't make?"

Once I had the temerity to mention to him something resentful of Al. Swami's defense was immediate and pointed. "Yes," he said, granting my point, "but you must remember one thing about Al; when he knows that something is standing in his way spiritually, he gives it up *at once*." It was not that Swami Ashokananda was enamored of hierarchy *per se*, but he respected the necessity and even the elegance of it, if I may say so. He came from roots in the Victorian era. In a lecture he gave, the *aesthetic* value of the monastic code was affirmed.

The young man who had answered my first ring at the monastery door was John, graduate in chemistry from the university. Regular attendee of lectures in Berkeley and San Francisco, John had, only a year previously, renounced under Swami's watchful encouragement, and entrusted his varied talents and bright intellect to the pursuit of Vedanta and the cultivation of potted flowers and plants on the roofs of the temple. Swami gave him some special technical assignments, one of which proved to be John's entire life work in later years: trying to join the "map" of the universe made by physics today and that of the philosophy of Sankhya-Vedanta.

When my permanence was settled I shared the room of an older man, a European émigré, who did not care much for me. He complained to Swami, through Al, that I was calling him by his first name, as I did the others, while in fact, being so much older, he deserved more respect. Swami Ashokananda sent this reply down the pipeline: "Is he prepared to call *him* by his last name?" The man often agitated for an outdoor life, one befitting his own conceptions of what a monastic life should be. It is characteristic of this swami that, remote as he might seem, he was listening. And when, shortly after, the property at Olema was acquired, he remarked in the hearing of all, "What a pity that Mr. B_ left just before we were to get the very thing he most hankered for!" The lesson for us was not lost.

There was also a part-time resident, a tall poetic young fellow, who made his living in the shipyards. He spent nearly every weekend with us, and before long Fran would renounce too. He became one of the founding workers at the Olema Retreat.

Our abbot did not live with us. He took all his meals alone in his kitchen, prepared according to his dietary requirements usually by the women devotees. He was always under the care of one or two physicians and did not shop around. Except for Al he seldom met with his monastic trainees. Yet, through the senior novice every detail of our life was regulated. As I see it now, the purpose was at least threefold: to introduce us to the ways of the

Indian monk, brought up in Hindu society; to prepare us for any future visit or stay in India, where things would be very different, and to make "gentlemen" of us in our own culture, with the day in view when we might have to take on a more public role. As Swami once told us, explaining why he almost never sent his "boys" out to visit other Vedanta centers, "Before you can go visiting you have to learn how to behave." True, but in his day that proficiency was evidently never attained and it seems to have been a hallmark of this first generation of monastic founders to prefer not to expose the tender green plants to the unfamiliar winds of other training methods. As one who subsequently flew in the face of this tradition I can easily see that the policy cut two ways: It fostered stability in a man; it also made him insular.

My picture of Swami Ashokananda in that first year was that of a gigantic being full of strength and power, dignified, a little formal in manner and approach, inwardly intensely affectionate, demanding much, giving much; stern and uncompromising outside, yet ready to do his all to protect us from any sort of injury. Jehovah in all his might could not have borne the wrath of Swami aroused; but, as Al often said, he was to us like a mother hen brooding over her chicks.

Swami ran a tight ship. Rising daily before five and showering at once was mandatory. It was a tricky procedure by which you arranged things so that you were ready for your turn at the one shower in this old-fashioned bathroom, and that, too, had to be quick. We had clothes set aside for the shrine room only; it was a question of getting into them and to one's place on time. After 45 minutes of group meditation we dispersed to our rooms, changed clothes and began individual reading. One was not permitted to go back to bed. Breakfast was at 7:30 and was ample, and if a scripture class (with which I shall deal in a later section) was being held, it took place then. All the remainder of the morning was devoted to study. Swami told us, "Maharaj (Swami Brahmananda) told Swami Yatiswarananda that when for some reason the mind cannot meditate or make japa, *study* is the thing to fall back on." He asked me to begin with the *Upanishads*, and one day inquired what I was reading. When I told him he said, "Yes. Don't just 'read' — *study*." And we knew what he meant: to take all the ideas apart the way he did.

Daily worship at the shrine was another of Al's duties, and lunch had to be prepared; otherwise manual work began in the afternoon. There was no napping or resting; we set right out for shopping, gardening, housecleaning or maintenance. We laundered, took care of Swami's personal service, watered the innumerable flowerpots and were expected back in our rooms quieting the mind by reading, half-an-hour before the evening service. Again meditation in the shrine room for all but the cook of the day. After dinner the last hour of the day was a group reading for which we chose some "lighter" book, such as lives of the incarnations and saints, passing it from hand to hand. Swami felt that no heavy study or deep thinking was appropriate before bedtime. "Eat well, sleep well, work well," he used to tell me. He took me to task in the very first week for eating too light a break-fast. "I hear that you eat two prunes!" he smiled. "You are going to build up spiritual power and that comes from food. Food is Brahman. So eat!" I had supposed that a small appetite was the sign of spirituality.

Reading was replaced by music one evening a week. There was a fair selection of the old 78 rpm's and an hour's program was made up by the one whose turn it was to choose, and turn, the records, and we all listened. All the music was Western and all classical. Swami Ashokananda believed we ought to keep our roots in our own culture and enjoy and be inspired by those things which had been meaningful to us, provided they were elevating. It is amusing to us now, but in true monastic fashion, solos by the female voice were discouraged! No sirens wanted.

Whenever anyone came into the monastery to live, or later, moved from one branch to another, Swami would ask him to rest — i.e., not undertake any definite schedule for a couple of days; for one who was into the 'grind' this could be austerity.

In those days we always saluted our abbot with the *namaskar*, palms together at our chest, when he approached or dismissed us, and we addressed him as "Swamiji." The first time he handed something to me — a book, I think — I began to extend my left hand. He quickly drew back and widened his eyes in that gesture of correction we knew so well. "The right hand," he said firmly. Another day I left my desk briefly and returned to find the opened book closed. Of course my place was lost; it was a flat book; how had it happened? Then I heard Swami's footsteps going on down the stairs to his office. He had walked past the room for some reason, seen the open book on the desk and shut it. The message was clear: Take care of your books and don't leave them open. We learned to see that he cared, in one way or another, about every little piece of material existence, but just why he did was not yet clear to me.

One morning someone failed to water a plant and he noticed it. "Did I not ask you to keep that plant watered?" Swami addressed the novice. "If you do not carry out such instructions you will regret it later. I once neglected to do something Swami Brahmananda assigned to me; to this day I am regretting that lapse." Naturally, by putting himself into the same category much of the sting was taken out.

On the matter of personal money Swami showed his firm adherence to the traditions. There was a cash box from which necessary purchases were made, listed, accompanied by receipts. We were not required or permitted to keep personal funds with us. From me Swami received my savings and insurance policy, putting them into safety deposit. When clothes were needed, they were bought by the Society. Swami Ashokananda disapproved of his monks wearing cast-off clothing used by people in the world, and asked us to be neat and respectably fitted-out, as he always was, in the mode proper to San Francisco at the time.

If our common life was regulated in this way, even more so were matters relating to the shrine room. The worship ceremony itself was brief, very simple. But the shrine and everything around it was scrupulously cleaned daily. The care exercised over items to be offered may be regarded today as bordering on the fanatical. There was a bench outside the room reserved for things pertaining to the shrine exclusively. This bench happened also to be located at the top of the first stairway. There was no more logical place for an unsuspecting workman to throw down his hat, or a first-visit college lad to set his textbooks. The bench had to be cleaned again. Eternal vigilance was the price of purity; moreover there was to be no posting of signs.

"The Four Pillars of Monastic Life" and Swami Vivekananda's principles in founding our order formed the subject of one morning's class. They must be included in our purview.

The Four Pillars of Monastic Life

I.   Spiritual Exercises — includes meditation, offering all deeds, speech and thought to the Lord, worship

II.   Character — includes moral virtues as well as virtues of will, determination, self-control

III. *Vidya* (Learning) — includes philosophical and psychological as well as spiritual; also cultural, economic, etc.

IV. Conduct — includes behavior; renunciation of ego; courtesy, monastic code, respect to guru and seniors, non-resistance

Swamiji's Principles and Plans in Founding the Order

1.   To have a college in the monastery

2.   The study of Sanskrit, particularly because it contains the most spiritual writings

3.   The study of science, lest we become antiquated, removed from modern knowledge

4.   Service to man by up-to-date methods, lest we become cut off from the stream of life

5.   Liberal policies — women to be freely admitted; obedience not super-strict

6.   All religions and paths (even future varieties) should be included and represented in the monastery, if not by each individual, then collectively

"No religious teacher," Swami Ashokananda remarked in closing the class, "has so well understood all the affairs of mankind."

"A monastic order exists," he pointed out on another occasion, "to train men or women to realize God; but it is not so simple as that. We must also conserve spiritual power and tradition for future generations. The current of spiritual wisdom follows the 'water law' — you can draw your share, but must not impound it. A great spiritual figure establishes a *sampradaya* [reservoir of spiritual power, working through an order]."

Any men's order interested in this continuity must formulate a policy regarding men-women relations. Swami Ashokananda had, after careful consideration, drawn his lines. In our American social life we had not encountered these and

had to get accustomed to them. Nor were they always spelled
out; it was an attitude, a mentality one soon learned to cultivate.
The devotees were there, in all the work of the ground floor —
arranging flowers, cleaning, doing office and magazine work —
and points of contact were inevitable. Moreover, John and I were
sent weekly to the Berkeley Temple, bag lunches in hand, to work
in the elaborate garden run by a master gardener and her helpers, some of them young girls aspiring to the life of the convent.
The work was the important thing; our relationships were limited to that. Other conversation was just not necessary. After a
time it became automatic. In the attitude Swami asked us to cultivate there was no discourtesy, no belittling or aversion. He made
one feel that everyone is worthy of respect, an embodiment of
divinity and to be treated as such. So there was no question of
scorn. And he built up from both sides, imbuing the minds of
the householder devotees also with the respect and awe accorded
even the newest of those who had renounced. Except for special
cases, the monks and the women (lay and monastic) did not
"know" each other in the manner of some centers, but they knew
about each other. A very subtle intimacy wove together the fabric
of Swami Ashokananda's extended family, though on a very high
plane indeed; for me, at least, it was a fact.

    This did not happen overnight. At one of the first evening
lectures in that first year, I had listened, charmed, to a violin
duet played at the service by a girl devotee and her teacher. A
musician's curiosity welling up in me, I walked from the back
bench where the monastery was supposed to sit all the way down
the aisle to the organ to ask the girl what piece it was they had
played. Swami was waiting for me on my return.

    "Why did you talk to that girl?" His ability to convey dis-
approval greatly exceeded his display of approval, and it came
out through his mouth, his eyes, his nostrils, the color of his
face.

    "To ask what the music was, Swamiji." I swallowed hard.

    "You are a brahmachari. You are wanting to be a monk!
Do you think you can do it if you do things like that? Never do
such a thing." I was stung. I had gone down so innocently. My
mind cried to me, "Unfair! What a small thing to worry about!"
I went off at once to bed with a hard lump in my throat and my

eyes red. But he for his part knew how many eyes in that auditorium had been upon us, and his training was merciless. I had yet to learn that, living around this swami, I would never find anything to be small again.

With our relatives, it was a case of breaking the attachment to family, an essential of the life. Relatives, if they wished to see us, were to come to the temple; that was the general rule. Each case he handled differently, and when a parent could not travel the man was sent there, but not for long and not often. Correspondence with family and old friends was not much encouraged. He did not want the disconnecting, however, to be done precipitately. One day he came to me and told me, "I have a letter from your mother. It seems you are writing home these fiery letters, picking a quarrel with all of them? Look. It is good to be full of renunciation, but one should not go around belaboring others with it. Don't you know what Sri Ramakrishna says about honoring the mother? Be firm, but be gentle, be tactful. Don't write more than you have to, and try to keep them in good humor."

I mentioned the Berkeley Temple garden. It is my conviction that it was an enchanted place. Before the Olema property was acquired, this garden was Swami's principal *tapovana*, his *karma-kshetra*, the field where the devotees could serve the Lord through hard and exacting work, building up their store of merit and expiating old sins. It was charged with the dynamic energy of six or eight eager and self-sacrificing souls, and provided them with visible short-term goals to achieve and enjoy. It was also supervised and cherished by Swami with the same kind of love for the plants that he had for his "children."

All that he had heard about Swami Vivekananda, all he had read and all he must have received through his unceasing meditation on him, must have gone into making up Swami Ashokananda's methods of training. He was uncompromising about what was expected of the candidate. So had Swamiji been. In a lecture Swami told us, "You think *I* am harsh; if you had been around in the time of Swami Vivekananda, you would have run away, such was his fire." We certainly didn't need it any hotter! But he was also ready to pour out affection and approval to the deserving and often the two dispensations were mixed together. One day I was to work with Al on some potted plants on the top roof. This was the exalted spot from which one could look all around on the world below: to the north, Marin County with its hills, mysterious Alcatraz Island holding its prisoners; beyond on the left, the Golden Gate itself, its majestic bridge emerging from the Presidio; to the right, Coit Tower, the Mark Hopkins Hotel — just peeking through a truncated view; and behind us the hill, a skyscraper of apartments rising above Pacific Heights and the spot of land already owned by the Vedanta Society and waiting for a new temple to be built upon it. It was glorious to be up there at all.

As I arrived on the scene, Al was in trouble for something or other and getting a dressing-down. Others were used to this, but I was new. As I listened to the verbal tirade I was amazed to detect, behind the words and the tone used, a deep-running river of affection and blessing. It was visible in Swami's eyes as well. Seeing me now, Swami turned, looked me up and down, and dropping completely his angry mood, addressed me in purring tones. "Don't you polish your shoes?" he asked. "It is not for vanity; it actually helps to preserve the leather." Like writing on the surface of water, is the anger of a realized soul — so the Hindus say.

On one of those occasions when he came to my room and spoke about the heritage of this monastery, he told me how hard Swami Trigunatita had worked and struggled to build up its traditions and what we owe to him; how unorthodox he had been, in some ways, how ascetic, austere yet loving; how every successor should try to change the patterns he inherits as slowly and as little as possible, in order to keep up the continuity of a center and make all older devotees feel that the values were being preserved. I am sure that all this had much to do with the way he masked with external severity his love for his monastics. In the later years he talked with me in an open, conversational way quite different from that of the first year. Others who were not privy to his ways surely saw those upbraidings as very grim affairs and despaired for the young men and women in training. Swami's very dear friend, Swami Vividishananda (then of Seattle) while visiting us one summer, said to our Swami after one of these scathing rebukes, "I plead for your students, Swami; you are so hard on them!"

"Swami," was the prompt reply, "it is true, but if they can stand me they can stand the world." Man-making was for him, as for Vivekananda, his highest priority. One saw here too the sannyasin's renunciation at all levels: Stand still, listen to the intent, give no excuses or back talk. "Give up this self-justification *forever*," he had told Al.

Such a thorough overhaul of living and thinking habits appears not to have been employed elsewhere in our Western centers even at that time, not to speak of today. I once described it to a casual inquirer as the fast track to God, if you can stay on. The subjection of the mind to the constant buffeting of external and internal reminder and restraint forces it to move out of the throes of *tamas* — laziness, inattention — to the gradual reclaiming of all facets of one's consciousness and conduces to the acquisition of that total awareness, the goal of all *sadhana* (the practice of spiritual disciplines). The consequent stress must be under the constant care and wisdom of the true guru. There is a best method, then, for every teacher. Swami Prabhavananda expected his monastics to achieve the same result on their own, through the deepening practice of japa and meditation, without "external" pressures, producing less habitual stress. Then the question becomes: Left to ourselves, do we get motivated to pull on the bootstraps? Certainly some did.

Al often had to finish the ritual before commencing a hectic day of business for the Society. One day it happened that Swami and I were alone in the house, others being already out on errands. Swami would have to do the worship. Something told me this was an opportunity not to be lost, and leaving my study I made a quick change to shrine clothes, went in and sat for meditation — and observation. Swami made no acknowledgment of my presence. Probably some preparations had been done for him. He was dressed just in his sport clothes and he finished the preparations. I wish I could report on how he performed the ritual, but at that time I knew nothing of those details. I did notice that as he waved the joss stick he kept his mouth open; later I learned he was breathing through his mouth lest he should savor the incense before it reached the Lord.

His meditation was unforgettable. He sat on the mat with

eyes closed and hands resting together on his lap; gradually his breathing became slower until I could not detect, strain as I might, that he was breathing at all. In this way Swami Ashokananda remained for a long time, until the "vibrations" in the room seemed to intensify so much I thought my head would burst. When his meditation was finished, he gave a deep sigh and then concluded the ceremony. We were ready at the same moment to leave the room. I thought surely he would go out first, but he paused, waiting for me to leave, and then came out. His teachings on worship are given in an appendix.

In those years he was performing the worship at each public festival, wearing the long lecture robe. Following the puja, Swami would sit on the platform to the left of the deity and chant while the devotees offered flowers. From the *Upanishads* and from the *Chandi* especially, he would go on and on. What an atmosphere it created! He was caught up in the festival mood and everything about him became magnified, as it were. His wit was sharper, his strength amplified, his interest in all around him keener, his love more warm and wide. He sometimes used these occasions of birthday celebration to take new steps in the Society's development, or give someone special attention. It was just at the close, for example, of Sri Ramakrishna's birthday festival, that he informed me of my assignment to special nursing for a period in the city of New York. But Swami also did a splendid job of puncturing sentimental balloons. One morning a devotee, more effusive than most, told Swami Ashokananda how thrilled she had been at the puja on the previous day. "Oh Swami," she bubbled, "I was simply in ecstasy! The vibrations just lifted me out of myself, they were so high!"

"Oh? And how do you feel today?"

"Oh, I don't feel anything today," she replied.

"The vibrations are even higher today," Swami said.

A man once told him that when he sat up near the front during Swami's lectures he saw amazing visions, etc. Swami told him in that case he should sit farther back in the hall.

Dignity was the watchword, even when humorous situations arose, none of which were lost on him. He rarely broke into loud or unrestrained laughter with his novices but was witty in a dry, subtle and ironic way. One affair was that of the double ceiling. He had asked John about the construction of a part of the temple building. The background of this was that, since coming into the monastery, John had undergone numerous humiliations — instances when, with all of John's scientific training and considerable practical experience, Swami had somehow been better informed or a jump ahead and had been proven correct in every contention. (John would sometimes quote to us Mr. Brown's great sigh of resignation: "God is always on the side of the swamis.") On this occasion the question was: Did a certain room have a double ceiling? He asked John to prove his assertion that it did. Swami was quite sure it did not. Crawling into a hole somewhere, with a flashlight, John demonstrated his knowledge of the facts. Swami Ashokananda appeared, for a moment, nonplused — then very quietly and resignedly said, "I see that you are right — as usual."

There was more laughter downstairs on the ground floor, where the "women workers" got a different sort of training. I will speak more of it later. He could be sarcastic. He once asked a novice to see that something belonging to him was returned. After a few days he inquired of the lad whether he had brought the item back to his, Swami's, room.

"Why, Swamiji, I left it here yesterday on this newel post (of the banister of the stair), thinking you would pick it up on your way up!"

"Do you think," said the Swami, his eyes popping and twinkling simultaneously, "that I live on this newel post?"

"No, Swamiji." Head bowed, heart lifted.

III. THE TEACHER

In India the genius of Swami Ashokananda's speaking and writing had been well recognized. As editor of the journal *Prabuddha Bharata* he had inspired the English-reading public to a keen anticipation of the next editorial, bound to enlighten, provoke or inspire. Dr. S. Radhakrishnan is said to have remarked, on hearing of the swami's assignment to the West, "It is a pity; India is losing one of her most original thinkers." Swami's discourses in the auditoriums of the Old Temple or Berkeley Temple were without comparison. He spoke on a wider variety of subjects than any other swami in the West, perhaps, ranging from the highly metaphysical (Vedanta and *Sankhya* — another of the traditional six *darshanas* of Indian philosophy) through the biographical and out to the secular contemporary scene (War and the Rise of the Universal Man, What Shall We Accomplish in the New Year?).

One habit of his seemed scandalous to people outside his orbit, but it was also the pride and delight of his devotees: He would speak for a minimum hour-and-a-half, often two. He really lost track of the time — and, when it came to his attention, ignored it. He had a topic to develop and it had to be done in the round. Rarely using any note or written quotation, he brought it all out from inside, *extempore*. Asked how he could do this, week after week, year after year, he replied, "You forget that I have been thinking about these subjects over many years." The audience was smaller on Wednesday nights, but on Sunday mornings a packed hall of 175 persons would sit, with overflow standing at the back and on the stairs, in breathless silence for nearly two hours, entranced.

In the case of the great teaching swamis I have known, the gurus, there seems to be a venue, a channel, or perhaps two, through which each distributes divine power, passing it along to the disciples and devotees. In one it may be through meditation, as others sit in his presence; in another, it may be through personal service, intimate contact, self-effacement; or rituals. Swami Ashokananda, I felt, used mainly two channels to make known this *guru-shakti*: the public discourses and involvement in the work of the center. He used a blend of jnana yoga and karma yoga, whose interdependence he illustrated with the example of taking a palanquin to the river for your bath. You can use the palanquin (karma) to get to the river, but then you must get out of the palanquin (jnana).

It is rather a pity that Swami lived into the age of tape recordings. They do him no justice, first, because his accent was strong and for many, required repeated exposure, although others had no difficulty at all. When the visual element is there, that handicap is more easily overcome. Second, the new equipment required the swami to stand still at the lectern whereas his natural style was to pace, like Swami Vivekananda, back and forth along the edge of the platform. Third, today's listeners are tested by a long speech, stripped of the movement, gesture, facial expression and personal presence.

The majestic bearing, the musical and resounding voice, the lion-like pacing as he elaborated a point, the use of his hands — all went to compose the drama. Just when things were becoming intense there might come a sudden pause — a joke, a tangential story or an abject confession — something to let everyone breathe once more. I well remember the instance when he suddenly spoke very softly, leaned over to the audience while discussing devotion and confided, "You know, God is a sucker for love." In 1945 in San Francisco there were still a few who, long ago, had heard Vivekananda and used to say that hearing Swami Ashokananda was nearer to it than anything else they had experienced.

It used to be said of another swami that whatever happened to be the subject announced, it always came out "God." In the case of Swami Ashokananda it came out Advaita - nondualistic. He always ended on a monistic note. Strength, self-effort, the need for same-sightedness, seeing God in all, the utter independence of the soul, the fact of man's divinity and potential for enlightenment, the needless delusion of ignorance — these formed the notes of the scale from which he would modulate and to which he would return. In discussing humility, for example, he gave an unexpected assessment: "Humility does not mean becoming a doormat; it means seeing greatness in others." The hidden implication, of course, is that since we are all involved with one another, if we learn to see the greatness in others, we cannot but be aware of greatness in ourselves, whatever the language we use.

Listeners were much moved, even overwhelmed by the swami's speaking. At one period I simply could not avoid the embarrassment of tears streaming down my cheeks — and I was not alone.

After the talk, Swami would stand to receive those waiting to greet him. Most would shake hands, or use the palms-together salutation; whatever the style, he would reciprocate. But he did not like the Indian custom of respectfully touching another's feet. Forbidding his Western students to do it, he resisted the attempts of unfamiliar Indian visitors to "take the dust" of his feet. He told us, the novices, "You are Western men. You are independent and have self-esteem. Why should you demean yourselves to do something totally unnatural to you?"

When he spoke on the great personalities, the incarnations, Holy Mother or any of the disciples of Sri Ramakrishna, he made each come to life enthrallingly because he had heard and remembered many personal details from his own life and the lives of his friends. Here, however, he had a little trick he used, which some of us discovered, of relating something about "a friend of mine," where he evidently felt it inappropriate to tell the experience in the first person. Such would be the devotion and force of appreciation for the personality being discussed that the listener might be inclined to wonder: Is Buddha, then, or Shankara dearer to the swami than his own Sri Ramakrishna? When the next lecture on the latter came around Swami would lay to rest the ghost of any such suspicion. Point after point would be piled up in his thesis that Ramakrishna was, after all, the greatest of the great. Ramakrishna's going into samadhi under certain *bhavas*, i.e., specific spiritual influences, he explained on one such occasion, was a sign of his mind's tendency to *soar above* that plane or aspect, not to stay in it. His mind was not caught for long by any bhava, but rose by nature to the highest if he was not careful. "The Master's problem," he used to remind us, ironically, "was just the opposite of ours — he had to learn to keep his mind down."

No one doubted that public speaking took a great deal out of Swami Ashokananda. It was well known to the seasoned students that he had a chronic duodenal ulcer. He seldom mentioned it but we knew there was no means of predicting when it would act up and interfere with his plans for the day. It was rarely, if ever, allowed to disturb a public class or lecture. Poking a finger into his abdomen now and then, he must have risen above the pain. More of this was seen as the years went by; then we knew the soldier was on a forced march.

The life of Swami Vivekananda, every detail of it, and his utterances, were the food of Swami's lifelong and continuous perusal, probing and pondering. He called himself Swamiji's disciple and aroused controversy thereby. He had not met Vivekananda in the flesh; nonetheless, he reckoned him as his

guru, not only in the general way we might all use the term "fol-
lowers," but as having received the great swami's *diksha*, initiation, during meditation. In an experience of extraordinary viv-
idness he felt the transmission of power from Swami Vivekananda
into his own being. In the lectures printed and circulated at the
end of his life, Swami Ashokananda gives his own account of that
experience and its validation. He seemed at times — in his lectures, in his personal instructions to students — to be but an
outer shell, a mannequin whose animator was Swamiji.

Let me include here a few fragmentary notes of Swami
Ashokananda's talks, that they not be lost from the record.

From "*Swami Vivekananda, Prophet of the New India,*" *a lecture
of 1945 or 1946:*

It is the speaker's conviction that Swamiji regarded the two phrases
of the vow taken by members of the Order as one whole, in spite
of the "and." (They are, "for one's own deliverance and for the
welfare of the world.") This is not the view of a number of monks
of our Order and elsewhere; it was not Shankara's view. But it is
likely that the ideal of non-action for an illumined soul was not
seen in India so much before Shankara. Witness the wonderful
movement called Buddhism! The Master's disciples had two
motives for their intense spiritual practice after his passing: to
become established in their realization of the Truth, and the loss
of the Master made them dive deep to find him *within*. It was a
great emotional shock.

Swamiji was a great scholar — don't be fooled. Don't judge
by the *Complete Works*. He purposely simplified things. And just
note Sister Nivedita's reactions and remarks, learned woman as
she was. See the subjects on which he spoke in America, only the
titles of which were recorded.

Did he not teach everything, all paths rather than just mo-
nism? Did he not accept everything? We will admit this, but after
accepting all that, he always reminded us of man's true Self.

Note from a class on Swami Premananda's birthday:

Swamiji was the only one authorized by Sri Ramakrishna *to
preach*. Sri Ramakrishna did not have any special message as such.

His life was his "message." Again, his message was Swamiji. In the *Gospel of Sri Ramakrishna* we find what he (the Master) said to those who came to him; they had already the Hindu religion and were traveling in those paths and he helped them. But the coming of an Avatar — do you understand what it means, in terms of all the problems of mankind? How comprehensive, how inclusive, how powerful must that message be? *That* he gave through Swamiji. Swami Premananda used to say that the Master could *not* be understood except through Swamiji and he said that he himself was "a disciple of Swamiji."

Note from a class talk:

Swami Turiyananda used to say that Swamiji was *always* in the transcendental plane, even when he joked and made fun. Never was a man so full of God. Swami Shivananda said Swamiji's pillow would be wet, many nights; the former often saw him put it out in the sun to dry.

Note from a class talk:

Just after Swamiji's death, Holy Mother wrote to a monk at Belur Math (the central monastery), "There is now not so much power at the Math; so you all must live very carefully."

Someone once remarked with surprise that Swami Ashokananda spoke more often of Vivekananada than of Ramakrishna. The reasons are not far to seek, as shown above. He felt that Ramakrishna's life was in every way extravagant — in its spiritual range, in the extraordinary manifestations of un-imaginable, encyclopedic experiences and the uniqueness of its purity — that it could hardly serve as example or model for us to essay. Vivekananda's was a more "normal" history and pattern of living, better available to us at our level. He would also quote the well-known dictum of Swami Vivekananda: "He led that great life and I read the meaning." He also told his brother disciples, "So long as I am on earth, Sri Ramakrishna works through me." Swami Ashokananda lived, breathed and bathed in Swamiji and built his life around the task of expressing him, but there was not in him any doubt about who was the incarnation.

Shortly after the day when I was told I might remain at 2963 Webster Street, Swami announced that he would begin to hold class after breakfast on weekdays, on the Sanskrit text *Vedantasara* by Sadananda. Recently this had been translated and published by Swami Nikhilananda of New York and portions of the translation brought out in the *Voice of India*, the Northern California center's periodical. Swami Ashokananda presented a copy of the book to each of us, asking us to read the verses in advance each day and to memorize the English as we went along. At the same time we were expected to take notes on what was said. If anyone neglected to do so he was gently advised that such notes would be useful to him later, something which indeed proved true for me.

Swami would read a *sloka* (verse) in Sanskrit and the translation, frequently finding it necessary to change the latter where he found it insufficiently literal. Literary factors were not in his mind. Then came the questions. "Don't ask me questions," he said at the outset, "I will ask them of you." He took up a phrase: "One only without a second," the text read. "Why is it necessary for the author to say both 'one only' and 'without a second?'" Swami would put his question to an individual at one side of the class, and if the reply did not satisfy him completely (it rarely did) he would gaze expectantly with his large eyes on the next man in line, to hear *his* answer, and so on around the semicircle until he got the whole answer with all the connotations he wanted. Only if it was still necessary would he add anything to the picture himself. It was his firm conviction that each of us had the divine knowledge within him, requiring only the right stimuli and moment to bring it forth. He did not pump knowledge into us, but only drew it out. If it would not come out now, we were left in such a stew of bemusement and self-examination that if we could sort things out they would never be the same for us thereafter.

In this process I learned more about myself and about Vedanta than in any other sadhana of any kind, before or since. I recall not only questions I had to answer, but those put to others also, and how it challenged them, turning dark pockets inside out, exposing typical weaknesses of thought, leaving the mind expanded. It was not brainwashing, but a washing of our brains.

Swami Ashokananda would get into the class mood if he was feeling well and seemed to enjoy it in a subtle way, his body rocking slightly in the armchair; his swaying was like the gentle movement of a great cobra resting erect. His voice became then very mellow, full of blessing. He seemed almost to play with our minds like a cat with a mouse. Once he was heard to say, while in this mood at a public class in Berkeley Temple, "I am just basking in the love of my devotees" — a most intimate thing to reveal, and for him, extraordinary. The following is a fairly typical monastery class exchange.

My turn came first and he asked, "What are the states of consciousness?" I replied apologetically that I had not studied that yet. "Tell me from your own experience!" he cried. The next question was, "Do you believe the soul has a past and a future?"

"I think so," I said uncertainly.

"Hut! Think so!" He glared. Then: "You see, it is all right to have tentative ideas, but not good to have vague ideas. Think everything out carefully." This "hut!" was a favorite expletive with him, used when someone was being a dolt or the reply failed to please him. He liked conviction. He would frequently ask me if I was feeling better, for I had chronic headaches. But often I was not very sure of that and would say, "I believe so, Swamiji," and this too would elicit a "hut!" In class one morning when I was unable to sustain my line of argument, he broke into a broad smile. "He is cornered," he said.

One day we received the monastery copy of the center's journal, *Voice of India*. This magazine appeared every two months; mimeographed, it sold from the book table and by subscription. It was a curiosity, being the first such journal I had seen in which every article except lecture transcripts was presented anonymously. Copies of the *Voice of India* are so rare now that it may be worthwhile to describe it in some detail. Al told us the history of it. In 1938 and 1939 Swami Prabhavananda and Swami Ashokananda were the editors. In 1940 the former had made plans to bring out his center's own magazine, and gave it the title *Vedanta and the West*. The name *Voice of India* was then used in 1945 by Swami Ashokananda for the Northern California journal.

A professional editor had come on the scene with whom

Swami was working closely. It was my privilege that summer to observe some of this work going on at the cabin at Lake Tahoe, and to discover, not very surprisingly, that the final form of every article was given by that erstwhile editor, Swami himself. The quality of the journal became widely noticed. But impressed as I may have been by my first encounter with it, I was unprepared for the many references made to the *Voice of India* in subsequent years by people all over the country who had been readers or subscribers. Some of the titles in one issue alone will give the reader an idea of what a compendium of history, philosophy, hagiography and poetry it was:

> *Buddha's Message to the World*
> *To the Fourth of July (A Poem)*
> *The Rig-Veda as the Source of Vedanta*
> *The Virus of Bigotry*
> *O Mother, Fearful, Beautiful (A Poem)*
> *India Transforms Islam*
> *Bayazid, Who Lost Himself in God.*

With the acquisition of the properties at Olema and Sacramento, Swami Ashokananda's time and energies were transferred to these channels; the production of the magazine halted and never resumed. A total of eleven issues had been distributed, from January of 1945 to November of 1946.

Early in his monastic life, while at Mayavati editing *Prabuddha Bharata*, Swami, using the *nom-de-plume* "Ananda," wrote the book *Spiritual Practice*, one of the few books in our literature to deal in detail with the way to live a life of renunciation *in the world*. Yet Swami regarded it as the product of an insufficiently mature period of his life and sometimes would discourage the reading of it, as it lacked the ripeness of his years in the West as learner, teacher and guru. He also made a translation, now in print and selling well, of the *Avadhuta Gita*.

Within the final decade of his life he allowed a few special lectures to be brought out in a private printing under his own editing, in booklet form. These are "Worship of the Spirit by the Spirit"; "Spiritualizing Everyday Life"; three personal reminiscence lectures, "Swami Brahmananda," "Swami Premananda"

On the porch of the Tahoe cabin

and "Swami Shivananda"; an intimate and fiery lecture, most appreciated locally, "Swami Vivekananda in San Francisco"; and finally his most important, definitive statement, the set of three bearing the collective title "My Philosophy and My Religion," now published under the title "When the Many Become the One." This last, widely read and admired, is even now carried about by some of his students like a bible.

Swami Ashokananda was an original. A number of his pronouncements and replies to queries, while not "heretical" certainly, were surprising — distinctive in flavor, not the party line. Let me give a few examples and defer for now any extended discussion of what constitutes his originality:

"Mind may be defined as the sense of otherness."

"Liberation does not mean that you will *not* come back to this earth; it means you will not come back involuntarily. One may choose to return."

Q: How could there be seven sages meditating in the "realm beyond form," as Sri Ramakrishna describes his experience of going there in search of (the future disciple) Naren?

A: There seems to be an area where there are no forms yet it is not the Absolute. Besides, there is a view that there are two "worlds" even beyond Brahmaloka, the highest heaven. Maybe the Master saw these sages on the edge of the Relative, not in the Absolute.

Swami: "Why do children always put things in their mouths and often swallow them? I think it is due to the natural tendency to want to put inside what seems to be outside. What does it mean, in the *Kathopanishad*, to turn the eyes inward? It means that the forces which are usually employed through the senses are gathered into the mind itself, becoming detached from the senses. There is the case of the mountain climber who suddenly rises above the clouds. Trying to ignore the Spirit is like trying to cover fire with paper! Truly higher powers *cannot* be used for lower purposes."

"Vedanta is not a theology because it has no dogma, no speculation. God is truly real — that is, he can be an object of perception. Then that perception must be of use to us — otherwise it is no different from hallucination. We must *know* Reality, but also must *enjoy* it. The next question is, how long can we enjoy it?"

"Matter can be defined as the ultimate in the sense of finitude. It is creativity that suffers most from this superficiality. So it is said that the individual (who *is* a product of superficiality) has not the power of creation. *Srishti-drishtivada*, the position that we see what has been created, is 'objective idealism': I feel small here. *Drishti-srishti-vada*, (we actually create what we see) is a higher view: To perceive is to create. This is the soul, or, in the third person, God. In either case, power is needed — in the first, power to reach Union, in the second, power to stand alone. Understand the hierarchy and evolution of power: Lowest is the power to achieve; middling, the power to resist; highest, the power simply to *be*." This description of power in its three forms was one of Swami's favorite analyses.

Another of his analyses was the *Stages in Spiritual Practice*:
(1)   Adjustment to externals — wishing everyone well

(2)   Physical adjustments — moderation in work, sleep, food
(3)   Moral virtues cultivated
(4)   Asceticism
(5)   Purification of psychic nature (ritualistic worship)
(6)   Devotional worship
(7)   Japa (repetition of mantra)
(8)   Meditation

IV. THE ADMINISTRATOR

Swami Ashokananda made elaborate plans for the new temple, drawing and redrawing them in minute detail. It is said that the final plans cost more, eventually, than the construction itself. The city's vulnerability to earthquake was always in his mind and what he sought was solidity, permanence, strength and the impression of strength. His relation with business people was an old-world one. He did not trust their promises and, dogging them, tried the patience of the architect and others who had to be hired. Once a project was on the boards he made it his business to go into every aspect of it.

Whether it was a piece of research for the magazine, a new variety of Pelargonium for the gardens or the purchase of a pump for the ashrama at Olema, he would send people to bring books from the library. In his office the shelves were laden with heavy illustrated compendia on flowers, fabrics, building styles. When the images for the New Temple were to be prepared by sculptors (who were devotees), he spent hours over a period of months going out to the studio to oversee the execution of the busts of Sri Ramakrishna and Swami Vivekananda, all but personally manipulating the arm of the artist for the effect he wanted. For the worker this meant being hounded through many a phone call until the project took that shape. And there were not a few who were sure it could never be done to his satisfaction. Some may even have suspected him of attempting to drive them to God-realization through sheer exasperation. But into all this badgering his maternal heart was woven — something very difficult to portray in print, probing into the well-being and conduct of his students in their various conditions of life, checking

on the carrying-out of his advice, cheering the desolate mind of
a shut-in, exhorting an apostate to come around again.

Swami's administering of his projects was somewhat se-
cretive. He did not believe in exposing to the profane and in-
quisitive what would one day be offered to God, and he abhorred
publicity, calling it "an opening for arrows."

Like Swami Brahmananda he preferred plants to animals.
A great variety of flowers and shrubs flourished in the temple
gardens: clematis weaving up a drainpipe, camellias, rhododen-
drons and azaleas galore; commoner plants — cacti of all kinds,
daisies and marigolds, lilies and chrysanthemums — and rarer
ones too: a fine Pleroma; whatever it was thought possible to
raise in the bay area. About most of them he knew more than
those who were caring for them. Camellias were his favorites. He
shared with the garden his precious time, examining, admiring,
studying the books, discussing them with Mr. Brown. A gardener's
gardener, for him these plants were very living things indeed.
Almost like a child, Swami would go up to them, bend over and
converse. "You are not looking very well these days; what is the
matter?" Or, "*You* have been a great surprise! We did not know
you had it in you to produce such a blossom."

At the East Bay branch of the Vedanta Society, located in
Berkeley, just off the university campus and sitting in the midst
of southside rooming houses, Swami tried to get everyone involved in the work of the center. Teachers, students, professional
people — all were asked to come for just a few hours a week and
weed or pick up leaves. Mrs. Messersmith was robust, vigorous,
and not a little formidable and dictatorial. She directed the garden with professional skill and dedication to the guru. But Swami
kept many plans and practical moves in his own mind and hand.

In that memorable year there was a funeral for all of us
to attend. Miss Sarah Fox, retired schoolteacher, president of the
Society and very close to Swami, had her farewell in one of the
funeral chapels of the city. The atmosphere of this affair raised it
above any funeral of my experience, before or since. Everyone
present remarked on it. Even the staff of the chapel were struck
from their proverbial pallor and unction by the vibrancy, the air
of hovering joy surmounting the whole occasion, and asked members afterward about their society and their faith. The darkness

of death seemed totally defied by the unseen current of conviction and sublimity pervading the service. But it was not all joy
for Swami. Even while chanting from the second chapter of the
Bhagavad Gita he broke down, his voice in tatters, one of the few
occasions when I saw him overcome in public by his private feelings. At a Sunday lecture months later he remarked that Miss
Fox (whom he had addressed as "Sister") had been the most spiritual person he had met in this country.

One of the properties owned by the Northern California
society was Shanti Ashrama, settled as a retreat in the beginning
of the century by a struggling but intrepid band of hardy pioneers led by Swami Turiyananda, another of Sri Ramakrishna's
disciples. Remote and in some ways inhospitable, Shanti Ashrama
suffered subsequent disuse principally because of the lack of any
extensive usable water supply. It serves well to illustrate the im-
propriety of criticism and carping, on the part of Vedanta students, regarding a place other than their own. I have heard Swami
Ashokananda chided *in absentia* for failing to develop this place
in the San Antone Valley where Swami Turiyananda had lived
and worked at the command of Swamiji. Ignoring those wonderful vibrations, he sought other property closer by, which he would
have to purchase. Long, careful weighing of many factors had
gone into Swami's decision: accessibility, the nature of prospec-
tive retreatants, development and transportation costs, the
property's basic resources and his own strength. The ensuing
choice, purchase and development of the retreat in Marin County
appears to have borne out the wisdom of Swami's judgment in
many ways. The fact that a piece of land was available close to
Camp Taylor, where Swami Vivekananda had camped in 1900,
played a large part in the decision.

Swami was strong on maintenance. He would allow nothing belonging to Sri Ramakrishna to become tacky, and regular
schedules of structural testing, re-bracing, repainting and refur-
nishing were carried out for all the premises. Of course the Old
Temple was the most demanding. One marveled, even years later,
that the Berkeley Temple looked as if it had recently been constructed.

For us, the ordinary members not in the ruling circle, the
closest view we had of how things were done was at the annual

business meeting. Whatever moneyraising was done at these meetings was accomplished through the voice of someone other than the swami. In fact, with all their vast undertakings and enterprises I never heard either Swami Ashokananda or Swami Prabhavananda make any public financial appeals.

But meetings for business were not the only annual assemblies: There was also an annual reception in June at which, in addition to music, there were appropriate remarks from the swamis and the reading of a paper. Assigned well in advance to some distinguished member, this disquisition on a controversial topic seldom failed to arouse intellectual expectation and excitement. "Who Can Pioneer a New Religion?" was the topic one year in the '60s, when gurus and cults were appearing on every side. These receptions were lively affairs, as questions from the floor followed the paper.

Swami once held a symposium with a group of some half-dozen of his most stimulating students on the lecture by Swami Vivekananda called "Is Vedanta the Future Religion?" This lecture, which had recently been recovered and reconstructed from the notes of Ida Ansell, had made a stir among those to whom it had been shown. The symposium was conducted in a series of meetings over many months and when an edited transcript of the conversations, all properly pseudonymous (even Swami was "Mr. Randolph"), came out in three issues of *Voice of India*, people were overwhelmed. The discussion had been frank, free, intellectually intricate and sophisticated. Devotees in other places and centers who have seen the rare copies of the magazine and encountered this symposium have marveled that there was ever a group discussion at such a level in a Vedanta Society. At the time it seemed to be nothing to out of the ordinary.

The *New Discoveries* books of Swami Ashokananda's student Marie Louise Burke, for which the entire career of Swami Vivekananda in the West was researched in detail, are the result of a literary collaboration of the most painstaking kind. I had the privilege to observe, only occasionally and from a distance, this relationship. The help Swami must have given Ms. Burke in initiating trains of thought and lines of pursuit; the loan of various arcane materials he had saved through the years; and the degree to which her discoveries may or may not have substanti-

ated conjectures he had entertained — all would make a wonderful story if some day it could all be told. I was awed and inspired by the little of it that I saw.

One day in Berkeley when a number of us were milling
around, something provoked Swami into blurting out vehemently,
"I do not care *anything* about *any* of you. All I care about is the
work!" I was shocked, but I doubt that anyone listening believed
it. Talking about it later we agreed on the hollow ring it had had.
Living around him was an experience of having our sentimen-
tality continually eroded; we became accustomed to it, and, as I
said, what was his work if not "man-making"?

He had his own ways of keeping his mind above all this
constant activity. Sometimes I rode with him as his driver took
him across the bay to give the Berkeley services, in the days before he had an assistant. Sitting just behind him in the car, I
could observe that his right arm hung down beside the seat, and
on the joints of his fingers he was ticking off, in the Indian manner, repetitions of the name of the Lord, all the way over the
bridge and up to the temple.

If I could summarize Swami Ashokananda and his work
in a single word, it would have to be *capacity*. He was a giant. At
the time of my arrival he was giving a lecture every Wednesday
evening in San Francisco, a scripture class Thursday evening in
Berkeley, and a class in San Francisco on Friday evening; Sunday
there was the morning lecture in San Francisco and one that
evening in Berkeley. In between were interviews, a dozen work
projects and plans, the monastery, starting a convent, the magazine, a Sunday school, public festivals, correspondence — and,
through all of this, the mercurial state of his health.

On one occasion someone was laying upon him effusive
sentiments about how thrilled she was by Swami Vivekananda's
rousing calls to service of the God in man. Had she, Swami wanted
to know, ever tried to put her love of man into a plan of practical
action? The lady admitted to being held back from that by various things. "Get in and *work* for people;" he said sternly, "then
see how much you love them." Now, I have tried to test this instruction over many years, puzzling over what Swami really meant
— whether the heartbreaks and rejections inevitable in human
service will cure one of a phony philanthropy complex, or whether

one's love is thereby actually expanded to the infinity of the Divine, like the Holy Mother's — and I hope to reach a conclusion about it before this life is over. Another of his potent mantras on this subject was, "What you want others to do, do yourself."

"The [new] Temple is progressing slowly," Swami wrote to me later when I was elsewhere. "The trusses are up, very soon to be covered with sheathings. Then roofing with slate tiles. So far things seem satisfactory. The structure is more graceful than I expected. It will take two or three years more before the Temple will be ready for Dedication." He dreamed great dreams for the Olema retreat. He would go up on the ridge of those two thousand seashore acres and describe its future, or to the "temple site" and envision aloud the temple to be built there one day.

When I returned to Northern California in 1958, after difficult years, it was to the familiar premises of the Old Temple. Looking out from the aerie of its roof I felt disarmed, pinned and held like a kitten by its mother's paw. And so thankfully! For those few moments all strife seemed ended, all problems blown away in the Marina breeze. I was "home." New men, some very well-educated, had joined; Swami had sent most of the older ones out to Olema and to Sacramento, the latest addition to the Society. But here was old Mr. Brown, and Al, now openly known by his Sanskrit name. So life in the Old Temple was much the same, except that there was this irrepressible energy of youth in the new recruits. Some found the way to weave their ebullience and love of fun right into the fabric of their spiritual and monastic adventure, and these were usually the ones who stayed.

Organized interest in Vedanta had appeared in the city and suburbs of Sacramento in 1948. Within two years, contributions made possible the purchase of a seven-acre plot, empty of even a single tree. On that barren rectangle Swami had ventured to start the construction of a branch center, sending a crew of the brothers who, by "practicing" at Olema, had now become proficient builders. More than seven years' work on this property was already behind them when I was sent there. After a few weeks, when I returned briefly, Swami Ashokananda asked how I was getting along. I think I grumbled about missing my friends in the Old Temple, the familiar atmosphere, rituals and services. I was hesitant to mention the Swami himself.

"That's right," he said cheerfully. "You will be less well off mentally, but you will be better off physically. Less headache. Is it not so?" I had to admit it was.

He had once told everyone, "You have to get splashed in the mud of Vedanta." Finding the "mud of Vedanta" atmosphere of brick and mortar at Sacramento, with its workshop and drafting table, somewhat culturally depriving, I suggested to the brothers that some of us meet in a wide-ranging discussion group, periodic and optional, to discuss issues of the day, etc., and some had readily agreed. It hadn't occurred to me that we might need permission. Shortly there came a personal phone call.

"Did I tell you to do that?" asked the familiar voice.

"No, Swamiji."

"No. Don't do that. This is not college. You see, all of you are living in an environment of hard work and raw materials. You must live *as close to God* as possible. *Create* the spiritual atmosphere there by giving all your spare time to the talk and thought of Him."

Another day he came on a visit, covering all the grounds and buildings with his probing and loving eye. "Do you make japa?" he asked me. I said yes, but knowing that my habit fell short of the level he meant. "Yes, you must. You *cannot* simply be a worker." And he branded the words on my mind with the fire in his eyes.

The Sacramento work went ahead, but not without sweat and tears, and yes, even blood, when a monk sustained a serious injury. Absent for nearly a year on special assignment, I received from Swami this rare and intimate acknowledgment of that dedication of the monks, an expression of what it meant to him: "Hope you will be able to return here as soon as Swami Madhavananda [whom I was nursing] leaves for India... After very hard labor the monks at Sacramento were able to finish sowing the lawn just before the rains seem to be starting. I cannot be too grateful to Dell, Phil, Jim and the others for this tremendous work."

In a sense Swami Ashokananda concluded his expansion work with the dedication of the New Temple in 1959. That building had been forced upon him by the eroding condition of the Old Temple, and the intervening years had taken their toll on his health. This dedication he set about with everything he could

muster. Host to nine senior swamis from around the country, he
planned all of their housing, food and entertainment, assigning
each a place on the program. Several days of ritual ceremony,
music and speeches ensued. Swami wore his Indian robes for the
ceremonies of each day (it was the first time I had seen them on
him) and led all the items on the program like an emperor. The
visiting swamis made numerous comments on how memorable
this occasion was becoming and what an atmosphere it was creating. If one had wondered at the sudden efflorescence of Indian ritual worship, so uncharacteristic of the tradition of his
regime, Swami would surely have replied as I once heard him
reply: "Well, if you are *going* to do ritual worship, why not give
Him your very best flowers, most expensive perfumes, your most
delicious food... Is there anything that is good enough for Him?"

The New Temple was strong, solid, impressive and re-
splendent. In that remarkable new auditorium Swami
Ashokananda seemed to draw a larger audience. By 1965, when
I left for India, the attendance when he spoke on Sunday mornings was commonly 275.

V. THE GURU

The question came up at an evening class, "Is there a
limit to the *samskaras* (impressions upon the deeper layers of the
mind) a person can acquire?" It was a Western question, no doubt,
for the Eastern idea is to drop off all past impressions, not to
speak of making more. Swami's reply, at any rate, was unexpected.

"Evil ones, yes, there is a limit; good ones, no limit. A
person can get better and better but not worse and worse; he or
she will get sick and rebel. Repentance is of very little value except as a preamble."

That we learn as much from our mistakes as from our
successes, if not more, was a favorite teaching of Swami
Vivekananda, who had told us not to repent. It was strong medicine and put my Christian habits on the spot. "All experiences,"
Swami Ashokananda was to write to me later in a letter, "are
lessons to the struggling soul. Let no experience, however un-
happy, weaken your resolve." His way was to talk to us, not in
generalities so much, as about ourselves. He may not have said
very nice things — indeed, things dreadful to hear sometimes,

when the ugly little self had caught his eye. But he addressed the Higher Self in us, appealing to it, never leaving us in doubt that he had our well-being and awakening always at heart.

So much of the attempt to live a spiritual life, especially in a close community, seemed to be a question of understanding other people. Why were they "that way?" What had got into them? We had been raised on psychology; I and many like me had the conception that the role of the master, too, was a psychoanalytic one with frequent consultations and analysis of the components forming our own nature and that of others. The idea that we are to put ourselves and one another in the framework of Divinity, and see all as Spirit, was revolutionary and demanding. Swami, lecturing, encapsulated it beautifully with a rhetorical question: "Isn't it much *harder* to understand a person in a superficial way — where he is so complex — than as the Divine, which is so simple, so beautiful?" There were many layers of understanding. Even our "depth psychology" was not nearly deep enough. But here we had in a sense been working too hard. Not that it is easy to "superimpose" the Divinity on all around us all the time; but by constant, patient practice, Vivekananda assures us, it can be done.

During the first few weeks in the monastery Swami asked me for the first time whether Swami Yatiswarananda had given me specific instructions in meditation. "He gave me only a general kind of instruction, Swamiji," I replied. "He did not actually initiate me." I had supposed initiation to be a formal affair. "Well, one day I shall give you some instruction," he said. And that is how I came to be initiated twice; for it was much later that I learned that the swami in Philadelphia had considered me his student. I had not known whether I should ever see him again, and I had, therefore, put myself completely in Swami Ashokananda's hands, no questions asked.

Troubled with a chronic headache, I found one day that it was taking a localized form. Swami happened to meet me as he came up from the first floor. As he asked me how I was, I told him. "Where does it hurt?" he wanted to know. I tried to describe it. "Show me with your hand," he said. I placed my palm on that side of my head and lo and behold, the headache, tension or whatever it was, immediately released. A blessing, neatly administered, and this was not the only such occurrence.

I had been a musician (which Swami knew) and one day I called up the stairway to ask him if I might go down to the auditorium and play the reed organ. There was a moment's pause before his reply came, gently but indisputably: "No. Don't play the organ. Not yet." The mind revolted. *Why* not? Such a simple, harmless desire — I was in the mood; what could he have against it? I had yet to understand that he had his own design for our lives, his own rate by which he was leading us forward; and when the time came to relax and the struggle could be lessened, it would be made amply clear.

There was, one morning, some indisposition due to which I felt much better lying in bed instead of getting up — a thing unheard of, of course. It was reported to Swami Ashokananda and after he had dressed for the day he came in and asked me all about it, the symptoms, etc. "But why do you not get up?" I gave some explanation. "No," he said, in very kind tones, full of understanding, "you see, you should go on with your routine. The body has a certain rhythm which it likes to keep up. It thrives better on that." Was this the secret of his own march?

Years later, when my spiritual sky was dark indeed, Swami wrote: "Let me tell you that nothing can happen to us which we cannot turn to our advantage. Never admit defeat. 'Struggle is God's gift,' Swamiji said. As long as you struggle onward you have his blessing. And whatever time may bring, it can make no difference to our innate divinity."

But was strength an easy thing to fathom? On a visit to the retreat at Olema, Swami accosted one of the novices. The man was tough, one of the hardest workers, known for his strength of will and unvacillating purpose. "What is strength?" Swami wanted to know. What the novice replied I don't recall. But Swami's words were, "No. Strength means being able to *bend*, as well, like steel. The strong can also be flexible."

I remember another occasion of feeling the drudgery of housecleaning (of which there seemed no end) when he happened to come along. He injected an air of lightness and brightness by showing interest in my humdrum work and asking me, "Work for the Lord purifies the body, doesn't it?" He said things of this sort in a tone of such certainty that if you hadn't known the fact already, there was now no doubt about it. But time proved him right. He knew that if one can somehow link every activity with the furthering of God-realization there would be every chance of escaping boredom.

It was a peculiar mood of renunciation mixed with rebellion that "took over" one day and sent me walking out the door, down through the Marina to the Golden Gate Bridge, then across it and into Marin County until I could walk no farther and, from exhaustion, dropped by the roadside near Sausalito. Coming to my senses, so to say, what was there to do but rest and walk back? I arrived at the monastery after dark, dreading the scene I expected. The brothers were obviously perturbed, and to them I gave some kind of explanation; what I really shrank from was Swami Ashokananda's reaction. He did not send for me that night. When we met the next day I was trying to prepare myself.

"I understand you went for quite a long walk yesterday," said Swami without any heat. I assented with an embarrassed grin, ready to tell all. "No, no," he simply said; then firmly but affectionately, "*Your* body is not for that." It was clear that the state of my mind was evident to him.

Swami Ashokananda favored shorter periods of meditation than the ones to which most of his students seemed to aspire. Often from the platform he would speak of those who, well-meaning and zealous but overambitious, broke through his instructions and landed themselves in difficulty. Over the novices in the monastery he could of course keep watch. At one period late in the first year Swami asked me to give up for a time all formal meditation and even attendance at the lectures. I found this — especially missing his lectures — to be a veritable austerity.

I spoke earlier about his blessings through his letters. Here is what he wrote in 1949 when the Southern California center had become my monastic home:

"I have been very happy to know that you feel quite at home at Trabuco and they also appreciate you much. I wish and pray, as I have always wished and prayed, that you succeed fully in realizing the purpose of the life which you have embraced. May Our Lord shower on you all His blessings!" It was not long before I wrote complaining of the attrition rate of our numerous recruits at Trabuco. "I am sorry about [those losses]," he replied. "The path of renunciation is beset with all kinds of difficulties and only a few make the grade."

Sometime before leaving San Francisco, filled with another upsurge, I asked Swami for a special interview. At this distance in time what I placed before him seems incredibly naive and quite in ignorance of the rules of the order. Straight off I laid it on the table: "Swamiji, may I take sannyasa (final vows of a monk)?" He was silent with a long half-smothered smile. He too must have found it incredible. Then patiently he went into a thorough discussion of the relative merits of living as a monk and as a layman, indicating the respective spiritual fruits of each. It can be summed up in one idea which I have never heard elsewhere. If you want spirituality for yourself alone, life in the world can be quite all right. You come to the source, get what you can, go off and put the seed into your own garden. But if you want to realize for the sake of serving others, of benefiting all mankind, then you have to renounce; there is no other way. Swami then explained the "mechanics" of the journey to sannyasa — the stages of probationer, brahmacharya, and then, if all went well and the order gave permission, the final vows. Up to that time I had not troubled myself with such formalities.

After interviews like these in his office, Swami often paused to gaze out the window, then would sit silent, eyes closed, for several minutes, before dismissing me.

Later in Berkeley after a class I approached him again seeking to join the order formally. I waited while his eyes bored holes in me. "Do you realize," he said, as if he had come from miles away, "what self-effacement that requires?" Of course I did not; but the rest of life has been a discovery of that. It may have been then or on a similar occasion I pressed him to know when I might have some "realization." His response is one I have found so remarkable that I have repeated it to numerous others: "Why don't you live as if you had *already* realized?"

Most of our personal talks in the middle years took place in his own bedroom where he would sit in his dressing robe at that littered desk and appear to be just chatting. It was here he

told me that Swami Shivananda had told him that all his visions
had been attended by the presence of light, and that this is one
of the hallmarks of a true vision.

But the conversation would often take a peculiar form.
Swami would spend a lot of time reciting the faults and failings
of old Mr. Brown and the difficulties he was having with him.
Apart from my sympathetic responses, I wondered what he was
getting at in relating all these matters. It was some time before I
learned that he noticed in me some things of a similar nature,
and had been instructing me in this way. Mr. Brown's failings
included licking an ice cream cone at the corner of Fillmore and
Webster Streets, and he, seventy-some years old, was the president of the Society! "There is an appropriate behavior," Swami
remonstrated, "for every age of life. One should always see that
one's conduct is in conformity with one's age and status."

In contrast is the following pen-picture sent to me in 1961
by one of the youngest and newest San Francisco novices. "Last
Tuesday evening I was raked lightly over the coals. Swami said
he owed my mother a letter for the 25 dollars she had sent him,
but kept putting it off as he was a lax correspondent. Then something like the following volley took place:

Swami, to me: "Do you find it difficult to get letters written?"

I (squirming slightly): "Yes." The yes would have made a
mouse stand its ground.

Swami (making a face of deep repugnance, then sternly):
"You be better than me! Can you do that?"

I: "Well... that's quite a task! But I'll try."

Swami (his frown covering a smile): "Yes... be infinitely
better than I am!"

Swami Ashokananda's women students were not like
women known to me before or since. This was true, I think, in
two senses — certain types were attracted by what he presented,
and, being influenced by his presentation, tended to become what
he expected of them. Discipline was characteristic of them all.
Librarian, typist, driver, gardener, musician, decorator, secretary
— whatever her function, each had responded to that call of the
swami to the spirit, or better, to the Divine Mother in her own
being, and to the degree possible, attempted to realize it. It was

clear that he, like Vivekananda, was not going to pamper the sex he did not consider in any way "weaker," and would not cater to the decrees of chivalry and society prevalent in that city. There would be no place for self-pity. Independence was as fundamental, both as goal and as practice, for the women as for the men.

We read of those pioneers whom Swami Turiyananda and Swami Trigunatita received and "tamed" at Shanti Ashrama. That has been passed down to an extent, it seems to me, through the years, and remains visible to this day in the women of this Society. No one now will know the sacrifices many of these unwealthy and even indigent devotees had made to cull an extra dollar or two for the Lord's work — a new hat foregone, an overcoat worn beyond its years. It was a lifestyle stripped of luxuries, frills and cosmetics, not only for the collection plate, but as a hallmark of a life's commitment to design, detachment and simplicity.

And what a capacity for work and study! On those evenings when no class or lecture took place Swami would be found once more down in the offices with these devotees, cajoling, consoling, inspiring, instructing — filling them with the *sraddha*, the positive attitude, and the *tejas*, the glow of austerity, which were the core of the Vivekananda ideal — and chuckling and laughing with them too. Discipline was not to be borne as a burden; lightness and cheerfulness of mind were to accompany tireless service. Swami told someone one day why he spent so much more time with the devotees downstairs than with the monks. It was because they had so little else. He felt that the men, after all, had the protection of the monastery with its nearly automatic routines and its bestowed atmosphere of sanctity and study. We were practically propelled into spiritual practice. But what did the women have, struggling for a higher life, swimming upstream against hostile or indifferent forces of family, work and world?

There were criticisms on the wind, as there always are — epithets like "amazons" and "de-feminized." Nobody paid any attention. Lives were being built or rebuilt. The bridging of diverse cultures was the business-at-hand in the process of being accomplished, and Swami Ashokananda was doing it in his own way. A few words of blessing and guidance from his letters may best summarize his leadership. "Wherever you live, may the Lord be ever manifest in your heart and guide and guard you!... It does not pay in this kind of life [monastic] to violate ways of this life; it is my conviction that the conventions of the life, which are obeyed all over the world by spiritual aspirants, should be followed implicitly. They are a bulwark against deviation."

VI. THE HOST

Swami Trigunatita, builder of the Old Temple, had planned the top floor as quarters for Swami Brahmananda, first president of the order, whom he had hoped to persuade to occupy it for at least some months. Whether Maharaj seriously considered it I do not know; certainly in India they had no intention of seeing their beloved chief off on such a sea voyage, involving a lengthy absence from headquarters. The floor was now used as headquarters for the swami-in-charge.

Swami Ashokananda's lifestyle and ours below, though equally simple and ascetic, were not outwardly synchronous. Swami never ate with us. It was his custom at Christmas to give each of us some rather elegant gift, usually clothing or a book.

The Old Temple, San Francisco

One year, I understand, when he asked John what he would like for Christmas, the latter replied, "For you to come down and eat the dinner with us, Swamiji." And he did. He had many dietary restrictions and ate at no set hours, but only when he felt hungry, or was told to eat — or perhaps when he remembered to eat.

The same was true of his sleep. Anyone awake in the night might hear the padding of his feet above, or the distant sound of the radio. Afternoons it was not uncommon to find him napping, but this might have been true at any hour of the day had we been in the habit of going up unannounced. He would sometimes spend the entire night in the study of his books, on his projects, or doing his own spiritual practices. Even less pattern was discernible as he grew older.

Swami's quarters consisted of a large bedroom, kitchen, bath and a smaller back bedroom leading to the roof gardens. It was his custom, whenever a brother monk came to visit, to stuff himself into this little room and leave the spacious one to his guest. Barring that, he left the back room in glorious disarray. "I have to keep one room like that," he told one of us. "Life is not all just hunky-dory." "Hunky-dory" came out in lectures also, bringing bright smiles to the faces of devotees. Swami often used slang expressions, some of which were gleaned from a faithful following of the comics section of the newspaper. The Bumsteads, Blondie and Dagwood, were among his favorites. He brought the house down one Sunday morning by interrupting the lecture to ask rhetorically, "Why is it — I don't understand — that Dagwood never *locks* that bathroom door?"

With a mind of his type out of which a two-hour discourse could emerge without a note, and keyed up for hours of the day to a pitch of highest discrimination, will it be any surprise if Swami had ways of achieving relaxation? In the modes available to him he clearly attempted to maintain the balance and vigor of a healthy mind. I mentioned his listening to the radio. He also had a turntable and albums, and liked music very much. He used to hum or sing softly any time of day. On the few evenings he was not downstairs he might play records — often classical Western music. The selection I best recall was the definitive Landowska recording of the Goldberg Variations for harpsichord of J. S. Bach. He had told Al that in Bengal he had had a room close to that of a European who played such records loudly and Swami had thus been forced to hear them; but after a while he gained some understanding of the music.

He would also play records of Bengali devotional songs, some of which sounded glorious to us as the strains wafted down from that distance. And when he joined his own full voice to the music, expressing an evidently ecstatic mood, it was a treat for the ears of the gods!

His silent source of relaxation and recreation was the detective story. Swami must have gone through reams of them. As I knew little at that time of the titles and authors, I cannot delineate his taste in mysteries — eclectic, I suspect. Some of the devotees knew his predilection and were able to keep him supplied. Sometimes books were offered almost ritualistically: "Swamiji, I bought this today; you please read it first and then I shall take it as prasad." He told someone that the mystery stories were valuable to him in exposing the nature of the human mind. As virtually all of them must have had a Western setting, we may well understand what this may have contributed to his ability to minister spiritually to Westerners.

I have heard that on the eve of Swami Ashokananda's ocean voyage to the United States he was given reminders by some of his friends and co-workers in India not to forget them. Some even hinted that in such a rich country he would be likely to get enough funds to be able to send some over for their work. Swami is said to have made it clear that he was turning his face westward. "All the funds that come my way I shall put back into the work there. Do not expect to hear from me; I am leaving India behind." That was his conception of where his duty lay. His ability to carry this out successfully must have been partly responsible for Swami's achievements in the West.

He remained in touch with a very few close friends. We get a small glimpse into his early life in India through one his oldest friends whom I met there, a fellow student in college in Sylhet, Swami Saumyananda. He described Swami Ashokananda as an intellectual giant from early in his life. He spoke of how he had organized classes for the boys of the poor cobblers of the village of Habiganj, raising their status conclusively. When no raft or boat was available, the future Ashokananda would jump into the river and swim to his classes.

In San Francisco and Berkeley I was witness to some of the visits paid by his best friends in this country, a most beloved one being Swami Vividishananda of Seattle, to whom, then in charge of the San Francisco center, Swami had come as assistant in 1931. For some years he came nearly every summer, and when this elderly Swami needed cataract operations Swami Ashokananda brought him from Seattle to the Old Temple and placed him under the care of the best surgeons in one of our fine hospitals. He asked me to nurse the swami, both in hospital and at the temple afterward. What fun they would have, teasing each other, speaking Bengali and "talking shop!"

The same fun went on when Swami Pavitrananda would arrive from New York as he too did almost annually. Swami Akhilananda from New England, though a less frequent visitor, was a great favorite with all and gave question-answering sessions which were much appreciated.

Readers who knew Swami Satprakashananda of St. Louis may enjoy an anecdote of one of his visits, related by E. C. Brown. Mr. Brown had among his assignments of those days the duty of standing at the back of the Old Temple lecture hall on Sunday to see that all went well. Swami Satprakashananda on this day was the guest speaker, but even before beginning to chant or talk he was looking steadfastly in Mr. Brown's direction while, with arm upraised, he opened and closed his fingers in imitation of a mouth. Mr. Brown fortunately knew just what to do. He ran up the back stairs (two flights), found the forgotten dentures and managed to smuggle them into the speaker's lectern at the other end of the hall.

Swami Vishwananda of Chicago made rare visits and Swami Vijayananda, on a trip north from Buenos Aires, stopped with us once in my time. Swami appreciated all of them. Taking them to the branch centers and showing sights of the city invariably made him noticeably more ill — "pulled down" was a favorite Indianism — after these fraternal get-togethers. The brother monks no doubt chatted for hours in their quarters; from below, all we would hear were the great guffaws which provided occasional punctuation. The story is told of Swami Vivekananda at Ridgely Manor in New York that a boy heard him laughing and laughing to himself as he passed Swamiji's room. Finally he looked in and asked the swami why he was laughing. "Oh, God is so funny," was the answer.

VII. THE RETREATANT

As that first summer approached, Swami reminded us that soon he would be going to the Society's cottage on the edge of Lake Tahoe for at least a month. A member of the monastery might accompany him on these summer retreats and one morning in class, looking at me, he said with a voice tinged with temptation, "Well, how would you like to have a vacation?" Quickly I replied, "Swamiji, I'd like to have a very *long* vacation — in samadhi." It made the others laugh and brought a broad smile to Swami's face, but that was not, of course, what he had in mind.

Carnelian Bay is a small area of the resort shore on the northwest side of that large lake. Most of the land is hillside and the cabin perched steeply, the porch offering a good view of the lake and the ribbon of highway passing alongside. Not far off a mere trickle of a mountain creek splashed precipitately to the water below. The high-pitched roof, discouraging winter snow, covered the ample parlor. There were two small bedrooms and just beneath the roof a loft big enough for a bed, reached by ladder from the parlor. It was a lark, to scramble up there to my own aerie whenever I had the chance.

Surprisingly, I was not expected to do anything for Swami. Devotees stayed in nearby cabins, prepared his diet, did the shopping and other things he needed. He told me what I had to do was to keep the cabin clean, dusting the parlor every day. I liked to sit inside, where he was, but he kept chasing me out when the weather was fair. "The fresh air," he said, "will strengthen your nerves, which are weak." So I made a place among the trees, above the road, where I had a kind of makeshift table and chair and spent my mornings in study.

One day I had to report to him an experience of difficulty with breathing during morning meditation. He gave me a searching look and, reaching for a copy of the *Bhagavad Gita*, handed it to me. "Begin memorizing the *Gita*," he instructed, "starting with the second chapter." The book was in Sanskrit and English, and trying to memorize it was my occupation at the little desk in the woods. The Sanskrit was difficult but I had only the squirrels to distract me.

It was the first time I had lived in close contact with Swami and it was a wonder to me. We did not talk much unless there was something particular to be said. One day he told me (as he often had) that I was weak and badly needed strengthening. Swami Vivekananda had put great emphasis on strength and I was distressed to hear this again. Puzzled, I parried, "Am I weaker than others at the same stage of development?" With that mixture of impatience and affection which was peculiarly his, he said, "It is your *body* that is weak! It has nothing to do with the mind. It is your nerves that are not strong; you must *eat*." Always he pushed me to eat amply, especially milk. He never liked novices to fast, so far as I know. I told him that Swami Yatiswarananda had told me no doctor could tell me how much to eat; that I would have to find that out for myself. But Swami Ashokananda apparently felt differently. "Oh, I don't know about that," he remarked. It was later I learned of the hazards of quoting one of these guides of ours to another. As this one had told me on our first meeting, the swamis are not all alike.

At this time the editor of the *Voice of India* was living in the next cottage, and she and Swami would begin working on the magazine in the morning, sitting for a long time on the porch under one of those huge umbrellas which covers a round table. In the afternoon he would take a walk, accompanied by one or more of the women. Those walks must have been spiritual calisthenics — powerful pedagogic episodes, with Swami sharing his inmost thoughts. My admiration for one devotee in particular was prodigious. I have seen her coming back at his side, weeping silently for what must have been some vigorous sandpapering of whatever rough edges he had detected. Many had this kind of training.

At Tahoe there was less of specific monastic routine. As Swami's meals were irregular, we ate separately. It was much later that I heard that one of his reasons for not eating with us was the fear that he might offend Western sensibilities with his different table manners. Often in the evening he would sit in his easy chair in the parlor, his head reclining and at ease, his eyes closed or half-closed, but not at all asleep. What was going on in that consciousness? Was he "meditating?" Difficult to say. The room had, however, an atmosphere suggesting communion with an unseen presence. As I look back I think to myself, where was India for him? Where were Swami Brahmananda, Swami Shivananda, Swami Premananda, where the precious memories and adventures of his spiritual life, if not in those moments?

Another book Swami asked me to study that summer was *Sri Ramakrishna, the Great Master*. He also asked me to make my own outline of it as I went along. He knew very well the means by which one could fix things in the mind.

Suddenly I realized he was washing his own laundry, by hand. This chore he apparently never put upon the devotees. I felt ashamed; why had I not thought of it? When I told him I would wash his clothes, he mumbled softly, "No, you needn't do that." I failed to understand why I shouldn't do this simple service. Maybe he was swayed by the Indian conception of us as well-bred and scholastically "qualified" — hence I might feel it beneath my dignity? So now I pressed him and urged it and at last he allowed me to wash them. These were beyond question the cleanest clothes I ever laundered in my life! I could not see a spot on them.

One day Swami called me to a closet and, shuffling some boxes about on a shelf said, "Here is something I believe you can use." The box contained a Kashmir sleeveless sweater — beautiful. It was his first gift and I wore it only with shrine clothes for 35 years until it was nearly in tatters.

We went for a picnic in the woods one day, quite a group of devotees having come for the occasion. It meant a stroll through the piney forest to a large clearing where we were to sit. On the way we came across an odd-looking little flower, perhaps a Dutchman's pipe, which had popped up all alone from the forest floor. Swami Ashokananda stopped, pointed, and commented to us, "See that. It is like what we call in India a snowflower, growing up alone where no one expects it, and out of season, and we liken it to some spiritual souls who just bloom spontaneously apart from company or culture." After we had sat down and the food was distributed, I attacked my plate with all the time-honored informality of a Western picnic. Swami frowned at me. "Wait!" he commanded. "There will be *Brahmarpanam* (the monastic blessing before meals)."

Mr. Brown came for a few days. He and Swami were old chatting companions and various topics came up. One night as we prepared for bed Swami said to us, "Now it is time to die our daily death, euphemistically called 'sleep.'" The old man reminisced one day about his guru, Swami Trigunatita, and about Swami Prakashananda, a disciple of Swamiji, who had succeeded him. "Yes," said Swami Ashokananda, "Swami Trigunatita was a lion; Swami Prakashananda was a lamb." Some articles in another magazine by Swami Atulananda had been emphasizing the role of Swami Turiyananda in the building up of the Society. Swami Ashokananda, whenever this was mentioned, would bring in what he felt was the larger role of Swami Trigunatita who, because in India he was less known, had been neglected in books and articles. One of his hopes for the future productions of the devotees was a proper biography of this swami.

The following summer, after a long illness, I was given permission to spend a portion of it at the Lake. Alone in the cottage for most of that period, I tried to intensify my spiritual practices and enjoy the balmy climate. When, after a month or so, I returned to the Old Temple and met Swami, he looked me over with evident satisfaction: "Yes," said he, "your health has improved."

Ten years later, in August of 1956, the "Tahoe retreat" was no longer the same restorative for him. Swami wrote to me in Southern California from his refuge by the lake, "My return to strength," he noted, "is being very slow this year... Well, I hope you are in good health and progressing spiritually. I have often thought of you here. The place is indeed very peaceful and helpful."

VIII. QUINTESSENTIAL ASHOKANANDA

Looking over the years and viewing the panorama of personality in the thirteen Indian monks with whom I have closely moved, I feel that Swami Prabhavananda and Swami Ashokananda belong in a special class. Theirs was not so much an adaptation to the West as it was the expansion of outlook into a wider world which breached all cultural and societal confinement. They identified with us and in so doing allowed more of

Swami Vivekananda's idea of the "universal man" to be embodied and visible in them. It was true to some extent of Swami Nikhilananda also, as we shall see later.

Swami Prabhavananda's case has been discussed in the previous chapter; his was a natural and perhaps an unselfconscious growth. Swami Ashokananda worked at it deliberately and, in the process, made it articulate. I would like to try to delineate the form this took in his thinking, and to formulate what seem to me those features which may be termed his uniqueness.

Swami Ashokananda did not favor the idea of Western devotees cultivating the gods and goddesses of Hinduism. He would tell some of the wonderful mythological stories and explain the icons, but did not sanction the use of hymns (such as are found in *The Gospel of Sri Ramakrishna*) addressed to Shiva, Durga or Krishna, either in the original or in translation. Rather, he encouraged the Society's would-be poets to write new verses for the magazine, underscoring the eternal and transcultural significance of these archetypes.

He did not care to have traditional images of such deities made and worshiped in Western centers. When some of the women began to take much interest in Indian food, he forbade the circulation of curry recipes among them. On this subject Swami was not totally consistent, however. Bengali that he was, he felt an irresistible attraction, seemingly, for the great harvest festival and solemnity called Durga Puja. We did celebrate this in the society, and in the Berkeley Temple he had placed a picture of that image, which was set up in the shrine and worshiped on those occasions.

In the brochure issued for the public opening of the Sacramento center he had written: "Vedanta is not a creed, it is, rather, the foundation of all creeds and religions — those not only of India but of the world; for it explains in rational terms the eternal laws governing all spiritual life and gives aid to all men and women in their spiritual unfoldment, whatever their individual religious affiliations and beliefs may be. It is, in truth a Universal Philosophy and Religion, belonging to no one race of people, but to mankind as a whole."

While explaining to us the details of the daily worship of

Sri Ramakrishna in the monastery shrine, he instructed us to add the Jordan to the sacred rivers, in that passage where their presence is invoked.

About Holy Mother he had some distinctive views. Not that he often spoke of her in public lectures. He always recounted with great reverence his own experience of having her darshan, in which she gave her blessing from a distance to an open gathering. But, like others of his generation, he had a concern to keep her image protected. He did not wish to have her photograph displayed in public view, and no picture of her was installed in either of the temples built under his regime. In both these shrines her worship was conducted daily as usual, but in the *Om* above the other pictures — taking that symbol outwardly, the worshiper was to visualize the Mother. Swami told us that modesty had been Sri Sarada Devi's outstanding possession; he could not bear to think that strangers, knowing nothing of her, might gaze upon her form with impure eyes; from that she must be protected. Moreover, this would be in consonance with her whole demeanor of self-veiling, retirement and aversion to multitudes and to display. When the third temple was completed, the New Temple in San Francisco, Holy Mother's was among the five sculptures commissioned for its sanctuary. I have never heard what guided his decision in this matter.

In this connection I am reminded that it was this swami, more than any other person I have known, who believed in the complete identity of a photograph and its subject and markedly carried this into action. Any picture of the enlightened ones he treated in this way. The photographs of our three honored ones in particular — and of other divine incarnations — were accorded the reverence, immaculate handling and worship which would be given to their living forms if present. He was consistent in this and asked it of all of us.

Some regard Swami as having broken new ground with his booklet, *My Philosophy and My Religion*. I never felt it quite that way. In the years I listened to his words it seemed that he gave fresh inspiration and an emphasis arising from experience, and that he played upon certain notes, in his exposition of Vedanta, rather than led the philosophy in any new direction. Nearly all of his presentation was to be found in that of Swami

Vivekananda, his hero and model. True, Swami would stress some of the more startling of Swamiji's pronouncements — such as "Don't seek Him; just *see* Him!.," and the unconventional portions of the lecture "Is Vedanta the Future Religion?"

Among the several Advaitic positions, although he expounded Shankaracharya's well and often, it was that of Gaudapada, the earlier teacher, that he seemed really to prefer. He was seldom content to elaborate the "story of creation" without coming to rest on the latter's *ajatavada*, the conclusion that there has never really been any creation at all. I think Swami was also more vocal on the importance of the ancient Sankhya view in the total Vedantic picture than most of the other swamis, and spoke on "Sankhya and Vedanta" approximately three times a year.

Like his guru he had studied Buddhism and the Buddha long and deeply. His devotion to Lord Buddha (as Swami Ashokananda always referred to him) was such as many a Buddhist might honor. His annual lecture at the birthday celebration drew people from various communities and affiliations and crowded the hall. It was invariably first-rate. Even today I can feel the reverberations of my whole emotional being as he described "the most compassionate man who ever lived," "the one religious prophet who was centuries ahead of his time and with whom we have not yet caught up even now."

With regard to Swami Vivekananda, Swami had some special views. They can be found in detail in the booklet *Swami Vivekananda in San Francisco* in which three of his lectures on the subject have been blended into one long article. In brief, Swami felt that Swamiji had actually concluded his message to the West in San Francisco; that the talks given there were, by the same token, the culmination of his message — it was here he gave out the "full truth," to one and all, qualified or not, uninhibited by the expectations of society, secular or religious. In that booklet we find some of Swami Ashokananda's strongest language:

> How can truth really hurt you? We get into all kinds of ruts of thought and make little patterns and molds for ourselves and continually cast our lives in them. All this antiquated stuff! Aren't new ways possible? How do you know this is the best your mind

is capable of? Because some ancient people did something, you think nothing better can be done? Then why don't you go on living in dirty old caves instead of skyscrapers? In everything else you believe in progress, in everything else you are seeking truth, but when it comes to religion, you think you must believe in what a man taught thousands of years ago; you think nothing else is possible.

He taught all the paths and the Advaita that belongs to all the paths. Who, for instance, can love God more than one who is Godlike? Only when you know you are Spirit can you have true devotion to God, the Spirit. You will feel that He is close to you, He is identified with you. He is your very own. Then moments will come when you will feel that even the little remaining sense of duality disappears. That is the bhakti he taught here.

I returned to the northern center in 1957 and was soon sent to Sacramento to help with the construction. One of Swami's occasional visits, which proved to be memorable, took place some time after I was settled in. Up to this time most of our monks — who, unlike Al, had never been in India — had felt only a tenuous link with the monks and monasteries in that country, with which our center was "spiritually affiliated." Now this was about to change. Swami Ashokananda asked all of us to come with him into the shrine room, which was at that time the site of the future foyer. There we stood in a row while he explained that it was proposed that at the time of the dedication of the New Temple in San Francisco most of us would be given the vows of brahmacharya, the novitiate, new official names ending in "Chaitanya," and would thus become members of the Ramakrishna Math and Mission in a more definite and secure sense. Swami gave the impression that this was not necessarily his idea or plan, though nothing to that effect was said. I think he mentioned that the trustee-swamis who had visited us the previous year had wanted it. This ceremony of formal novicehood had, we knew, been instituted already in the Southern California center but we were not expecting this. Then Swami added, almost acidly, "And I suppose I will have to give you the rosaries and all that." He proceeded to demonstrate how the beads were to be moved through one's hand and how to keep count of the number told. He seemed to me that day a man who was giving ground.

He and I used to have arguments (if such they can be called) about pacifism, Gandhi's methods, etc. Of course I made no concerted attempt to uphold my end, recalling Mr. Brown's observation about the swamis holding all the cards. Swami was no follower of the Gandhi doctrines, though he admired the man and his "soul-force," about which he used sometimes to speak publicly.

When people who did not know Swami Ashokananda have asked if he became "Westernized," I have found it difficult to reply. He dedicated himself to becoming so in certain ways. He had put down virtually all his roots here, where he had been posted. He read scores of American books, picked up slang and colloquialism, talked with young and old, met hundreds of Americans and studied their ways. But his monastic habits; his preference for simplicity in food and routine; his austere and irregular hours of sleep; his insistence on doing much of his own "service"; and probably his basic patterns of thinking did not change much — they were perhaps as Indian as when he left his land. Of course as a karma-yogi, a man filled with practical acquaintance with a technological society, keenly interested in things scientific and mechanical (albeit as a layman), Swami was a man of the West, and as one whose principle it was to adapt himself, he was ever ready to learn and use what the West had to offer. He was truly humble in this respect and never stood on a platform of racial or national superiority. He had said of the Catholic monastic orders that they had been in this business a long time and what they had learned was not to be taken lightly. They had influenced his own techniques as an abbot, it is safe to say. But the term "Westernized swami" seems to imply something else, and it might better have been applied to some others. Swami Ashokananda always retained an "old-fashioned" aura about him.

Other people, I found, experienced quite different aspects of his nature. I was surprised to meet a young fellow at the university who told me Swami had been an occasional visitor in his home and had frequently dandled him on his knee when he was very small.

Here is a rare and frank account of Swami Ashokananda's,

dealing with his introduction to the mother house, Belur Math, in words slightly different from those already published:

> There is a popular Bengali song, "Who can find Thee, Lord, except he be drawn by Thee?" When I was a young boy at high school, I had no particular interest in or feeling for God, religion or any of those things. But we had one instructor who was sympathetic to the Ramakrishna Mission and from him we used to hear a number of stories, etc., about Sri Ramakrishna. One day he arranged for a friend of mine and me to go to Belur Math to visit the place. That was in 1911 or 1912. It was the Master's birthday and we two went there for the celebration functions and all that. And while we were there I experienced a great upliftment of the mind, felt that God and religious things were true and should be pursued. But the moment I left the grounds all this feeling disappeared. I felt and thought just as before. Then, as we were coming home to our village from Calcutta (we came by train but the station was ten miles from our village: this we walked, as that was nothing to us in those days), the convictions I had felt at the Math suddenly returned to me in force, almost overwhelming, like a cloud hovering over the spot and pouring its rain upon me. And that feeling and certainty has never left me since. That you would have to call grace, wouldn't you? "Who can find Thee, Lord, except he be drawn by Thee?"

IX. PULLING OUT

From New York, where Swami had sent me to attend on Swami Madhavananda, I made regular reports to Sacramento. Among these I find the following paragraph:

> These days I am wondering whether all our men realize what Swami Ashokananda has done for us. The creation and maintenance of the kind of atmosphere which obtains in our monastery is a thing so marvelous and difficult of achievement that I never cease to wonder that we can take it for granted. I have now seen enough of Vedanta in America to know that the opportunity we have been given is virtually unique. I do not see, frankly, how the spiritual depths can be sounded except in silence. It is in the abyss of withdrawal, in the great chasm of the undisturbed, that

the Profound is found. What a place he has made for us! Have
you any idea? That spiritual climate for which the devotees and
monastics wait hours (meditation time) and for which many persons wait months (summer retreatants), that climate is ours, nearly
all day, every day, all year long. Nor do I see how one can catch
the pearls that lie on the bottom when middle-age is robbing one
of half one's divine strength. All this has been ours, in our youth,
through his grace — and His, of course. We should not waste a
single hour of it.

At the end of 1965 I had left Sacramento for India. Al,
now Swami Chidrupananda, wrote to me in September of 1966
concerning Swami Ashokananda's health and the latter's concern for mine:

> Swami received your letter informing him that you were laid up
> in the hospital at Narendrapur with jaundice. The news has made
> him very unhappy and he is much concerned. He is sure, how-
> ever, that Swami Lokeswarananda will do the very best for you.
> He urges you to follow the doctor's directions to your utmost,
> even though it means that you are not able to carry on your
> spiritual practices as you would wish to. He says to bear in mind
> that the Lord will recognize your inability under these circum-
> stances.

> Swami told me to explain that he has asked me to write you for
> him, to avoid delay: his letters nowadays are few and far be-
> tween and are always long-delayed replies to the ones he re-
> ceives. He urges you to be very careful and thus gradually you
> should be able to adjust to the Bengal climate. If this does not
> come about, the Math authorities will surely do the best for you.
> And don't forget, he says, that Sri Ramakrishna is also looking
> after you!

> Swami has been at Tahoe since August 16 and will return in five
> days more. He does not seem to have improved noticeably, he
> says. Blood pressure is up and down and this makes his head
> uncomfortable. The doctor gives hope that his head may feel
> better at sea level, however, where there is more oxygen. Let us

hope so... Swami asks that you keep him informed of your condition. If you are unable to write yourself, try to have someone else
send him a few lines....

It was a year later that Swami Shraddhananda of the Sacramento center sent me the following report: "I have bad news
for you," he reported, "Swami Ashokananda had a bad setback
recently and the doctor advised hospitalization for special tests...
As a result of poor circulation of blood in the brain his thoughts
and words are partly incoherent."

In January of the following year I heard again from Swami
Chidrupananda. "Swami Ashokananda received your letter... a
few days ago, in which you have told him your problem with the
Bengal climate and food and your reasons for asking to be returned to the West. He has asked me to reply because, as you
have doubtless heard, he had a mild stroke on December 6 and
at present, writing would be a quite difficult chore for him. His
left arm and leg are considerably affected and the right side is
weak. Physical therapy will be resumed this coming week... which
will put things more on the mend." And in February he added,
"Swami is still confined to his bed, with special nurses, since he
cannot yet move about unaided. The physical therapy treatments
are helping him, but it is and will continue to be a long and slow
process. We can only hope for the best." He was also plagued by
a chronic hiccough the doctors were unable to arrest.

But Swami was not about to give up, and with characteristic toughness he held on, more or less in this condition, for
nearly two more years. The end came in December of 1969. I
was in the London center when I received this account of it from
a beloved brother monk:

On the afternoon of Saturday the 13th, at St. Mary's Hospital in
San Francisco, Swami Ashokananda left this world of ours — left
it much the poorer. Perhaps you have heard. The diagnosis was
heart failure. Swami had received three transfusions and had just
licked a virulent infection of the kidneys; the doctors thought a
good recovery was likely. Yet the infection, together with all the
antibiotics Swami was given, had drained him of his last ounce of
strength. The day before his departure Swami Shraddhananda

and I paid him a visit; he lifted his right hand feebly, for us to shake, but didn't speak. I stood at his bedside for ten minutes or more while Swami Shraddhananda held his hand and stroked it gently, now and again speaking a few words to him in Bengali — a touching sight. Had I known that Swami Ashokananda's end was so close at hand, I would have put my head at his feet.

It is as well that he did not. The convention in India is that a holy man's feet are not to be touched when he is on his sickbed. The letter continues:

Sometimes, such is the sordidness of the world, it seems almost impossible to believe that a man of selfless dedication, burning sympathy and absolute moral integrity could actually exist. Such great ones are so extremely rare! Yet Swami Ashokananda was one of these select few, as those who knew him intimately will attest. He was, to me, a saint, living at a great spiritual altitude, on the uplands of the mind; and he was a marvelous force for helping others to reach those sunlit heights. One thing he never lacked, but *never*, was tremendous spiritual enthusiasm. He was consumed with eagerness to do Swami Vivekananda's work, and he did it beautifully — always with a vigorous intellect and with all the strength at his command.

Swami Nikhilananda

MOTHER'S PARKSIDE PATRICIAN

SWAMI NIKHILANANDA

I. UPPER EAST SIDE

In 1961, when the birthday of Sri Ramakrishna was being celebrated at the New Temple in San Francisco and the crowd was still enjoying refreshments, Swami Ashokananda unexpectedly drew me aside and asked if I had ever lived in New York. I racked my brain to think what odd piece of information he might require of me about a city I had only passed through.

"Would you like to live there for a few months?" I was speechless. Swami went on to explain that Swami Madhavananda, long the respected general secretary of the Ramakrishna Order, now retired because of poor health, would be coming to this country for medical treatment. Swami Nikhilananda of New York, who would be his host, did not have enough personnel at his center to give the patient proper attention and had asked Swami Ashokananda to lend them a novice.

"And I am proposing to send you, if you think that agreeable. You have done some nursing, isn't it?" I had been a hospital orderly, raised in a family of physicians, and a few years previously had done a little nursing for the Berkeley swami; so it was settled.

I made a full report back to the monastery in Sacramento of this, my first long air flight. From New York's Idlewild Airport Swami Nikhilananda's two assistants escorted me on the long drive to the Ramakrishna-Vivekananda Center on the upper East Side. They were Swami Budhananda, Indian, his assistant of the time, and Swami Atmaghanananda, his American disciple, a jolly pair ready with just the right sort of remarks for a nervous new-comer. At the center, a four-floor pile of vertical activity — so different from the one I was used to — was of 1890 vintage, its original dark woodwork and decor intact. Swami Nikhilananda, its presiding spirit, proved the soul of affability, affection and helpfulness.

It was but ten months that I served Swami Nikhilananda, and for that I received eight years of blessing. The letters he wrote to me in the years that followed are filled with the gener-ous expression of his satisfaction and gratitude. His relation to me was less that of a conscious teacher to a student than of an older brother to one much younger, but how much I learned from him! The first of these letters was one of welcome:

"You will no doubt derive an inner satisfaction," he had written, "from attending on a person like Swami Madhavananda. I believe this will compensate you for all the discomforts and inconveniences which you will find at our small Center... He is reluctant to accept service from others, but we shall manage the whole thing through the grace of God."

One by one appeared the other members of what was to be my "family" for nearly a year: Countess Colloredo-Mansfeld, Swami's secretary and widow of an Austrian nobleman, who had an apartment a few blocks away; Al, a young physician who had moved out to a hotel to make room for the visitors; and the hired cook who came in to do the dinners. They seemed so competent that I wondered a little that it had been necessary to borrow me. But there were manual labors a novice could do, not expected of swamis, and in any case they were all busy. I had been urged by the monastic brothers at home to press the older monks for their reminiscences of the first disciples of Sri Ramakrishna. The American swami now warned me that here such questions were not much appreciated; memories must come up spontaneously. They very soon did. At the evening class on Good Friday, Swami

Nikhilananda told of the passing away of Swami Brahmananda and how he had said, near the end, "I am floating on the banyan-leaf of faith down to the ocean of Brahman."

Swami Nikhilananda promptly put things into perspective for me by explaining that I would find things different here; that he had never wanted to start an "ashrama" and did not like to have a large group of people around him. "This place is a book factory," he ventured. In fact, his literary output was prodigious; it included his justly celebrated English rendering of the *Gospel of Sri Ramakrishna*; a four-volume translation of the Upanishads; and several other scriptural translations and biographies that, taken as a whole, represent an irreplaceable contribution to the Vedanta movement in the West. But a book factory? Perhaps, I said to myself, but also much more. His own quarters took up all but the hallway of the second floor above ground. At the back was a large bedroom with bath attached. Adjoining it a dressing room and closet led into the study or living room at the front of the house. In this study we had tea in the afternoon; here private interviews were held and so were the deliberations of the triumvirate which operated the center: Swami, his secretary, and Swami Atmaghanananda. The last-named was referred to, with true East Coast formality, as Mr. Moffitt, which was a bit shorter; Swami Nikhilananda addressed him as "Moffitt."

Swami's books and papers were in the study, but there was a large writing desk in the bedroom and it was on this that most of his books were written. Although I had met the swami before, in California, here I saw him for this first time in his own element. I could think of no comparison except David Copperfield's first captivation by the presence of Steerforth.

We began on a high note. His important guest was not expected for a week or so, and Swami took me with him to Douglass College in New Jersey, a part of Rutgers University, where he was conducting a course in Hinduism. It was surprising to see him wear a gray Nehru cap and a lighter gray *sherwani*, the long cloak seen on Congress Party dignitaries, for this assignment. It was decorated with his gold watch chain. To this class of about 20 students, men and women, Swami spoke in a disarming and informal way, seeming to become just one more college boy again. He moved from desk to chalkboard, sometimes sitting on the desk, feet hanging down, keeping up a running patter on the Hindu concepts of God. On the question of how we can ever "know the knower," he charmed all with his illustration of the dancing girl who can cut all kinds of capers, but whose limitation is that she cannot climb upon her own back. He aimed his material at their level exactly and was able to make it so clear and simple that I was in awe:

"Recall Plato's cave allegory: The prisoners know there is a reality, back behind, but are compelled to look only at its shadows. After samadhi a person *acts* because of *seeing* duality, but does not take it to be real; that person sees also the unity. Can he enjoy the world? Yes and no... not the way we do, but better. Our life is, after all, full of false fear (the rope taken for a snake) and false expectations (water in the mirage). Do we not enjoy the magician's show? We go to it knowingly, knowing that we want to be fooled. But is he not a fool, who, coming home, asks in all seriousness, 'How did he get that rabbit out of that hat?' — such is the scientist."

He seems to have caught the mood of the '60s.

The intellectual coolness and serious detachment which he manifested from the pulpit in his center were not present at this affair. "Our modern idea is to get everything the first day. I once met a Jewish gentleman who told me, 'Don't be disgusted with us Americans. We judge everything by a time measure of 175 years. But you come from a land where time is measured by thousands of years.' He was right."

Douglass College, at the conclusion of this course, held a tea to which were invited all Swami's previous students there and some faculty members, and he was voted their most popular lecturer. The citation presented to him read as follows:

SWAMI NIKHILANANDA, philosopher, student, teacher, translator, monk, man of good will, ponderer of the secrets of time, being and destiny; master of the folklore of a people and of the highest achievements of Indian intellect; we honor you as a teacher, who, coming to live among us thirty years ago, has shared with America the wisdom of the East, its philosophy, its habit of reflection upon man's resources for transcending the spirit of man into the realms of the eternal. You have lectured at the great American universities, placed students of our own Douglass College deep in your debt, and won our unalloyed respect and gratitude for your intellect, your warm humane concern, and for the Ramakrishna Order which ordained and commissioned you to be our teacher and our friend.

Therefore, moved by unbounded admiration for work so ably done, your friends and debtors of Douglass College do now bestow upon you — unofficially, but with all the love of their hearts — the title which we feel becomes you!

TEACHER PAR EXCELLENCE
May 16, 1961

Swami was right in his element with the great and famous. Scholars, college presidents, writers and musicians, doctors and clergyman — not always his students — were his good friends, and it was no uncommon event for us to see or hear him talking with persons of distinction. When he showed them through the rooms he did not ignore devotees who might be sitting there, but rather made it a point to introduce the latter to anyone he thought they might like to meet. He had been host to Dr. Radhakrishnan, later president of India and Indira Gandhi, who is known to have visited him on her own as well, more than once; among his students were numbered such names as Chester Carlson, inventor of Xerox, J. D. Salinger, Joseph Campbell, Mrs. Max Beckmann and others I do not now recall. In the beginning I was a bit wide-eyed about this, but I would remind myself that before Swami Turiyananda and others of the disciples got his ear and his heart, Swami Nikhilananda had been a highly political journalist, an agitator for independence. It was natural for him to be where the action was.

Now we were on the alert. Swami Madhavananda would be arriving soon.

We met Swami Madhavananda on the appointed day and as we drove back from the airport these two brother monks, guest and host, seated in the rear of the car, were swept into conversation in Bengali. Both were disciples of Sri Sarada Devi, the Holy Mother; the general secretary was not only the older but had also been a mentor of Swami's, yet the relationship was that of close brothers or the best of friends.

Swami Madhavananda was to be at the center for a week before entering New York Hospital for removal of a benign tumor of the brain. His bed faced a large photograph of the Holy Mother. It was she who reigned here. One might say that if in San Francisco it had been all Swamiji and in Hollywood all Maharaj, in this establishment it was all Holy Mother. Both swamis told us of their first meetings with her and their subsequent opportunities for darshan. These have been widely published. With becoming modesty Swami Nikhilananda told us that Holy Mother appeared to him in dream and requested him to write her life "for the West." No such book appeared. A second time the dream had come and he had not treated it seriously; he stalled. Now it was her *Life* which lay on Swami Nikhilananda's desk as a work-in-progress; after a third occurrence of the dream, Swami had taken up the pen to carry out what he now saw as a divine command. Downstairs a bust of the Mother, a creation of Malvina Hoffman cast in bronze, graced the entryway to the auditorium's main floor. It was fascinating to me to live among those who had taken for granted that God had incarnated this time jointly in male and female form.

II. HARRIED HOST

From before the arrival of our guest the disruption of Swami Nikhilananda's daily routine began, and for the ensuing year he was to know no respite from the attention and anxiety occasioned by this undertaking. Possibly the heavy financial drain — all transportation, hospital, surgeon and other medical expenses — was the least of it. The emotional and nervous strain brought on in the supervision and care of an often reluctant and occasionally uncooperative senior monk as guest and patient greatly aged the swami, as those of us moving in his orbit could see.

Up before dawn and at his writing desk for an hour or more was the usual routine. Then came his bath, after which he would enter the tiny shrine room. It was one of the distinctive features of this center that there was no place for regular group meditation. Accustomed to such an element, I missed it; I would sit either in my room or on the platform of the auditorium, facing the Hoffman bust of the Master there. Others meditated in their rooms, while the shrine, adjacent to his room, was Swami's own. After returning to California I mentioned to Swami Ashokananda that I regretted the absence of a common shrine and daily worship at the New York center. He saw no importance in it, commenting that a center can have quite as good an atmosphere as any other, without that.

After about half an hour Swami Nikhilananda would be ready to go down for breakfast, sometimes served him by Al, before he went off for doctors' calls. The atmosphere on these occasions could be tense, as this "luckless" disciple seemed to have the knack of drawing down upon himself his guru's frequent blessing in the form of ire, spicing his eggs and toast with scoldings or arguments. Old tendencies were hard to remove. Said the swami: "If you drive a screw into the wall by twenty turns, you cannot just pull it out with one tug."

Countess, as we referred to and called her, would arrive by mid-morning and begin taking care of the day's correspondence. If it was not heavy there might be time for a walk before lunch. Swami would go out with a very brisk step and head held high, his face tilted a little up. Many was the time I saw in him, I thought, Swami Vivekananda (who is said never to have seen anything lower than a telephone wire) — the lofty bearing and good looks, relieved by puckish mischief in the sparkling eyes. A walk, however, seemed to require a cane. It was tempting to think this was just the New York look, but I believe he had fallen a time or two, and there was the possibility of an unfriendly dog. At his height, and wearing in winter a long coat, he cut a fine figure on Fifth Avenue. Vladimir Horowitz lived across the street and we would often see him walking; his figure was the only one that could offer comparison.

Either Moffitt or I put lunch together. The kitchen was an old-fashioned small one scarcely separated from the spacious dining room. At meal time the formality with which all life in this part of the city seemed to be affected was visibly intensified. The high-gloss table (having perfectly matched extending panels) was laid with fine china and silverplate. Cloth napkins, the glasses placed on coasters; spoons and forks and plates for each course as required. Swami Nikhilananda quite evidently had known, or had acquainted himself with, the ambiance of a staunch Victorian family of breeding. A bell rang to summon us to meals and, arriving at the table, one paused behind one's chair until the head signaled the seating. At night the cook served table. Swami loved to find an excuse to tell a story and for him it was easy to do so.

"An English preacher was called to account for the fact that he spoke in casual conversation about his not believing hell to be eternal. 'A few Sundays ago,' said the objector, 'you said in your sermon that that is what God does: He sends the sinner to eternal damnation.' 'Well,' said the clergyman, 'that is what He does in his official capacity; but what he thinks as a private individual is something else.'"

Swami would take a nap after lunch, unless some peculiar ripple had got into that day's program. Tea was prepared by Countess and served to us all in Swami's study. It was the social high point of the day. We were expected to be present, and Swami was often at his most scintillating here. "You speak of social service? Out of every miserable dollar you give a poor man in charity, with fifty cents you preserve his miserable body and with fifty cents you destroy his soul. 'Going about doing good' soon becomes more going about than doing good." Occasionally the conversation would be so engrossing as to last out the afternoon, but more often this was a period for visitors, interviews, or just reading, or another walk.

The cook would have come in to prepare the dinner. Her roots, I discovered, were in Trinidad and must have been both African and Hindu. She was a good and noble soul who performed her work well. She would turn out standard three-course dinners with hotel-style desserts. She and Swami Nikhilananda had one of those relationships which, while never compressing the appointed distance of employee from employer, nevertheless vibrated with the subtle chimes of a deep and affectionate mutual admiration. Eva knew little, probably, of what the center was all about, even less about Vedanta itself; yet no one had had to tell her who — or what — Swami was.

Except on the two class nights nothing was scheduled after dinner. We retired fairly early.

One must imagine all of the above being broken up daily by the arrangements preceding, attending on, and seeing through, the presence of Swami Madhavananda in the house, in the hospital and in convalescence, to appreciate what an undertaking this was to be for the New York swami. He confided to me later that one of the reasons he had had to send for me was that they were all a "sickly bunch." "Each of us here has something wrong with him," he added.

There was a memorable dinner before our patient went off to the hospital — a party, it should be called, since we had a rare guest, Swami Pavitrananda, who presided over the Vedanta Society of New York, on the other side of Central Park. We had looked forward to this for several days with much expectation. He arrived just in time, and was seated to the left of Swami Madhavananda who, since his arrival, had occupied the head of the table for meals. Our host sat on the latter's right and the rest of us in our accustomed places. I don't know how it was possible to eat anything for all the entertaining conversation. Swami Nikhilananda began it.

"One swami in India, a longtime attendant of Holy Mother, always used to insist that real devotees will always go to some *loka*, some higher world, after death; devotees of the Master to Ramakrishna loka and so on. Then when one would ask him, 'Suppose I don't want to go to any loka, just to become absorbed in Brahman, beyond all lokas?' the reply would be, 'Go to your Brahman. After a while you will become bored with that, and come to Ramakrishna loka.' [To Swami Madhavananda:] What do you think about it?" There was no reply.

Swami Pavitrananda picked up the thread. "We once asked Swami Vijnanananda (a disciple of Sri Ramakrishna and a president of the order) about this. He said, 'I don't understand much about this loka business; I feel that if I can remember the Master here, this is Ramakrishna-loka!'"

Now Swami Nikhilananda: "Once we were puzzled and worried, because both Master and Mother have said that if there is the slightest desire left at the time of death, you cannot get liberated, but will have to be born again. I went to Swami Shivananda and told him, 'You see, here I am, I have no samadhi or anything, and there are these desires, this and that, to write a book and so on; now does this mean if I were to face death now, there would be no liberation for me?' Swami Shivananda replied, 'In the course of public work many little desires come up and have to be worked out. It is not these that are meant. Look, do you suppose that when death approaches you, and Sri Ramakrishna comes and appears to you and leads you by the hand, you will remember those trifling things and be drawn by them? Of course not. This is called the grace of the Lord. But if one has any deep-seated attraction for something that is very worldly, that is another story.'"

(To Swami Madhavananda): "I have another idea about these lokas. Now you tell me if I am wrong. I am thinking that *satya loka* (highest of the heavens) is divided into territories, as it were, so that when Christians go to heaven they reach the Christ-loka and so on with Krishna-loka, etc."

Swami Madhavananda: "Why not the same place, seen in different ways by the different devotees? What need for geographical divisions?"

Swami Nikhilananda: "No, I think some kind of distinction like this must be. Well, tell me another thing. Arjuna, in the *Gita*, had the vision of *Viswarupa*, yet he had to be born again as Yogen Maharaj [Swami Yogananda, another of Sri Ramakrishna's disciples]; Mathur Babu [a patron] served Sri Ramakrishna so much and had his grace, yet he had to be born again. How do you explain it?" (The other swamis laugh loudly.)

Swami Madhavananda said: "That the vision of Viswarupa is the highest realization, that is your own interpretation."

Swami Nikhilananda to Swami Pavitrananda: "Well, you are giving lectures all the time; how would you answer it?"

"I would find some trick to get out of answering," he replied. (More laughter.)

Swami Nikhilananda: "Well, Sarat Maharaj [Swami Saradananda, another disciple] told me once, 'It is better to go to hell through your own action, than to go to heaven climbing on the shoulders of another. For if you lose that support you will fall, but if your own efforts got you to hell, you can again climb up by them.'"

Swami Madhavananda now added his own terse comment: "I should think it would be better first to go and see what kind of a place that hell is."

The topic of evolution was raised. Swami Nikhilananda said, "You know, when Swamiji was lecturing in this country, one report came to India of a lecture in which he had said that in the Hindu idea of reincarnation, there was no retrogression — no descent lower than manhood for those who have attained it. People thought, 'What is this? Has he become so Westernized? Has he forgotten the testimony of the *Upanishads* themselves?' A later lecture reported him as saying the opposite, that there is retrogression and all that — the orthodox view. The people of India talked again. 'Is he so changeable? Do his views keep shifting like this?' No one knew what to think. So Swami Akhandananda [another disciple of Sri Ramakrishna] asked him about it directly. He in turn raised the question with Goodwin, the stenographer who had recorded the lectures. Goodwin replied, 'Swamiji, in the first lecture I felt I had to keep you from appearing a fool. In this country that idea would never find acceptance, what with all the ideas current of evolution. So I recorded it in that way. Later, when I had had time to absorb and digest more of your ideas, I saw it in a different light and recorded it as you were giving it.'

"Somewhere Aldous Huxley has written very cleverly to this effect: that Darwin and others never intended the idea of an atheistic, mechanical evolution. The generation coming up wanted to interpret it in that way because they wanted to live a sensuous life and this made it so much easier, without God. In fact, one might say, the doctrine was simply a God-send for them." This brought laughter all around.

III. RACONTEUR

I wondered why, as the center was not poor, we had to put a price on some small tracts kept at the book counter and intended for new inquirers. Swami answered my question with an anecdote. It happened, some years before, that he was with other tourists at the top of the Empire State Building one day at about noon. Suddenly a woman came up, grabbed him by the wrist and led him away. Pulling him, too startled to resist, to a microphone, she there informed him that from this moment every word he said would be broadcast. She proceeded to interview him in the usual manner and when he had explained his profession, asked if any collection was taken at the center, or how otherwise he made his expenses. Swami replied that a collection was taken and other donations were made. She appeared astonished and asked how he had become so Westernized as to do this; she had thought all Indian teachers abjured money in exchange for their teachings. Swami, never at a loss, confided, "Well, I'll tell you something: I have found in this country that even a good thing you cannot give away; but even a bad thing, if you sell it, people will take it."

He had a fund of stories that was justly famous. It never ran out. Those at his own expense, like the above, were as delightful to him as the rest. When he narrated one of his tales you laughed till you wept, and not only the first time. Countess was particularly vulnerable and that was fortunate, for she had more occasion to hear them than others. I wonder if, in the ten months I was there, he exhausted his repertoire. Perhaps. It did not seem to matter how many times he had told it, if there was one person present who had not heard it, out the story would come — and sometimes even *that* stimulus was superfluous. It did not matter how well you knew the lines, so funny was Swami in the telling. The anecdote of Alex Munthe's in *The Story of San Michele*, his wanting a shave on board ship where only a mortician's helper was present to give one, was, even in numerous repetitions, far more amusing than the original writing. "A grouchy person," he used to say, "can never be spiritual. A certain basic contentment must be there." There is no question about it at all, he was the most stimulating conversationalist I have known. Swami often seemed to me to be a grown-up naughty boy. I should have to vote him "Person most fun to live with." Another episode of his early years in New York concerns a dinner party to which a friend had invited him. In after-dinner talk a lady of the party said to Swami Nikhilananda, "You seem to be a very intelligent man; how does it happen you never became a Christian?" How his eyes would sparkle on relating this!

He told serious stories too, of course, like the following incident to which he said Swami Akhandananda had been witness. On the day the Master gave up his body he had said, early in the day, that he would eat two eggs, an item unusual for him.

They were prepared for him, but in the ensuing events of that dramatic day the eggs were put aside and he never ate them. After the passing, Naren (Vivekananda-to-be) said at one point, "Well, I am terribly hungry; what is to be done?" Finding those eggs, he ate them on the spot. Swami Akhandananda had felt that with Sri Ramakrishna's lifelong identity with truth, his words were always fulfilled, and this was the way it had to be done, and it showed there was no difference at all between him and Swamiji. Swami Nikhilananda on hearing the story had expressed astonishment that Swamiji could have felt hungry at such a time, but Swami Akhandananda replied, "Well, that is the way it happened."

With his elder brother monk in the house, Swami Nikhilananda frequently came upstairs and chatted with him in Bengali for hours. I do not suppose the swami really thought his scholarly and self-sufficient guest could become bored, but he certainly made this appear the one thing most to be dreaded. So he urged him again and again to fix his gaze on the television screen, a thing Swami Madhavananda was at first not at all inclined to do. After all, he had his monastic training and habits, and in India, no such toy.

On an evening during this week, Swami Prabhavananda of Hollywood arrived to pay his respects to the old swami. With him, then, commenced the list of the many visitors who were to honor the distinguished monk. The swami from California spoke on Sunday to the Vedanta Society, across town, while our swami was giving the service for his own flock at the observance of the Thrice-Blessed Day of Lord Buddha. After the service I happened to meet Swami Nikhilananda on the stairway. There had been the traditional serving, to the congregation, of *payasam* (a rice pudding) after the lecture. Swami himself had donned an apron and prepared the sweet for the occasion. "Well, Swami," I remarked, "I have had many kinds of payasam in my Vedantic life, made by various persons, but I have never tasted a better one than yours today." At this he burst out laughing and, before the rest of the household, to general merriment and my own intense discomfort, replied: "He praises my payasam to the heavens, but not a word about my lecture!" Before any rejoinder could come to my lips — some temporizing, face-saving remark — he came out with this: "He is thinking, 'I hear the best lecturing ever, every Sunday in San Francisco; what can I say about his lecture?'" Ah. Monastic life is indeed a glass house, as Swami Ashokananda was wont to say. This may be a suitable point at which to observe that Swami asked me to go to the Vedanta Society on a Tuesday evening to hear the scripture class of Swami Pavitrananda; he just thought it was the right thing to do. And he sent me in a taxi.

Now came the grand day for moving our serene guest to the hospital. Bronson Ray, outstanding brain surgeon of the day, had been engaged through the consultative process. New York Hospital, while not one of the world's largest, certainly looked so to me, and its staff, equipment, food and privileges seemed superlative. We installed Swami Madhavananda on the sixteenth floor of the private-patient section, which was more like a hotel than a hospital. Room 1620 was the same one Swami Nikhilananda had occupied, some years before, during his own bout of surgery, and among the doctors, nurses and orderlies some of his old friends remained. Like so many of those acquainted with this popular man, they now sought his company.

Suddenly I had to learn my way about town on my own. I would leave the center early, ride by two bus lines and arrive to attend the swami for the morning. Trees were now in leaf, and lawns appeared where no one could have imagined them. From the top of the hospital it looked as if some great goddess had dropped green lace handkerchiefs all around, embroidered here and there with the pinks and lavenders of azalea bushes. It was necessary now and then to take a taxi. They were at least three-fifths of the vehicles on the street, driving at breakneck speed through the smallest chinks imaginable. Clearance meant literally fractions of an inch. I would close my eyes and take the name of the Lord. There was nothing else to do, until the curiosity to see just *how* narrowly one can miss got the better of me. Space in New York seemed to be worth more than life itself. One day I saw a church used by three different congregations — an ethnic one on Sunday morning, a revivalist in the evening and an offbeat Jewish congregation meeting on Saturdays.

At noon Swami Nikhilananda would come, have his lunch in the cafeteria, and let me go home. In the afternoon the younger swamis might visit. I would return by five o'clock and remain until after nine, sometimes going home with Swami, if he had returned. No king or queen (and this hospital had hosted some) could have had more attention than this silent, unassuming monk from India. A covey of white-coated doctors was examining him — dermatologist, neurologist, three or four surgeons.

Following the operation (discussed more fully in the next chapter), Swami Madhavananda was even more docile than before. It was difficult to give credence to Swami Nikhilananda's private prediction to me that our patient would become more difficult to handle as he recovered. However, he knew what was going on in that mind and saw the resistance to the swami's plans for attending to all of his disabilities. Swami visited every day, often at evening with a devotee or two. He would inquire into everything with concern and chat with the older man for an hour or two before we took leave. One night he spoke at length, mostly to Swami Madhavananda but also for our benefit. I give it here as closely as I can remember.

"Swami Vivekananda," he began, "was a man of another plane. We try to put him in our own mold and explain his life thereby. But it is impossible, it is ludicrous, he was entirely of another order. Once two admirers of Swamiji in India were conversing, one waxing very emotional, saying 'Oh, if Swamiji were only here now, to see the plight of our country!' The other was Holy Mother. She said, 'Don't say that. He would have been in jail if he were here today. Things have come to that kind of pass. And I could not have stood it. I just could not have stood it.' Swamiji was an unsheathed sword. And how he felt for mankind, we just cannot imagine. Once at Balaram Bose's house he was with Hari Maharaj (Swami Turiyananda); he just became overwhelmed with man's misery and condition — he wept and wept until his emotion spent itself into a song which he began to sing.

"You know, people who saw him once, never forgot him. One year at Lake George I was vacationing with Swami Yatiswarananda and Swami Satprakashananda. One day, walking near the lake, I stood for awhile until I noticed a young sailor hovering near me. I wondered what he could want. Then he came up and showed me his wallet. In it his name was printed, and his first name was 'Ceylon' — I forget the last name. He said to me,

'My father was also a sailor and went to Ceylon and liked it so much he gave me that name. I don't know much about Indian things; my wife knows more. She reads books on it. Would you like to meet her? I replied 'Certainly.' So he brought her. She had read *Raja-Yoga* and some other books, and was a devotee-type. She had had asthma, and by practicing some of the simple breathing exercises had overcome it. She spoke nicely with me, but she said, 'You should meet my mother-in-law, because she *met* Swami Vivekananda.' The mother-in-law was called over. She was a little old lady over eighty with eyes so bright they looked like coals, and there was a great pride about her. What she said was, 'Yes, I went to hear one of Swami Vivekananda's lectures in Chicago at the fair. I was taken by my mother when I was about sixteen, but I can see him yet. He would stride up and down the platform and every now and then would come to the edge of it and look at me. I was sitting right up front. He would emphasize a point and then finish by looking in my face. Much later I wondered a lot about my religious beliefs and felt very confused about things. At that time I came across his *Raja-Yoga*, and everything seemed to fall into place.' Then of course I told her who I was and that we had a center in New York. When I asked where they lived, she said in Brooklyn. I suggested she come up to our service some time and gave the address. Then the old lady looked at me with her burning eyes. 'Do you think,' she said, 'anyone who has heard Swami Vivekananda needs to go to anyone else?'

"A man came to Swamiji, a man who was always getting sick with one ailment or another. He asked Swamiji what he could do about his poor health. And he got this interesting reply: 'If you can get to the point where you can say that you have never done anything in your life which you need to regret, then you will always have good health.'"

IV. COMPANIONS

Swami Madhavananda's operation had resulted in a slight impairment of the cerebellum, which houses the sense of balance. The task of his recovery now lay before the patient, his nurses, therapist, host and attendant. Every factor was taken into account. Countess Colloredo-Mansfeld (Swami sometimes called her by her given name, Mabel) was a woman of New England with the charm and manners of the graduate of an aristocratic college. She had married a member of the old Austrian nobility, so was connected with the Hapsburgs. The young man had given his life in the war and left her with two children, now grown. There was an air of European sophistication about her, perhaps, yet her basic simplicity and absence of any self-importance were obvious and spiritually exemplary. Countess dealt with each of us with friendly solicitude, courtesy and gentility. Her placid countenance would be ruffled only by the humor of Swami Nikhilananda's reiterated jibe quoting Oscar Wilde. "Countess, you know," he would tell anyone in her presence, "can resist anything — except temptation." She had had her apartment renovated during our patient's hospitalization, had moved to a hotel and now invited Swami Madhavananda and me to occupy her quarters, the reason being that the house had a "lift," saving him the trouble of stairs. It was so announced to our convalescent. "One week," Swami said to the figure on the hospital bed. "The doctors say about one week and you go there. So, better make up your mind to it, as you will have to be ready, you know."

"Tell the Old Man," was his summary reply, referring to Sri Ramakrishna. His eyes and teeth were giving him trouble, as every one knew, but these repairs would have to wait until fall, for we were all going out of the hot city for the summer.

The move was duly made and from that apartment we took our daily walks, accompanied occasionally by Swami Nikhilananda. One morning the latter, using every argument conceivable, finally persuaded Swami Madhavananda to vary his customary route into the park by returning in such a way as to pass the center on 94th Street. The house displays two flags hanging high out over the sidewalk, that of the United States and a white one bearing the seal of the order and name of the center. As we approached the building, Swami remarked with the pardonable pride of a boy showing his favorite toy, "Now, is it not nice, seeing our flag flying there on the front of the house?"

"Hmph!" snorted the other, "Advertising!" It was a "Peanuts" cartoon.

It was now late in June. City temperatures were 88°F. and going up, and it was humid. The patient was making rapid progress. Plans went ahead for the move to Thousand Island

Park, the center's summer retreat on the St. Lawrence River at the very northern edge of the state. Everyone now had to be busily engaged. Swami Budhananda, a little older than I, had a good physique and could be counted on to help in various ways. A studious and quiet Indian who spent most of his time in his room, he often served in wiping dishes and was good for jolly camaraderie especially on walks in Central Park. It surprised me that he too had a health problem — an old injury to his knee or leg. I once mustered the nerve to mumble something to Swami Nikhilananda about the number of times his assistant had been replaced. He rose to the occasion. "Yes," he said, "I have trained many a man, and sent him on to better things!"

Swami Atmaghanananda or Moffitt was older — early fifties at the time — but a real live wire. He could be up and down and all over the house in a jiffy. A published poet (*Atlantic Monthly*, etc., and two volumes of verse), he shared the verbal and literary expertise of his guru, with whom he had lived for many years. He was Swami's right arm. Moffitt's taste in music, classical and highly refined, revealed itself at the services on Sunday mornings, as he sat at the piano in the back of the auditorium, performing Frescobaldi and the like in a most professional manner. Now he had gone ahead to the Vivekananda Cottage at the Park to make preparations, and to plant some flower sets in the little garden so that our summer stay would be graced with blooms.

V. THE SUMMER PARK

It took the entire day to make our way up to Watertown on the St. Lawrence, taking a short detour to see Clayton, a village from which an ancient little steamboat takes mail and passengers over to Thousand Island Park. This was the way Swami Vivekananda made his first trip there. The full history of the Vedanta involvement with Thousand Island Park has been recorded in several places, among them the introduction to Swamiji's book *Inspired Talks* and the Indian journal *Vedanta Kesari* (Aug.-Sept., 1963). We have only to set down here the way it was told by Swami Nikhilananda himself. Amid the scattered glacial rock which studs the bowl of the St. Lawrence and is known as the Thousand Islands lies one much larger than most, named Wellesley. For this was, at the turn of the century, the province of the Methodists. The settlement which formed at one of its harbors was a principal summer camp of the church, the colony being known as Thousand Island Park. Unable to avoid altogether the secularization of that America, it has lost its denominational and missionary stamp, but the Park is still a corporation, tightly held and regulated by descendants of those who occupied these fragile wooden summer homes in Swami Vivekananda's day. Lacy with Victorian "gingerbread," these attractive seasonal homes surprise us with their stamina, their ability to be reborn in May with an air of patient abiding and welcoming.

Those familiar with Swamiji's life know of the summer of 1895, when, fed up with the lecture circuit and public appeals, and longing for the forests of the sannyasin, he gladly took up the invitation of a student of the city classes, a Miss Dutcher, to spend some time at her cottage there. The six-week period was utilized by the swami not only in rest and recreation but also — and for this America must be profoundly grateful — as a retreat in which to prepare a dozen seekers for deeper spiritual adventure, leaving in their notebooks the priceless pearls of the *Inspired Talks*.

Miss Dutcher's alarmed reaction to the Vivekananda she discovered on retreat (probably to the Advaitic mood so evident in him on this "holiday") has also been well remembered. The little hostess disappeared into her room and was hardly to be seen. But just who Miss Dutcher was, what happened to her or her now famous cottage — even just where it stood — was not known for half a century.

These facts came to general knowledge in 1948 when Swami Nikhilananda decided to investigate. When the house was located it was found to be in a desolate state indeed. Tumbling, shaky, decayed as only such buildings can be, it was in the care of a neighbor who was about to scrap it for firewood. Miss Dutcher, it was learned, had owned it until, no longer able in her advanced years and poor health to make the annual journey, she had given it into the keeping of her nearest neighbor, a Miss Otis. Miss Otis, approached by the swami with his purpose, and identifying himself, startled him speechless by producing the first line, in Sanskrit, of the "Nala and Damayanti" episode from the

epic *Mahabharata*. She was, it seems, a classicist, had a doctorate
in Latin, was familiar with Greek and Sanskrit, and had become
a permanent resident in the Park.

As nearly as it can be worked out, the original cottage
consisted of two large rooms downstairs and four small upstairs
bedrooms. Before Swamiji arrived in 1895 Miss Dutcher had
completed the new wing, said to have been built for him, consisting of three rooms stacked up, with an outside staircase. At
some later period the large kitchen and north wing were added.
The house was host to 12 people that historic summer, and at
meals they must have been quite squeezed into the dining room.
Where they all slept is a mystery; perhaps some had rooms in
neighboring cottages. It is probable that Miss Dutcher rented
rooms out to summer tourists, else why build them? We do know
that the rooms used by Swami Vivekananda stood empty for some
time in his memory. For many years this house was unused except for a period when a caretaker stayed in the basement rooms.

Miss Dutcher had been a homespun artist, painting in
oils and watercolors and setting the canvases out along the path
to the top of the hill so that summer visitors who climbed to see
the view would be attracted; their price was modest, about two
dollars. At the time of the finding of the cottage there were at
least three persons still living on the island who had seen Swamiji.
One was the carpenter, builder of those extra rooms, who with
his son had the monopoly on construction in the little settlement. Aged over 90, he remembered well the colorful man from
India and had made his acquaintance. Then there was one, described as "a funny old lady," who told them she used to see the
swami walking down the village road in his orange coat and his
turban. Often she had wanted to go up and just shake his hand,
like any friendly little girl. "Stay away from him," her mother
had warned, "he is a heathen!" A third was a woman who would
sit on her porch and watch him go by, but never dared speak
with him.

On my first wandering through Vivekananda Cottage I
thought it a veritable rabbit warren of little rooms, passages, hidden closets, stairs running in all directions. Scarcely any room
seemed to have true right angles any more, if it ever had. And
the marvel was that anyone had been able to go on living in this

place without improving it. I had California standards, to be sure.

Certainly the charm of the original slapdab summer cottage construction had been preserved, because it felt like 1895.

*Swamis Madhavananda (l.) and Nikhilananda
at Thousand Island Park*

Moffitt told me they had spent thousands on restoring it even to this condition; no doubt the builder's charges were high. A trap door could be discovered in the floor of each room. But if the roof leaked and the doors stuck, it took not a whit away from the overarching sense of peace and dedication pervading the place.

Vivekananda seemed to be living here still. So far as is known, the only furniture remaining from his day was the dark, heavy dining room table with its numerous leaves. I held this piece in great veneration and would never sit down to it without thinking of him and those who had been around him. On this table he had laid the special dishes of curry he loved to cook for his companions. On the walls were several oddities. One of Miss Dutcher's surviving oil landscapes hung there, and one of her watercolor paintings. There was a portrait of Tantine — Miss Josephine MacLeod — painted by, of all people, William Ernest Hocking, the philosopher, who knew her well and had heard Swamiji at the Parliament of Religions in 1893. There was the original manuscript of Vivekananda's poem, "Peace," found at Ridgely Manor, New York, and another frame holding the original of "The Song of the Sannyasin." The story goes that builder Mitchell's young son had been hired, at the time of reconstruction, to remove a heap of refuse from the attic. The boy found a poem in longhand lying on this heap; it seemed to him interesting and peculiar and worth taking home to examine at leisure. So it lay in his dresser drawer for several years before it occurred to him to offer it back to the swamis. Swamiji's scratches and penciling are there to awe us with authenticity.

Miss MacLeod had come to the cottage, we were told, after Swamiji's passing away. Perhaps she stayed in his bedroom for about four days, tucked away there, weeping and grieving. Things have a way, sometimes, of coming to us just when we are most in need of them. A few words of Maurice Maeterlink came to her eyes. He had written, "When a great man you have loved dies, do not spend your strength in weeping at his grave. Spread his message and carry on his work." It pulled her up directly and turned her thoughts in the direction they took thereafter.

That bedroom of his had become the shrine room now, complete with Indian carpet, the usual pictures, busts, harmonium, flower vases and bolsters. One recalls that it was out on the little porch adjoining this room that the group of retreatants had sat in the moonlight and summer air to drink in Swamiji's outpouring which went on sometimes till dawn. He would go down from his quarters by the back stair, now removed, and walk up the path leading to the hilltop where lie the large rocks he was wont to rest upon for reflection and meditation. One such is now pointed out as the site of the samadhi in which he evidently lost himself. The rock is spacious and flat, rising from between two old oak trees and commanding a view of the island's valley, now a golf course.

One of the stories told us by Swami Nikhilananda in these first days of our stay concerned Swamiji at the palace of the Nizam, the ruler of Hyderabad. As a rule the Nizam did not rise from his seat to show respect to anyone else. At Swami Vivekananda's arrival he did so. Asked by a courtier how this had happened, the ruler replied, "This world which I am clinging to like a dog to a bone, he has spat out. That is why I could not do otherwise." Swamiji, telling this later, said that he had gone to the Nizam partly to seek financial help but when this was reported to him, he said with a smile, "I had not the heart to ask him for any money."

Summer at the Park always brought to Swami Nikhilananda the "community" he never wanted. Devotees began to come even before he arrived, having rented cottages or rooms thereof, or hotel rooms, the hotel being an oversize Victorian cottage like the rest. Swami had initiated the practice of holding an annual seminar, the equivalent of a retreat, and this year was to be no exception in spite of his great preoccupation with the older swami. For the seminar, people from around the country had gathered. Mr. & Mrs. Chester Carlson came; two physicians from different parts of Canada; a Christian minister, student of Swami's, who had lost more than one pulpit through speaking about Sri Ramakrishna; the sister of the man who had given the property for the Sarada Convent in Santa Barbara; people from Ohio, Virginia and other states. That year there were 21 of us.

These devotees went in and out of Vivekananda Cottage constantly, attending the daily vesper service, using the shrine room, browsing at the library shelves, volunteering for the cooking and housework. For Swami Nikhilananda to meet them all was to wear himself out. He tired of duty. "Duty is all well and good," he told us, "at the human level, but it always creates frictions: 'I don't really want to do this!' Swami Vivekananda said, you know, 'Duty is like the midday sun that scorches the tender

plant of spirituality.' Do the same thing out of love, not out of
'oughtness.'" If that beehive of activity became too much, Swami
would have to escape. He had bought, some years before, another cottage, situated at the bottom of the hill. It had been
named Vedanta Cottage, and in past summers he had lived there
in order to minimize disturbance to his peace and his writing.
For it was here he would remain for hours, at work on literary
productions and lecture preparations. Next to the cottage was
Sri Sarada Kutir, bought for the use of serious women students
by an earlier secretary, Mrs. Elizabeth Davidson, whose name
was never mentioned without the deepest respect. Countess had
improved its facilities and life there was regulated. Sometimes
the ladies would invite the swamis to dinner.

The Vedanta Cottage would be needed now for Swami
Madhavananda. We established him in the larger of the two bedrooms. He and I had a living room, kitchen and bath to ourselves here, and enjoyed the quiet so clearly sacrificed by our
host. In spite of this, Swami was to say to me, near the end of the
summer, "Lake Tahoe [the retreat of the San Francisco center]
and other mountain places, fine as they are, I find stimulating;
but this place gives me *serenity*. I am very happy here." If there
was anything Swami Nikhilananda did not require, it was stimu-
lation.

He often spoke of his association with Swami Turiyananda,
who had sympathized with his collegiate passions for politics and
journalism but had turned his thinking in a quite opposite direction; Swami felt it was he who had provided him with the
rationale, the intellectual support, for his eventual choice of the
life of renunciation. "Once Swami Turiyananda went out for begging his food," he related. "Getting nothing at all and feeling
tired and hungry he sat down. Suddenly he thought of the verse
in the *Gita*: 'I am in the sun, in the moon...' and he felt identified
with the Whole. He lost all hunger and thirst and fatigue. Of
course he was a great ascetic."

He told us one day of an incident about which he had
heard from the same great swami. The latter was sitting in the
Master's room with him one afternoon, when suddenly a boy
poked his head in the door and asked the Master if he had a
knife. Sri Ramakrishna kept quiet. "I say, have you got a knife?"

The lad went on: "My friends and I are having a picnic in the temple garden and we need a knife."

Sri Ramakrishna looked hard at him. "Will you bring it back?"

"Yes, I'll bring it back."

A second time: "Will you bring it back?" Of course he would, came the assurance. The Master told him there was a knife on the brick under the bedpost; he might take it. "But be sure to return it." After the boy had gone out toward the trees the Master jumped up, ran to the door and shouted after him, "I say, don't forget to bring back the knife!"

"Are you crazy?" said the boy, "We'll return your old knife!" During the following hour or two the Master interrupted the conversation at intervals to ask Hari Maharaj if he thought they would return the knife. Hari Maharaj was thinking, "This man is a poor Brahmin's son; no doubt that is why he is so much attached to a measly penknife." But he said nothing. When the hour advanced beyond four o'clock it became evident the boys would not return.

"It is as I feared," said Sri Ramakrishna, "they have not brought the knife."

Swami Turiyananda consoled him, offering to buy another. The Master told him, "No, you just go and find that knife." Good disciple that he was, he obeyed at once though he knew that to look for it in a big jungle was sure to be hopeless. Then the Master came to the door of his room and called. "Just go over to that grove of trees there and under the largest tree you will find a heap of potato peelings. Under the peelings you will find the knife." So it was. (Swami, in relating the story, opined that this was not psychic knowledge but good surmise.) Back in the room, the disciple still did not express what he was thinking. Then the Master asked him to put the knife back in its place. "No," he commented, watching, "you have put it back dirty. Wash it, wipe it so it won't rust, and, closing the blade first, put it on the brick. You see, I keep this knife just on that brick, next to the right hand post of my bed. In the morning I will reach down to get the knife, to cut a twig for cleaning my teeth. If I find it open I may get cut; if I find it dirty or missing I will be upset; I will then be unable to meditate and what kind of day will I have? So

I have told you to do all these things in that way."

"But, sir, how did you know that he would not return the knife?"

"You see, when the boy looked in I saw that one shirt button was not buttoned and his hair was running in all directions. I knew at once that he would not return the knife."

The story instantly threw light on how the kind of training I was exposed to had come down to me. "Those who really enjoy meditation," said Swami Nikhilananda, "live a very disciplined life. Not a single unnecessary word they utter, nor make a single unnecessary move, because these later become distractions in meditation."

A happier story was the one about Holy Mother's disciple named Chandra who is described in the swami's biography of her. He is the one who always requested of her only prasad, though he knew her to be the great Dispenser of Boons, such as devotion and liberation. In the days after Mother had left this world and her birthday had become a grand festival, Chandra at one such celebration watched carefully how the prasad was being passed around. On this occasion it was a popular type of sweet called *gaja*. The brahmachari who served Chandra moved on quickly, to his surprise and chagrin. "Hey, you fellow," he blurted out, "I wanted another piece."

"I cannot give you seconds. Each is to get one," replied the server.

"What! What do you say? I... I... why, Mother used to feed me gaja with her own hand."

"I'm sorry... I have my instructions."

"You, you were made a brahmachari only yesterday, and you refuse another piece of gaja to me, an old-time devotee, who ate from Mother's hands?" All day he could not get over it. At night he was given a place to sleep which happened to be in a storeroom. It was hot and he was tossing and turning, just chewing over the insult. "What, they gave me but one piece on Mother's birthday, of all days." And with his foot, extending it this way and that, he touched some kind of jar. "What is that?" he thought. It proved to be a drum stuffed full of gaja which had gone undistributed. "Ho-ho, you fools," said Chandra to himself, "you thought you could cheat Mother?" After eating all he could, and stuffing more into his pocket, he went home before daybreak. "Thus did she fulfill the desires of all," was Swami's comment in ending his narration.

VI. IN THE VIVEKANANDA MOLD

My time being much taken up with our patient, I missed most of the life and thought centering around Swami Nikhilananda at the upper house. But such good stories as I heard I fortunately wrote down. Here is one about Sarat Maharaj (Swami Saradananda), another disciple of the Master whom Swami Nikhilananda had served and loved and who had shared it with him.

One day Swami Vivekananda was scolding Sarat Maharaj. He was doing it as only Swamiji could do. His voice was cutting and merciless and he went on and on. Suddenly a devotee passing by came in to pay his respects to the swamis. Swamiji's tone changed at once. He became soft and sweet and chatted with the visitor, raising little topics as one does — the very picture of benignity and graciousness. Before long the visitor departed. "Well, where did we leave off?" Swamiji inquired of Swami Saradananda. "Let us begin again."

Once Swami Akhandananda had made Swamiji very angry by the way he had written something in a journal article. Swamiji gave him a scolding of the same sort, and for punishment sent him into a corner, like a schoolboy, with his face to the wall. "Now you sit there and meditate till you get some sense in your head," he decreed. Meanwhile, in the same room he struck up a conversation with some devotees present. He brought the topic around to fishing and got deeper and deeper into it. Now, Swami Akhandananda had been very fond of fishing in his premonastic days, and Swamiji asked one of the men, "Do you know that kind of fish (giving the Bengali name) which thrives in East Bengal? How big does that fish get, do you know?" The devotee did not know. Swamiji asked again, from one devotee to another, "Do you know how large that fish grows?" At once, from the meditation corner two hands were seen to come up in the air, under a shawl, showing a certain length. "Hey," shouted Vivekananda, "this is your meditation! You rascal!"

The rock garden at the cottage was more extensive than

I had at first realized. Moffitt had designed it expertly. There were splashes of bright color on three sides of the building, blossoms all coming out simultaneously. The vegetables were neatly confined in an area at the bottom of the huge rock one sees in the original photograph of the cottage. (It is apparent that that photo was snapped from someone's perch in a tree; no other place could have given that perspective.) In addition to begonias and petunias, hydrangeas and many kinds of lilies were now poking out from the pockets and crevices in the large rocks, along with rarer bergamot, salvia, Funkia, balsam, phlox, mullen pink, Platons, platycodon, ageratum and wild flowers. Ferns were there, too, and even odd fungi like the Dutchman's pipe seemed to spring up as boons for the gardener's good offices.

On one occasion there was a visit from Gayatri Devi, of Cohasset and La Crescenta, ashramas founded by Swami Paramananda but subsequently separated from our order. She was invited to have her meals at the Holy Mother Cottage and there treated the ladies to Bengali songs. Perhaps it was this visit of hers that sparked off Swami Nikhilanananda's little anecdote about Swami Paramananda, her uncle and mentor. It happened in Cincinnati, where Swami Paramananda was speaking some twenty years after his first visit there, which had taken place very early in his career. This night the hall was filled. One old gentleman came up after the lecture and shook the swami's hand. "Well, now, you know," he mused, "I happen to have heard your father in this same hall about 20 years ago. You do pretty well as a speaker, sir, but you're not the equal of your father. My, how he could preach!" "In this case," Swami Paramananda replied, "I and my father are one." Such a story, told by this superb storyteller with his sparkling eyes and mastery of timing and anticipation, would make one's day.

Swami related to us an encounter he had had in Ireland. In the town of Killarney he stood one evening in Killarney Park, dressed in Western clothes and without clerical collar. Two priests stood not far away, one an older man, the other about Swami's age. Approaching, he engaged them in conversation. "Can you tell me," he asked the younger, "just what Christ meant when he said "Love the Lord *thy* God with all thy heart, mind, soul and strength?""

"Well, now, what do you think he meant?" was the priest's rejoinder. Swami replied that to him it meant Christ was telling each man to love *his* God — his idea of God — with his whole heart, whatever that ideal might be, throughout the world.

"Indeed!" said the older priest, "We have preached on this passage for many years, but never heard it put like that."

"That is what it means to me as a Hindu," Swami persisted. The talk went on. The fathers now asked him if he wouldn't like to visit their cathedral, pointing to a steeple nearby. A meeting was set for eight o'clock in the evening. Swami Nikhilananda went to the church, this time dressed in his clerical suit (a very Catholic-looking outfit, black with clerical collar). The old priest greeted him. "But are you a minister?" he said in surprise. "I had no idea."

"I am. I am a monk." The father, bemused, led him into the sanctuary and Swami prostrated himself before the altar.

"Now why did you do that?" the priest asked. "That is not your God."

"Is it not? Do we not worship the same God? Can I not see God in your shrine? I worship the Christ just as I worship all forms of God." After a while the priest commented that the swami's life seemed in a way richer than his, in that he was able to appreciate many ideals.

"I cannot do that," he said, "I cannot, for instance, see God in your gods." They went then into the study and the talk went on, regarding doctrines, scriptures, Sri Ramakrishna — until it was close to midnight. As Swami rose to take his leave, the father saw him to the door. "Brother," he said, putting his hand on the shoulder of his guest, "we shall meet again; if not in this life, then in heaven."

Perhaps Swami had explained to the priest what he had given us one day: "The gods? Their only proof is the scriptures. Does the new space science give us new evidence? There is talk like that. Creation, you see, is the seamless garment of the Creator. Or, a pyramid; very solid or dense at the base; as you go up, the matter becomes more rarified — it is pure Spirit at the top. Some gods are eternal; they coexisted with the Creator. Some are procreated. Some are men who are God-become. Like the peers in England, some being hereditary, some elevated. 'Animism', the term so often used by Western scholars, is not a good explanation of the Hindu idea, because the real power is Brahman Itself, delegated as it were. These natural forces also control our various sense organs. The gods are the custodians of social welfare."

In these early weeks of the summer Swami was putting the finishing touches on *Holy Mother*, writing in his study, which was beneath the shrine room in Vivekananda Cottage. Each day in mid-morning the households of the three cottages would assemble in the living room of Vedanta Cottage, as the author sat at a small table, reading to us from his manuscript. Swami Madhavananda would sit in a large armchair and was solicited at intervals for comments or criticism. August and silent, he seldom had any to offer unless it were in regard to some error of fact known to him. Swami Budhananda was the most frequent commentator; he seemed to feel it incumbent upon him to play the gadfly role and did it as best he could, but it was difficult to fault this writer.

The seminar was to last two weeks. Some devotees had taken their entire year's vacation for this. They would drive or walk from their cottages to the bottom of the hill and trudge up the steep oily dirt road which leads to the cottage porch. Swami Nikhilananda discoursed, in the manner of the *Inspired Talks*, freely and informally from the Upanishads. He was using his own published translation. Lest anyone suppose that Swami Nikhilananda might be "known" from his books, or even from his lectures in the city of New York, let me hasten to say I saw a different man, just as I had at Douglass College. In the seminar there was a vitality and an inspiration not seen elsewhere in his life. There was also a feeling of relatedness to the audience which did not come easily in other environments. Explain it as one will, attributing it perhaps to the influence upon him of that special milieu, we were galvanized. There were sharp and penetrating questions he fielded handily. His approach was fresh. In the gathering were physicians, a dentist, an inventor, teachers, clergy and an editor from one of the prominent publishing companies; one does not pull much wool over the eyes of such a company. It was only later that I learned that Swami's incarceration had prevented him from sitting for his B.A. examination, his regret for which can be appreciated when one knows the value placed on degrees and titles by the Indian people.

In the afternoon we would return for singing and meditation. On one day only did the strain of the load on Swami's mind become clear to everyone: he absented himself, asking Swami Budhananda to take over. My notes, such as they are, of the remarks made in these discourses, are offered below as unstrung gems.

Beethoven said, 'I wish I could express one millionth of the music I feel inside.' One person said, when people were praising a great painting of a sunset, 'We are surely seeing only third-hand'; i.e., the original sunset was not visible to mortal eyes.

There is a story of Leopold Stokowski and an Indian *veena* player. The former was so entranced with the latter's music that he requested him to play for tape recording that Stokowski might take it back with him. The Indian musician declined. 'I know,' he said, 'you will go back to your country and put on my tapes to accompany some cocktail party.' We must not vulgarize the sacred. In India everything that is considered music is regarded as religious. Reincarnation is just 'in the blood' of every Hindu. According to us it is the necessary corollary of the immortality of the soul. And without the latter, only ethics is left, not religion.

Hindus mean by 'the world,' all the worlds, not just this one. Therefore rebirth is postulated because so many persons die with their desires unsatisfied. Reincarnation gives much consolation for the living of our life, much calmness. People in America are excited now about reincarnation, hoping for further enjoyment. But the Hindus do not want to be reborn.

The mango falls. It is ripe. But the mango has a seed for another mango tree. The difference between death and dream is that in the latter the *prana* does not leave the body. Where do the materials come from for the new body? We do not deny heredity nor environment but — note! — we believe the soul *chooses* just those elements which will help it to manifest the blueprint already given by its past — those which we need to fulfill our unfulfilled desires. We don't pass the buck to our parents or our teachers or to society.

The soul has no contact whatever with the body. We lead our daily life by mixing up truth and falsehood. Evolution means that the soul is involved, for some reason or other, in matter, and is struggling to get detached from it. Every soul that comes into this world is provided with a round-trip ticket.

A woman brought a month-old baby to C.G. Jung and asked for "preventive psychoanalysis' for it. "I hope it is not too late..." she said. "Madam," Jung replied, "you have already wasted ten months."

Two paths are offered to the dying person, the familiar and the unfamiliar, which leads to Light. Jung favored the practice of detachment after the midpoint in life; but Plato said we should practice detachment through the whole of life. Yes, old age is too late.

The ethical person's life is based on 'oughtness.' Ethical laws are a sort of device by which we live harmoniously in a discordant world. It is like the band of porcupines arranging themselves in a sunny spot. All reciprocity, however politely couched, is just that. Ethics can punish, but never redeem, never bring perfection. If you can make a person conscious of his or her own Divinity, having seen it yourself, then only can you redeem that person. But a student must *follow* ethics, up to a point.

Is the river afraid to flow into the sea? The chrysalis to transform itself into a butterfly? How funny that would be! Even in the waking state, we are in another kind of dream state; does anyone want to dream all the time, however pleasantly?

A study like this helps us to stretch our consciousness. Realization? Well, that comes from God, through grace. But we can help you just to get out of this little circle: *my* family, *my* business, *my* center... Teachers *can* give samadhi and other experiences. But can you stand it? It may be like the janitor winning the sweepstakes! Our body, mind and senses must be prepared by spiritual disciplines. And will you really enjoy what you have not earned?

Since we know realization is really just a matter of "waking up," why use the word "attainment" at all? Only for the sake of the ignorant. It is also like purifying water by means of alum; you don't create new water.

Remember that the Taj Mahal, St. Peter's dome, Plato's philosophy, rockets and satellites, all have first to be conceived in the mind. Purity, too, is in the mind.

"Neti, neti" — this negation process is like a servant entering a strange, dark room to find his Master where he lies asleep. Light has to light even the sinner for the committing of his crime. Sometime he may discover, 'I have been going down and down, with such speed!' If he can just change his direction, he can go with the same speed.

Every object of our perception shows these five characteristics: *asti, bhati, priya, nama, rupa*: isness, consciousness, dearness, name and form. This list goes from closest to more remote relationship; form is the furthest from our true being. Self is the cement that holds all these together.

A road is full of broken bits of glass. Instead of removing it all before you walk, bit by bit, remove the big chunks and put on a heavy pair of shoes (love of God) and then go over.

For our lunch and dinner the elderly Swami Madhavananda and I would journey up the hill to join the main household. Access from the road to the dining room was gained by a long flight of internal stairs. Swami Nikhilananda made the mistake of calling the patient's attention to the railing he had had installed from top to bottom. "Please use the railing, Maharaj," he would say. "You will find it much easier, both mounting and descending. We have put the rail there just for you, you know," and so on. Swami Madhavananda would not so much as lay a finger on it.

To relieve this and other frustrations Swami Nikhilananda

resorted to exercise. Thousand Island Park was a walker's paradise. A veritable fairyland of water vistas, gem-like rocky green islands set in crystal currents; shower-born toadstools springing up as edible umbrellas for the squirrels, brown and black, who ran in complacent abandon everywhere over the rocks and tree roots. Swami knew all the nooks and crannies. He had been so often on the boats which toured the Islands that he knew the guides' every line of patter. There was a cove along the river front, reached by one of the lower roads, where he and others so inclined would gather on hot afternoons for a plunge. And he went out walking with one little group after another, as the mood struck.

Such an hour would be the right one in which to recall, for his companions, a pair of experiences from his ample storehouse. One concerned a time he had been put up at the home of a husband and wife who were spiritualists, but on whose susceptibility to higher ideals he had endeavored to play, by means of various remarks and suggestions. At the time of his leaving they wanted to make him some gift. Swami could think of nothing he needed and said so. No, they insisted, he must accept something and they were going out to look for a suitable present. When it was presented, unwrapping it Swami found it to be a fancy barometer. "Oh," he said, as we do under such circumstances, "a barometer! I've always wanted a barometer." He already had one. "See!" exclaimed the wife. "Didn't I tell you? I told you there in the shop that the spirit was telling me, 'He wants a barometer.'"

The second anecdote is about a couple who used to come to Swami for counseling. In nearly every interview, separately each would say about the other, "Swami, you have no idea how much So-and-so means to me. I just live for him (her)." They would make quite a fuss about it. After some years the husband died. At the widow's next visit with him, Swami inquired kindly how she was getting along now. "Swami," she replied, "it's the first time since we married that I am able to sleep without a Luminal." But Swami also had this to say about marriage: "In the Hindu view marriage is not a confession of weakness nor a concession to sin — it is sacred and mandatory (for all but defectives and freaks). It is important to satisfy physiological and psychological cravings. Hindus found this out long before Freud."

Weather along the St. Lawrence was perplexing to a Californian. Summer lightning and torrential downpour would be followed in a day or two by lovely hot sunshine, when the steam would rise in clouds. In the last week of our sojourn I had the privilege of typing for Swami one chapter of the new biography of his guru, Sarada Devi. The book was now nearly ready for the printer. When it appeared in finished form he sent me an inscribed copy. That week also added substantially to the collection of anecdotes.

Swami was once scolded by Swami Turiyananda for 29 consecutive days. It was after the young man had clearly made his choice for the life of the monastery; now the older began to take just the opposite tack, berating him for his decision to renounce and go off to be with the monks of Mayavati, one of our Himalayan outposts. "Such a promising young man," the revered Swami had said, "such a bright future! What a lot of good you could do for India, with your gifts of reporting, writing, political analysis, etc." The two would go out walking and this harangue would go on and on. It finally wore down the younger man. One day Swami Turiyananda started out alone. Seeing the new renunciate following him, he called out, "What do you want?"

"Well, Maharaj, if you feel so strongly that I have made a mistake, and don't want me to..." "Hup!" The other eyed him sternly. "No courage of his convictions!"

Swami Brahmananda was friendly with the distinguished religious leader Vijaykrishna Goswami, who had been close to Sri Ramakrishna. Once, probably during the swami's younger days, they were out on pilgrimage together. Vijay had a number of disciples, one of whom was accompanying him in his austerities. Night came and they made camp. Next morning Vijay greeted Maharaj with a peculiar remark. "Never make a disciple," he said.

"Why do you say that?"

"In the middle of the night I was rudely awakened by a pounding upon my chest. It was this fellow, who had climbed up on me shouting 'Give! Give!' 'What do you want from me? I asked in alarm.' 'Give me realization. Give it.'"

I doubt whether I have ever so much regretted the close of a summer. The inevitability of farewell and departure, famil-

iar though it is as an aspect of "maya," had a special poignancy
here at the Park. As Swami Nikhilananda had said, "One day
you find out that you were born alone, and must go out of this
world *single file*." But here one could not simply pack up and
exit; camp had to be broken, the dwellings put to bed for the
winter. There was an eerie air about it. Mattresses were hung
over chairs, moth flakes sprinkled on floors, lamp cords pulled
from sockets, windows and doors nailed shut and a brick placed
over the chimney. It all looked so final! The shrine room was no
exception. Cloths were draped over the statuary; one had somehow to think that the Master, the Mother and Swamiji would
now go into hibernation, so to speak. To make it all the more
ironic, the sun came out in a cool breeze to grace our departure
with one of the finest days of the summer.

VII. WEARING DOWN
    The holidays had passed and with them the calm waters
of our collective mental stream, untroubled by decisions. As we
reached the white water of disturbing uncertainty, the strain on
Swami Nikhilananda returned. All the medical opinion he could
glean advised him to have the rest of Swami Madhavananda's
treatment accomplished in the United States, and here he was,
trying to go ahead with the arrangements. But it was more than
the senior swami could bear, to think of money again being spent
on his body, when, as he so often said, he *could* eat, he *could* see.
Why not wait a few years; work of equal quality could be done in
India by the doctors and dentists there.
    His host had other problems as well. It was Rosh Hashana
and the celebration of their New Year by millions of New Yorkers
had closed many businesses and offices; it had not been possible
to get hold of the eye surgeon. More treatment meant hospitalization once again and further nursing. I was expected at my
home base. Would Swami Ashokananda extend my leave?
    Once again we settled in at 94th Street. It was the first
Sunday of the new season and Swami was using for his sermon
some of the material prepared for the seminar. Over lunch he
brought up my name.
    "He knew my lecture was the same stuff I gave at the
seminar, rehashed; so he didn't put any money in the collection

basket." Following his instructions, I never did.

"Just thank God, then," offered the older monk, "that he didn't reach in and take anything out."

Swami came up to me one day to say, "You know, I have been wondering for years why it is that the hair on my head remains black, but the hair of my beard has turned gray. But now I think I know the answer." Naturally I was all ears. "It is because I have given so much exercise to my mouth and so little to my

Ramakrishna-Vivekananda Center of New York

brain."

Various swamis and devotees were passing through the city now, visiting Swami Madhavananda. One was my own immediate superior, Swami Shraddhananda of Sacramento, who, though housed at the Vedanta Society across the park, would come to us for dinner each evening and at other hours as well. It was a fine opportunity for me to collect news from home, and I took it. About this time there was on Swami Nikhilananda's schedule a trip to Philadelphia, to lecture at the University of Pennsylvania on "Man and His Environment," one of a series on the subject. On returning he made some comments on the difficulty of finding precise equivalents for idiomatic expressions. It seems there was an elderly lady who had been one of the students of Swami Saradananda in his days in America. She visited India and one of our swamis there told her how Sri Ramakrishna had compared Swamiji and Swami Saradananda. In Bengali it is "they are like the pot and its lid," but in his mouth it came out "like the cup and the saucer." This miffed the lady, who thought it a very unfair comparison for her guru and never got over it. Swami Madhavananda, hearing the story, said that someone should have told her, "We always drink from the saucer, not the cup," and that would have placated her.

Someone had telephoned Swami Nikhilananda one morning, identifying himself as one of the staff of the *Encyclopedia Americana*. He needed information about Asvaghosha, author of some of the earliest works of Sanskrit literature. Swami asked if the *Encyclopedia* was going to contain any entry on Ramakrishna or Vivekananda. The staff member thought well of the idea and invited him to lunch, finally asking him to write an entry on Vivekananda.

"You know," he confided, "I have a special interest in that, because of a family connection." He went on to explain that there was a British General [Sir Charles Napier] who made history in the war in 1842 by capturing for his government the province of Sind. It was done against the wishes of the East India Company. His fame lay in the telegram he sent to headquarters: the one word, in Latin, *peccavi*, i.e., "I have sinned." The General came to the United States to offer the Confederacy his services as a mercenary, but was too late. The war being nearly over, he found a wife in the form of a fashionable southern belle and settled down. She was a prominent society lady who knew Swami Vivekananda and used to tell her family tales about him, stock stories in the household. She had taken him to plays, concerts, soirees. "And I," said the speaker, "am her grandson." He then tried to persuade the swami to take a hand in the writing of all the entries on India. Swami thought it would be too much for him and declined.

One afternoon Swami led me with an air of mystery to a large pile of faded ochre-colored cloths on a tray. "Can you re-color these for me? It is one of the first tasks given to a new brahmachari in India." I gulped, guessing at the yardage involved but also cognizant that this might be one of the few things I could do for him in the way of personal service. My experimental methods of handling this, with two bathtubs, etc., proved disastrous. The hour was approaching for my taking Swami Madhavananda to the Vedanta Society for the evening. Close to panic, I ran to Swami Budhananda's room and with a simulated calm put to him a question. "Swamiji, at what point can this dyeing process be halted and resumed the next day?"

"Oh, it can't be at all," was his cheering answer, and he asked me to explain the problem. Soon both of us were washing and rinsing, stretching and dyeing, in pails of water with alum and powdered rock dye, until the bathroom was a thorough mess. The appointed hour now struck, and alas, I had to leave the swami to finish the task. I had told him I would clean the bathroom, but on my return found it all done. It was the largest of the numerous debts I could never repay him.

Moffitt had said it rightly. Incidents about the first disciples could not be prized out; they simply fell out as the spirit moved. We were told that Swami Adbhutananda, the disciple who was even more destitute of learning than the Master, often had penetrating and remarkable illustrations to give about spiritual matters. After a talk which Latu Maharaj, as he was familiarly known, had given to a group of devotees, one of them asked him how the *jiva*, the individual soul, realizes (the Bengali word used means "to catch") Brahman. Latu Maharaj after a moment replied, "As a string of a sitar catches the tune played on the sitar, so does jiva 'catch' Brahman."

In the preface of his translation, *The Gospel of Sri Ramakrishna*, Swami Nikhilananda acknowledges Margaret Woodrow Wilson as one of those who edited it. They had formed a bond of warm friendship, the swami and this youngest daughter of President Wilson. It was she, he told us, who had insisted on their retaining, in places where he might have chosen to vary it, the literal equivalents of the Master's original expressions, *e.g.* the phrase "woman and gold." She felt he had a strong obligation to the world to keep this whole translation as literal as possible. (In recent years a whole new controversy about this has arisen over the exact equivalent of the word *kamini*; "woman" does not meet the criteria.)

Miss Wilson relayed to Swami a family episode from her father's last days. One afternoon long after Versailles and the subsequent struggle with Congress over his Fourteen Points, her father was sitting on the lawn in an armchair, chin in hand, mulling over the turns of fortune. Margaret silently crept close to him and simply insinuated herself undemandingly into his presence. She had been his favorite. Wilson acknowledged her with a pat on her hand and soon spoke aloud without breaking his mood. "You know, Margaret, I have been thinking — all that world cooperation. It can come only from the bottom — from the ground up. *That* was my mistake. I tried to superimpose it all, from the top."

Returning to the matter of his guest's program, Swami Nikhilananda won the battle of the teeth, and now bid fair to win that of the eyes as well. We were off to the dentist, and very soon Swami Madhavananda was shown the plastic mold of his own gums and palate, cradled carefully in the hands of one of the most expensive of the city's dentists, who was visibly moved with pride and ecstatic appreciation. "The eye makes its own beauty, doesn't it?" put in the office nurse, mercifully, and surely more Vedantically than she knew. The complicated denture was promised before Thanksgiving Day and that seemed another mercy. It may have been in this reception room that we had a much longer wait than anticipated; even Swami Madhavananda's vast patience was tested. I picked up a magazine and began to read. This drew from Swami Nikhilananda the comment nearest to a personal criticism that he ever gave me. Shaking his head, he said, "I see that you really are a Westerner, after all! Faced with this wasted time, you *must* have something to read. You could have decided to do japa and that would have put you in a different mold."

November had crept up on us and with it, winter weather. The decision about a cataract operation could be made only at month's end. It began to look as if we might all be together for a winter in New York. Diet was becoming a problem, for our patient had tired of the bland American flavors often doctored or denatured for his benefit, and for my cooking he had lost whatever graciousness of accommodation he may at first have had. One opinion was that this fastidiousness was a new sign of independence and therefore of improved health. Swami and Swami Budhananda, both men of his part of India, pitched in to prepare curries and the like to tempt him. We even secured imported ingredients from out-of-the-way shops. Swami Nikhilananda was not unaccomplished in the kitchen. His stock of dishes was considerable and he turned out favorite items with expertise. One day, after a spectacular culinary flop of mine, he put himself, ever so gently, in my shoes. "This 'Peace Corps' business is not so easy, my boy. Don't you see how difficult it is to bridge disparate cultures?" I had many years ahead of me in which to test it further for myself.

Two of his reminiscences might be *apropos* at this point. Gurudas Maharaj, the first Western swami of the order (his formal name was Swami Atulananda) had related to him that when he was a newcomer in India he went through trying days at Belur Math, when homesickness nearly overcame him. He was feeling out of place, that he had not been accepted by the Indian community in which he had decided to place himself. On one such day there was a large public celebration, and on a bench in the center of the gathering sat Raja Maharaj (Swami Brahmananda) and Swami Saradananda. Suddenly Maharaj called to him, asking him to come and sit beside them on the bench. All the dark clouds of his mind were blown away and he felt immensely gratified.

The other incident took place during one of Swami Nikhilananda's routine walks in the streets along Central Park. He came upon (as he described it) a group of urchins. Puzzled, they studied him for a moment. "What nationality are you?" ventured one.

"Indian," said Swami, just as abruptly.

"Indian! Then where are your feathers?"

As the snow and ice appeared Swami did all he could to persuade his brother to wear an overcoat, scarf and mittens for his prescribed daily walk. The latter served as immovable object to this would-be irresistible force. He had already accepted the indignities of "longies," wool shirts and stockings; more was superfluous and that was that. The clash of wills reached such a point that the rest of us began to feel that if this winter passed without Swami Nikhilananda having a heart attack at seeing Swami Madhavananda go out without his overcoat, we would be fortunate indeed.

VIII. WINTERING OVER

Finally in December it was back to New York Hospital for our long-suffering patient. Cataract was to be removed from both eyes. It mattered little that our former room was not then available and that the smaller one we took had no fine view; he would not be able to see it. To entertain him, and us, Swami Nikhilananda went on dispensing from his inexhaustible fund of tales. The following set we may term the Famous Persons Department.

Winston Churchill had real admiration for Jawaharlal Nehru. He once told Nehru he wished he could have gone with him to America to introduce him there. Nehru smiled. "What would you have said?"

"I would have said, 'Here is a man completely honest, free of fear, free from malice.'" At this point in the story Swami Madhavananda chimed in with: "... and therefore unfit to be a politician."

Swami had a friend who, with his family, lived in Princeton, not far from Albert Einstein. The young son of this family had an encounter with the great man. Einstein at the time was wearing no stockings, which was a matter of much comment by the children of the neighborhood. At last Denny, aged about seven, mustered the nerve to approach Dr. Einstein. "Hello. Why don't you wear any socks?" he asked with no beating about the bush.

"My young friend," the sage replied, "I am 75 years old and at that age I can do *just as I please*."

It seems that Swami's devotion of time and talent to the works of the Indian philosopher Shankaracharya was not merely a matter of his own admiration but owes something to Somerset Maugham as well. Swami had asked the writer what he thought would be the best contribution a translator like himself might make to the thought of America. "Popularize Shankara in the West," Maugham had thought. "We have our various religious philosophies — Aquinas, the dualistic ones and so on. We have no counterpart at all to Shankara."

While on a tour of the Holy Land, now Israel, Clarence Darrow, famed advocate of Darwinism in the Scopes Trial, arrived at the edge of the Sea of Galilee. Enticed by the sight of the tour boat, a standard tourist attraction, he inquired of the boatman the price of the complete tour. "That, sir, comes to $200," replied the man, who may have thought he saw a well-padded American.

"Two hundred dollars! My," said Darrow, "the price must have gone up tremendously of late!"

"Oh no," came the hasty reassurance, "that has been our standard price for the last 2,000 years."

"Ah, I see..." said Darrow, "no wonder Christ got out and walked!"

A picture of Sri Ramakrishna was kept in their parlor by a man and his wife who had been coming to Swami's lectures for some time. This was their first interview and the wife was explaining how devoted her husband had become. Now they kept the Master's photo and showed him reverence. "And you know, Swami," she went on, "when you spoke several weeks ago on that verse in the *Gita* about 'whoever offers Me a fruit, a flower, a leaf or water — that I accept, the pious offering of the pure in heart,' well, Walter took it right to heart." Swami Nikhilananda was nodding at all this and muttering "Fine, fine."

"But there's only one trouble: you see, I keep some plants in the window box and there isn't a leaf left on those plants!"

So thorough was Swami's comprehension of Swami Madhavananda's nature that when he inquired of me whether

our patient had at any time told me of his deepest spiritual experiences, I suspect it was a bit of leg-pulling. He must have
known it to be as improbable as any such confiding on his own
part would be.

Christmas had come. Our Christmas service was held at
8:30 at night, with Moffitt offering appropriate music at the piano, Swami Nikhilananda reading the Biblical account and following it with a fine homily on Christ and what is a true Christian, and closing with St. Paul's discourse in Corinthians, 13th
chapter. We sang carols. Lastly and unexpectedly Swami stood
again and brought forth *extempore* a moving expression of faith.

"Though I shall not live to see the day," he began, "I
cherish the hope that it will come, when the Christians will celebrate in their churches and the Jews in their synagogues, the
birthdays of other incarnations and prophets."

The next day, while shopping downtown in a crowd, I
lost my wallet to a pickpocket. The subway crush was unbeliev-
able; only later in India was I to meet anything comparable.
People who would never speak to one another anywhere had to
hang around each other's necks. This was the cosmopolitan city.
Chagrined to have Swami hear of my negligence, I conveyed it
to him through someone else. I was rewarded not with scolding
but with some of his surprising store of pickpocket jokes. Several
days later back came my wallet, cards and all in the mail, minus
the money. I hastened to Swami with this glad tiding. "Well, that
just shows you," he said, turning the glow of his ever-beaming
countenance upon me, "in New York even the pickpockets are
gentlemen; and in San Francisco even the gentlemen are pickpockets!"

There was sufficient time for another festival before we
were sent on our various ways. It was the Birthday of the Holy
Mother, and as she was guru here, I expected the observance to
be one of utmost reverence and intensity of devotion. So it was.
In the reception room at the front of the house an altar was set
up and the photograph and footprints of Sri Sarada Devi worshiped in a lengthy service. Swami Nikhilananda served as
prompter while Swami Budhananda performed the ritual.
Thirty-five devotees gathered to watch and participate, a goodly
number for a week day. Swami Madhavananda was among them

for a time, which was a departure, he said, from his custom of late, in India. Swami closed the function by asking us all to go up to the senior swami's room and "take the dust of his feet." This we did, one by one. Prasad was served in the form of a meal catered by a pair of professionals who were also devotees. At the public lecture held the following Sunday, with an attendance of 110, Swami got through a fine oration on Holy Mother without breaking down at all. I admired his detachment and told him so, adding that I knew Swami Prabhavananda, for instance, could never speak on Mother without breaking down. "Oh, I broke down too," he said, "at the very end." I doubt whether anyone knew it.

Swami Nikhilananda wanted the older swami to speak from the pulpit at a Sunday service. Time was running out and the guest proved obdurate. The persuasion attempt ran on for days; I witnessed only a portion of it. It was a surprise to all that the swami ultimately agreed. He delivered without notes a vigorous, well-phrased speech lasting nearly half an hour. The satisfaction this gave to Swami Nikhilananda and the rest of us may easily be imagined.

On a cold night in January, we drove to the airport for the flight Swami Madhavananda had so long yearned to make. To save our much-beloved visitor — who was soon to be president of the order — a long walk, he was taken by wheelchair down the long ramp to the boarding area. Swami Nikhilananda and devotees as well as Swami Pavitrananda and a group from his center gathered around to have the final darshan. Next day I packed my things and was physically though not mentally ready to return to Sacramento. It was not easy. I had made myself too much a part of the center and had become "attached." There was consolation in the knowledge that the master of the house would now sleep in peace and quiet.

IX. FINAL STROLL

By the end of the month Swami Nikhilananda was off to Jamaica on a badly needed winter holiday. His first letter attests his generosity. "I want you to know," he began, "my sincere gratitude for all that you have done for Swami Madhavananda... For your loving service you will get the blessings of the Master and the Swami.

"Another thing I want to mention... when Swami Ashokananda said that he would send you to look after Swami Madhavananda, I clearly told him that your work would be solely confined to Swami's service... We made you do things for the Center... I treated you the same way I do Al and Swami Atmaghanananda. I hope you will not cherish anger against me. I am truly indebted to you for fully participating in the activities of the Center." He went on to tell me how restful a place Jamaica was. He was enjoying his vacation by swimming daily and taking long walks.

Dear Countess, what can I say, that the readers of this memoir may share in my gratefulness for your help and sympathy, your dignified yet ever good-natured demeanor and sisterly affection? How shall I explain what your presence meant in the drama of that memorable year? Countess Colloredo-Mansfeld died of cancer only a year or two later. Her letter from Jamaica, where she was attending on Swami, traces him for us there:

Swami is really looking splendid once more. The sun, swimming, walks and abundance of tropical fruits, and gentle climate, are benefiting him. Yesterday we had been here two weeks and he promptly began work again. He is writing the article for the Vivekananda Memorial volume in India. In any case that is why I am answering your letter for him, with all his news.

We appreciated how very different life with us was, from anything you liked or had been used to... Perhaps you do not know it but Swami Nikhilananda prayed for you each day humbly and lovingly all the time you were with us and until he knew you had safely reached Swami Ashokananda's care... Behind everything you see in Swami lies the biggest heart in the world. But perhaps you too discovered that.

All our Centers are different, yet behind the diversity all of us are seeking the same goal. It is that unity among us which counts, and creates the loving relationship we felt each time we had the joy and privilege of being for a time with a brother or sister from another Center.

She signed the letter "Nishtha," her Sanskrit name.

In May it was Swami Budhananda who wrote. "Swami Nikhilananda wants me to tell you," he relayed, "that this summer you could come as our honored guest to Thousand Islands. Perhaps he wanted to assure you that with no Swami Madhavananda to look after, there would be no occasion for you to shoulder sudden and unforeseen avalanches! I pointed out that you might not be had that easily, not because you would not like to come, but because you belonged to a place." (Of course he was correct.) He continues: "Swami Nikhilananda's 1962 lectures on Sri Shankaracharya's philosophy were very well attended at Fordham University. On the first night more than a hundred persons attended... Among them were teachers of philosophy and religion from other colleges also... In introducing the Swami to the audience the Father said that fifty years ago they would not have ventured to invite a Swami to speak on Shankara at a Catholic University. But of late they have decided that other religions exist, and so dialogue is necessary for subsistence! He also admitted that this study of Shankara has helped him to understand Thomas Aquinas better. There were lively and perceptive questions and lively answers too... Some nuns attended the lectures."

By June the center had received copies of the *Holy Mother* biography from the printer. It must have been a day of rejoicing. Swami wrote to me on the 7th that he had just mailed me a copy with his loving greetings penned therein. He asked me to let him know how I liked it. He was about to leave for Europe to visit, among other countries, the Soviet Union. "But do not worry about this visit," he assured me, "I am going as a *tourist*." He mentioned too, for his own and my special enjoyment, the fact that he had sent to Swami Madhavananda a pair of spectacles from this country, costing $100. The swami had been disgusted at this "unnecessary outlay," but had admitted that the glasses were lighter and gave him better vision than his own pair.

By summer Swami Madhavananda had been inaugurated into the presidency of the order.

"You have often been in my mind since I returned here," Swami Nikhilananda wrote from Thousand Island Park. "This vacation I am staying at the cottage where you and our President Maharaj stayed last summer. Everything is just the same as you saw, the same Ayodhya (capital of Rama's kingdom in the *Ramayana*), but no Rama or his devoted servant Hanuman. Some of the villagers inquired about Swami Madhavananda and one asked if he were still alive... My Russian experiences were very interesting though exhausting. Instead of spending five weeks I left after two, but I would not have missed it for anything. I have every intention of going there again — but always as a tourist."

In the winter of 1962 he went to India to see his old friends and of course one of them in particular. After giving me news of the president he went on to say, "I have decided to stay at the Belur Math till March 10th, when Countess, Al and I will leave for New York via Europe, reach home in mid-April. I have not yet been able to adjust myself to the Indian climate. It is difficult at my stage of life."

Countess' letters were pleasantly philosophical and ruminating. This one was her last:

"Yes, you are right: Swami has indeed had a 'rough road.' Perhaps it must be that way in last births and especially if you are a teacher... I suppose sickness is the austerity for monks who have to live in the world with comforts and cannot practice *tapasya* in the classical sense. In any case, Swami's heart attack would not have been detected unless Al had had his cardiogram machine at hand. What it did was to prove that Swami had had several earlier mild attacks even prior to 1960, and that these had been overlooked in the turmoil of events... In any case, he can lead a normal life now, only avoiding as much as possible stairs, hills and the heavy responsibilities of running all the routine of a center."

I should have mentioned earlier that Countess was actually one of the swami's best critics as regards his writing. One day he told me, "One of the secrets of good writing is to 'murder your darling.'"

"What does that signify, Swami?" I asked.

"Everyone has some pet habits, peculiarities cultivated as fancies, which need to be seen by others and killed on the spot. For instance, Countess knows that I like to stick in little French phrases, mostly to show that I know what they mean; she makes me take them out. So I say, 'murder your darling.'"

The following spring news was sent in detail by Moffitt:

The Swami Vivekananda Centenary Dinner held last Thursday exceeded all our expectations. U Thant was marvelous. He was thoroughly familiar with the Mission's work in Burma and had evidently read a lot of Swamiji's life. He called him one of the greatest men of all time and said that what he had preached about religious 'tolerance' must now be applied to the political sphere. He also said that Swamiji taught the very difficult matter of getting to know who you are in the simplest possible terms. Etc., etc. The general effect was solid and impressive. Vincent Sheean was very lively and said among other things that Swamiji acted with what must be one of the greatest examples in religious history, in not mentioning his teacher for two years during his speeches in this country... Ambassador B. K. Nehru inaugurated the whole thing, in a few very dignified words, as the representative of the Republic of India, and mentioned the fact that Swamiji had caused a revolution in people's thinking during his generation. Also there were messages from President Maharaj, Dr. Radhakrishnan and Prime Minister Nehru. Swami Nikhilananda spoke last and made a very fine effect on everyone. We had engaged a room to hold 225 people (more than we ever had at any dinner before) but the requests for reservations kept pouring in, and we had to have a second room to take care of the total of 267. The Voice of America had two men there taping the whole thing for India and the U.S.I.A. had a photographer and a reporter present.

We now have only the Consulate celebration, the Community Church and the Asia Society, to get through, before we call a halt to temporary activities. Note: Present at this ceremony were Swami Pavitrananda and a number of his students, Swami Sarvagatananda [Head of Boston and Providence centers] who canceled a class to come, and Swami Nityaswarupananda [of India] who flew across the continent to be here. Numerous other notables were there, including Dr. Harrington of the Community Church... Dr. Amiya Chakravarty, Miss Malvina Hoffman, Mrs. Lillian Montgomery [who heard Swamiji speak a number of times], Mr. Joseph Campbell, etc.

I had a letter from Swami himself later in the year. That was 1963. He was not feeling very strong, he said, and told of an operation he had had performed in May. "Swami Madhavananda has been pressing me to come to India for two or three months this winter. Though I am not particularly keen about going there, perhaps I shall go during the first part of December and return the first week of April. If I go to India, Countess, Al, Mr. [Chester] Carlson, and Mrs. [Max] Beckmann will accompany me.

"On October 4th the Indian Embassy in Washington is arranging a Vivekananda Centenary Celebration Meeting. Dr. Grayson Kirk, President of Columbia University and I will be the speakers and the Ambassador will preside. I hope you are well."

They went to India as planned. "One of the highlights of my visit," Swami wrote after his return, "was the privilege of being allowed to spend some time every morning and evening with the President Maharaj. He was very affectionate. After leaving India, Al, Countess and I spent two weeks at Capri, one in Vienna, five days in London and two or three days in Rome and Naples. As we traveled by air, we had to limit the weight of our luggage, so I am sending you only a trifling gift as a souvenir but with a lot of affection...

"Perhaps you know we have a new assistant who will be arriving here on June 4th. Swami Budhananda is going back to India. He will spend quite a few months on the West Coast, so you will see a great deal of him.

"We are planning to leave for Thousand Island Park on June 30th. I always associate the place with you. As I told you, if you ever visit it again while I am alive, you will be treated as a royal guest. But if you feel restless or uncomfortable leading such a life there, you can cook three meals a day besides raking the leaves, watering the gardens and so forth."

Unfortunately I never had that opportunity. The news he had to send me in December was very sad:

"I am recovering from a heart condition for which I was hospitalized about a month ago. The old cancer of Countess Colloredo has come back. This time it has affected her lungs, bones and other parts of the body. There is no hope of recovery. It is only a question of time. We are all very distressed. She is very courageous. I know she will have eternal rest at the feet of the Master but our loss will be irreparable." When the end came, in March of the following year, Swami wrote me that he felt blessed that she died in peace thinking of the Master and Holy Mother.

It was a year of sadness. Our former distinguished guest and patient had but a short time to serve the order as its head. He gave up the body just at the close of the Durga Puja festivities and before I, who was on my way to India to meet him, could get clearance for travel. Swami Nikhilananda's letter was brief and taut with his own grief. But he added, "I am looking forward to seeing you in New York on your way to India. I have been requested to send through you three sweaters... I had sent Swami Madhavananda some special eczema ointment which I am afraid arrived only a day or two before his passing away."

In India, in spite of the special arrangements made for me, a Westerner, I was experiencing culture shock and, having lost through death the two persons whose company I had most sought, Swami Yatiswarananda and Swami Madhavananda, I could not resist availing myself of Swami Nikhilananda's ever-sympathetic ear.

If Swami Madhavananda had not come to America he would have died within two years and suffered excruciating pain. Well, we must practice surrender to the Lord. I am still puzzled about Swami Yatiswarananda's mental depression or noncommunicative mood. Do you have any idea about it? Anyhow, you were fortunate to have been with him at least for a few days. I am very sorry but not at all surprised about the difficulties you are facing there. Perhaps time will heal most of the things. I know the conditions of India. Every time I visited I experienced great emotional upheaval. Think of the Lord and he will guide and protect you. I hope you can visit the Belur Math frequently. Also pay a visit to Kamarpukur and Jayrambati (birthplaces of Sri Ramakrishna and Sri Sarada Devi respectively) and spend a few days there. You will have inner peace. Above all, look after your health. If you become sick the whole thing will be spoiled. I am sure Revered Prabhu Maharaj (the new President) and Revered Bharat Maharaj (Manager of Belur Math) will help you in every way possible. You are a child of our Master; He will give you courage and patience. My leg is improving, but not yet normal. I can walk only one block. The cold weather is not ideal for this kind of ailment. I believe you are getting better food at Narendrapur than you can expect at the Math. The ashrama there is located at an ideal place. Swami

Lokeswarananda (the Abbot) is a real sadhu, completely devoted
to the ideals of the Order. Please convey to him my love and
namaskar. Can I do anything for you from here? Do you need any
money? Then do not hesitate to let me know. Do not feel too
miserable. I am sure after a short while you will feel all right.
Please write to me whenever you can.

To me, every line of the letter seemed to be soaked in his
understanding and readiness to assist. Time did heal many things.
When I heard from him next, in May of 1966, I had gone off
during the school holidays to Barlowganj in the foothills, for a
darshan of Gurudas Maharaj, the first American monk of the
order, who was past 90. The swami wrote:

I am glad you are in Barlowganj, escaping the heat of the plains.
The company of Gurudas Maharaj is certainly uplifting. He is an
amazing person. I saw him twice while I was in India and he left
an indelible impression on me and my companions. Even if he
doesn't talk, spend as much time as possible in his company. I
hope he is not suffering much, but he has infinite patience and
sweetness. He is living in a spiritual world where he feels the
presence of Sri Guru Maharaj [Sri Ramakrishna], Holy Mother
and other disciples of Sri Ramakrishna. To be able to serve him is
a rare privilege. Stay there as long as you can.

I understand your difficulties in India about the climate and
the food. That, I anticipated.

...Surrender yourself completely to Sri Guru Maharaj. Let him
do whatever he wants. You will have peace of mind. I hope you
will not grumble too much, as that will upset your inner peace.
You know how much we all at the Center like you... Don't be in
any hurry to run away from India. While there, visit as many sacred places as possible. If you decide to come back to America
you will have many precious memories to cherish.

My health is improving though there is a trace of swelling still
and some pain which I disregard. This is the fag end of the work
year; naturally I am tired, but due to the grace of God, during the
last one year, which was not an easy one for me, I did not miss a
single class. Do feel free to write to me whenever you can and tell
me if I can do anything for you.

It had not been possible for me, however, to avoid debilitating illness. From the hospital where I was being treated for jaundice, I wrote to him, knowing he would hear of it sooner or later. He replied promptly from the Park that he was sorry to hear of it and then went on to say more about Gurudas Maharaj, who had recently given up this life of 97 years:

"I am happy to know that you met Swami Atulananda. He was really a wonderful monk. He gave us the example of putting up with all difficulties without grumbling. Everyone among my American friends who met him in India was impressed by his serenity and gentleness. I believe his first visit in India was in 1906 when he was initiated by Holy Mother. The second visit was around 1911. When he tried to practice austerities at Rishikesh he consulted a Western doctor, I believe, who said to him that if he wanted to die in India he should stay there, but if he wanted to live he had to return to America. He went back [to India] about 1924 or 1925 and lived there until his death. He always took care of his health. I lived with him in Mayavati for a long time. We were very good friends." The purpose of his reciting all this history was not lost on me. But there is more to his letter.

"We are returning to New York on September 8th. I have been very busy this summer writing some articles. I did not have a single day's rest. I swim practically every day in the river, take physical exercises and feel not too bad. This place recalls to my mind many of your memories. Now Swami Madhavananda has gone. Both you and I have lost a genuine friend who cannot be replaced."

I had aired with him the questions surrounding my petition to the authorities to speed up the taking of my vows. These were the counsels he offered: "I believe you will get your vows this year. I prayed for you this morning. Do your duties and surrender everything to the Master. He never lets down his devotees. He will fulfill your desire, and you have the blessings of Revered Swami Madhavananda Maharaj. I feel he is not far from us and is thinking of our welfare. He was the most compassionate person I have known. I am sure Swami Lokeswarananda will take care of your case with the Math authorities. Again, I say, please keep well."

Swami Nikhilananda's letter of May 10, 1967 combines political comment, sardonic humor and portents of the coming end.

"I understand that Dr. Hussein has been elected President of India. The Congress Party had to be loyal to its ideal of secular India. I don't know if this will solve our problem. Thanks to 1000 years of foreign domination the Hindus have forgotten their spiritual heritage. I don't care whether a Hindu or Christian or a Buddhist becomes India's president. Whoever can propagate the universal religion of Vedanta in India and abroad will be the right man, according to Swami Vivekananda. I am afraid we shall have to go through a long period of stress.

"For a change I am going to the hospital... for an operation of double hernia... If everything goes well I will be in the hospital for three weeks, finally going to Thousand Island Park the third week of July. My doctor is not worried nor am I. If anything happens you will read about it in our Bulletin. I was very interested to see your article in our London magazine... Don't you plan to return to the United States? You will stay in India, perhaps, until you get your sannyasa.

"...Somehow I feel that my active work will soon be over."

There was more for him to do; six months later he chronicled some of it for me. "I have been in Thousand Island Park for the last two weeks but I am still very weak. It seems that though my physical strength is building up very slowly, my mind is not able to think serious thoughts. Some are saying it will take me about a year to get more normal mental and physical vigor, but in the fall I shall have to face the duties of the Center and also teach a graduate class at Temple University, Philadelphia, where I have been appointed as an adjunct professor of Hindu religion. I shall have to go there once a week. Under normal circumstances I would have been very happy to teach at the University but now I feel distressed at the very thought of it.

"There are quite a few students here now. More will be coming. We have our daily meditation at the Vivekananda Cottage and we read from the life and teachings of Buddha at night.

"I hope you are feeling well and getting accustomed to the Indian way of life. You have not mentioned to me about your future plans... I have gone through several serious operations in the past but never felt such depletion of strength as I now do... I suppose my age stands in the way of quick recovery. Countess said to me just before her death that my active life was over. I would like very much to retire as soon as arrangements for the Center can be made. If I have any mental vigor left when that time comes, I would like to devote my time to writing. Let me see what the good Lord has in mind."

Swami dictated another long message within the month:

"I take a short walk every day and according to the doctor's advice paddle in the river about fifteen minutes a day. My brain is not yet quite active... I have been writing to Belur Math about an assistant and I also intimated to them that I am planning to retire from active work from September 1968. I am now 73 years old. I have not yet got any encouraging reply from Belur Math. Apart from my illness, I don't want to manage the Center after that time. I doubt whether I shall last that long. So my whole future is rather uncertain... The Vivekananda Cottage has become a place of regular pilgrimage. We meditate there every afternoon and after dinner read the *Gospel of Sri Ramakrishna*.

"You will be glad to hear that my last manuscript, *Immortality*, has been accepted by George Allen & Unwin. The book will be published in the spring of 1968. I hope you have enough to eat in these days of scarcity. I also understand there is political confusion in Bengal. This confusion is now going on everywhere in the world."

Things move slowly in India. Some of his problems were being addressed by midsummer of the next year, when he wrote to me in London. For me, too, affairs had been shifting, and I had decided to accept a proposal to be a worker at the London center, leaving India even before having my sannyasa vows. Swami was happy to have the account of the pilgrimage to South India I made before I left. "You have seen more sacred places," he commented, "than most of our Swamis. South India has preserved Hinduism. It is too bad that the heat pulled you down. I am not surprised. I hope you will feel very well in London. There you will have opportunities for expansion of your head and heart.

"My trouble is old age plus high blood pressure, a heart disturbance and a few other things. The doctor has asked me to take complete rest. Perhaps you have also heard that Belur Math has agreed to send me a new assistant. I understand he may come to the Park sometime this summer. That will hasten my recovery but I do not know for certain when he is coming. I am sure you will enjoy your life and work in England. How is Swami Ghanananda [the head of that center]?"

Swami Ghanananda was not at all well, and in fact he preceded Swami Nikhilananda in exiting this world. He passed away in November of 1969, a little more than a year after my arrival. Despite Swami Nikhilananda's declining condition, his letter in reaction to this news reveals the person of judgment and feeling he invariably was.

"Your letter came as a great shock. The death of Swami Ghanananda is not only a great loss for the Ramakrishna Mission but it is also a personal loss to me. We had known each other for a long period of time. We both took brahmacharya the same day... from Swami Shivanandaji Maharaj. Every time I was in London we saw each other. It is a relief to know, however, that his period of suffering is over. According to your request I have informed the Swamis on the East Coast, in Chicago and St. Louis.

"Swami Ghanananda had suffered for a long time from various ailments. In a sense his death is a relief for him, but we are all human beings and the death of a friend moves me very much. His name will always be remembered as the founder of our work in London.

"There is nothing more to write. I hope you are well. My health continues to be the same. Please accept my love and namaskar and convey the same to the other inmates of the monastery."

It was the last word I had directly from this beloved, much older brother, who scarcely ever dealt me a cross word or cutting remark. All I knew of him were the sparkling wit, abiding care and the charm of his insouciance. Others, I saw, experienced other sides of Swami Nikhilananda's nature, as his students. They were fortunate in their own way; I feel fortunate in mine.

News of his condition thereafter was always sad, but not depressing. The devotees reported that in spite of his silence and nearly complete retreat within, there was a radiance, a hallowed presence they felt when around him, and everything I know leads me to hold no doubt about it whatsoever. I could only be happy, in fact, when I learned that he was at the Park, his great love, and sitting at dinner in the Holy Mother Cottage where I had often seen him, when his time here was over.

Swami Madhavananda as President of the Order

"EXCEPT YE BECOME AS A LITTLE CHILD..."

SWAMI MADHAVANANDA

I. INTO THEIR HANDS

It was on a Saturday in April of 1961 that Swami Madhavananda stepped off the plane in New York's Idlewild Airport. He had made the journey from Calcutta alone, knowing full well what faced him on arrival. Despite a warm welcome from brother monks and devotees of the Ramakrishna Vivekananda Center, he was soon to be hospitalized, thoroughly examined and scheduled for brain surgery. A tumor, understood to be benign, had been creating pressure at the back of his brain. Swami Nikhilananda had put forward the funds and arranged the entire affair from his headquarters at the center. To be more accurate, he had insisted upon doing so, to all concerned. After long persuasion Swami Madhavananda, who had retired temporarily from his active service for many years as general secretary of the Ramakrishna Math and Mission (the chief administrative post), had bowed to the pressure from all sides.

As he approached us from the airplane, dressed in a gray suit of Indian cut and a gray cap, he walked with a slightly rolling gait. The greatest change in his appearance, since I had last seen him in 1956 when he visited this country in company with

Swami Nirvanananda, was his gain in weight. We later learned
that this was in part a side effect of one of his medications. During the trip home from the airport to the center, where he was to
stay, I was on pins and needles, grasping for a first impression
indicating what sort of immediate future was in store for me. I,
too, was a guest at the center, after a fashion, on loan from the
Vedanta Society of Northern California to help in his service.
The hint I was looking for was not long in coming, and I was at
once set at ease. Swami Nikhilananda had been talking with the
swami in Bengali, but now remarked in English that his servant
had arrived and would do everything for him.

      "You know," Swami Madhavananda replied with a straight
face, "we have a saying in India that when a horse is brought into
the party, even seeing it at a distance the hiker begins to limp. So
it will be with me." Wry, dry humor was characteristic of him,
and it set the tone for our entire relationship.

      His room, a large one at the back of the top floor, was
ready with a new bath installed. I had been given Al's room just
next to it. Moffitt had left the large room and squeezed himself
into a small one at the other end of the hall. Swami Nikhilananda
had asked us to put the large television set, still something of a
novelty at the beginning of the sixties, in a corner of the swami's
room — "to provide entertainment," he said.

      The ensuing days Swami Madhavananda spent very qui-
etly, apparently doing nothing. It was a marvel, and a perfect
model of what the scriptures tell us, how he could simply sit in
his armchair, hour after hour, seemingly perfectly content. If one
attempted to help him with dressing or eating, he would break
into a sweet smile and say that he really did not need any help.
From his quarters below, Swami Nikhilananda would often come
and they would chat for hours in their native tongue. Swami
Pavitrananda came from the Vedanta Society on the west side to
visit him on the very first day, and they talked for a long time.
Otherwise, Swami Madhavananda spoke very little; but always
there was that smile and angelic expression. His flexibility in
these first days was impressive: Every question, every choice, he
met in this way, like a child too happy to care about unimportant
things.

      Swami had been in the United States twice before. As

mentioned, in 1956 he and Swami Nirvanananda had accepted Swami Prabhavananda's invitation to be present at the dedication of the temple in Santa Barbara and had participated in that ceremony. On that visit, after spending some weeks in the centers of Southern California, they toured other Vedanta centers of the country on their homeward way. More importantly, Swami Madhavananda had had charge of the San Francisco Vedanta Society for two years, from 1927 to 1929, before being urgently called back to India. Here he was, back in American life after 32 years! One has to consider, too, the slower pace of change in India for that period in order to appreciate properly the constant comment going on in the swami's mind as the scenes of this new environment and new day passed before his eyes.

Swami's reputation as a monk of austerity and severity, difficult to approach, was known in advance. But I had no idea of the awe with which he was commonly regarded in the order, even by senior swamis; nor that there were monks and brahmacharis even afraid of him. My ignorance was my salvation. I had no fear of him and proceeded to behave almost as would a professional nurse.

One evening at dinner he was informed by Swami Nikhilananda that due to his presence many tasty items were being brought into the house, dishes never seen there before. At this, Swami Madhavananda told of a religious festival in Rome for which the image of the Gesu Bambino is carried in procession through the streets, seated on an ass. On one occasion, he said, the people were shouting and throwing flowers and confetti. The ass began to think that all the to-do was for him; so he stuck out his ears to take it all in, and then decided to stand still, the better to enjoy the adulation. It was then the people let him know loudly just what his place was.

Another day Swami told me of the little boy who was told by his mother that God is almighty. He asked her what that meant. "Well," was the reply, "it means he can do anything."

"Then can he put the toothpaste back in the tube?" It threw Swami into a gale of giggling. A marked contrast to his usual seriousness, this is the way he reacted sometimes, when we were alone, to amusing things he would recall. On occasion I had to beg him to stop laughing so that I could hear the end of the story. I watched carefully and observed that he never laughed at new jokes; perhaps he had to take them in and mull them over to appreciate them. Also, in the presence of others his reaction to humor was always restrained and seemingly mirthless. So these were exceptions to the rule of straight-faced solemnity.

Late in April we got Swami Madhavananda admitted to room 1620, high up in New York-Cornell Hospital on First Avenue. The room was large, light and cheerful as hospital rooms go. Through the northern window other sections of the hospital occupied the view. But the large windows on the east looked over the East River, where it flowed around Welfare Island on the left and ran down past the gleaming rectangles of the United Nations on the right. From these windows the visitors, nurses and attendants of the swami could often enjoy diverting and beautiful scenes and describe them for him. Because of his post-operative condition and also because he suffered from cataracts, he saw very few of these sights himself, although his bed faced in that direction. Telling him about them was one of the highlights of the day. I remember the city fire department used to put men through training on Welfare Island by having them fight fires set in abandoned buildings there. This was fun to watch and interested him. And on the Thrice-Blessed Day of Lord Buddha, when night fell, the full moon of May rose — a huge golden disk — and hung before us for hours.

The room had been occupied on a previous occasion by Swami Nikhilananda, who had made a number of friends in the hospital. Now three private-duty male nurses, one for each shift, had been retained for Swami Madhavananda, in deference to his Indian and monastic mode of life. It was a novelty, as male nurses were scarce. All three proved to be excellent with him and he enjoyed their jolly company. Therefore, although spending most of my day at the hospital, I had very little actual work to do, serving chiefly as errand boy to and from the center, selecting his diet and keeping an eye on all the arrangements. Swami showed the floor nurses, who were women, more formality, but always great regard and courtesy, and he slowly became accustomed to them.

He was thoroughly calm and resigned at the prospect of going into surgery for a difficult and risky operation, no doubt partly because of his confidence in Dr. Bronson Ray, perhaps the outstanding brain surgeon in the city at that time and a student of the late Dr. Harvey Cushing. Chiefly, of course, he was calm because as a man of self-knowledge he had nothing in particular to fear. His spirits were very good. At one meal, when the hospital food was more than usually flat and the salt in the shaker had become damp and recalcitrant, he told a little story.

"In one of the Indian villages, in a large joint family, a member died while the paterfamilias was away on a trip. There was a big quarrel about the disposal of the body. Some said only cremation would be proper, others favored burial. Finally it was left up to the eldest son to make the decision. After due deliberation, he ordered burial, on the reasoning that if Father should come home and be angry at the decision, it would still be possible to cremate; but not vice versa. Such is the case, you see, with the salting of food in cooking."

It was amazing to see the troop of doctors attending on him, as they marched in the morning, a procession of white coats and spectacles. He seemed to feel much gratified. There was a doctor for his skin irritation, a neurologist and three or four brain surgeons. Later he would have eye doctors as well.

Swami's operation was a long one, occupying hours. He described the recovery room as a bare, cold place from which he thought he might never be delivered! It fit well the traditional Indian descriptions of hell. In a few days he had made the shift to convalescence. Now it was time for that adjustment which was to occupy him for the remainder of his American days and indeed the remainder of his life - the adjustment from a bed-psychology to a walking one.

Swami Madhavananda's post-operative condition was for a long time one of considerable lethargy. We had to urge him to stir about, practice walking and sitting up, which tired him. Swami spoke little and seemed unable to do much but lie inert. It was amusing to see how the nurses behaved. "Swami" meant almost nothing to them, "senior monk" or "secretary of the order" little more, so they were able to cajole him, pat him on the back when pleased with him and so on; nor did I attempt to instruct them otherwise. At this point Swami Nikhilananda predicted to me that our patient would become more difficult to manage as he recovered. This was hard to believe, seeing his docility, but later it proved to be true. His host came to the hospital every day to visit him, usually in the evening, and examined all the proceedings with great solicitude. Swami Pavitrananda visited frequently, always in the morning; but he was a bit unfortunate, because by late morning Swami Madhavananda, still affected by his medication and fatigue, was often asleep shortly before the swami arrived, or soon after. A disappointment to Swami Pavitrananda, this was an unexpected boon for me, as he and I held in hushed tones several long conversations I found very rewarding.

It had been impossible to remove the tumor without slightly impairing the cerebellum, that adjunct of the brain proper which houses our sense of balance. For this reason Swami had to be "taught" to walk again. The conditioned reflexes natural to us since childhood did not all spontaneously arise in him now, when he attempted to walk. One of the first exercises the doctors assigned him was to push an empty wheelchair through the corridors, three times a day. He did not want to do it at all. But how courageous he was! There is nothing about the corridor of a huge American hospital that makes it a congenial environment to a man of his nature, fifty-some years a monk. Women are everywhere, nurses bustling by, visitors staring curiously, wondering who he was and of what race and why the wheelchair was empty — but along the hall he would go, dressed in hospital gown, dressing gown and slippers, pushing this empty wheelchair! How many times one felt pained to have to urge these things upon him; yet he knew it was necessary, and called his training "dinning it into the brain."

We were most fortunate in having as Swami's trained therapist Mr. E. Brown of the hospital staff, a man of utmost skill, patience and kindliness. He handled his patient with maximum adroitness. He explained to the swami that in the latter's present condition he was attempting to move his entire left side and then the entire right side when he tried to walk, whereas the only way we maintain balance while walking is to lift simultaneously the left arm and right leg, then the right arm and left leg. Swami recovered this natural sequence eventually, but only after great difficulty.

On the first morning in the therapy room Mr. Brown was

asking him to try walking, holding to parallel bars fixed on either side at arm height. "No, Swami," he would say, "*right* arm, left leg. No... that's the wrong arm." Then with his genial smile, "You are a very strong-willed person, are you not? Rest now." Coming to me he whispered, "Has this man been the head of his order, by any chance?" Smiling, I replied, "Something very like that. He had been giving orders for the last 30 years; you are the first people to be giving *him* orders in some time." Said Mr. Brown: "It gives me a strange feeling... But I... I *have* to do it."

"Of course," I answered. We saw this in all his medical relationships: that although Swami was rendered more or less helpless, people could not help feeling the power and authority of his personality.

II. RECOVERING

Toward his customary religious practices Swami had an attitude in the hospital which was puzzling to me. He never used his rosary though it was just beside him. He did not read his holy books, nor ask to have them read.

"Would you like me to read to you from the *Gita* or anything?" I would ask. "No," he would mutter, "not now." Nor did he ostensibly practice meditation. Finally I commented on it wonderingly.

"Probably the hospital atmosphere is not compatible with these things," he said. "It is better not to 'make a show.'" That he never did. I began then to realize how careful he was to appear ordinary and unobtrusive; we all realized, too, that his release from the hospital would do wonders for his morale.

One day some letters from devotees and monks in India were read to him. They were full of hopes and prayers that everything might go well, that his recovery be quick and certain. Swami Madhavananda brushed it all off with one brusque comment: "Tell them to pray that I may have devotion to the Lord and faith in Him."

Another day Swami Nikhilananda told him, "One week. The doctors say about one week, and you go home. So, better make up your mind to it, as you will have to be ready, you know."

"Tell the Old Man," said Swami Madhavananda, meaning Sri Ramakrishna.

All plans had been carefully laid for the day of his release. The stairs at 17 E. 94th Street would pose a serious problem until his legs were more seaworthy. The secretary of the
Ramakrishna-Vivekananda Center, Countess Colloredo, lived on
92nd Street in the top-floor apartment of a building which had
once been famous. It was "The House on 92nd Street" in an
early mystery-thriller film of that title. Because it had an elevator (referred to in our circle as a lift), Countess had magnani-
mously offered her quarters to the two of us, renovated the entire two-bedroom flat and moved out to a hotel. Although the
view from the parlor was just a city street, the sun came in glori-
ously and it was settled that in this pleasant place the swami and
his attendant would live until stairs could be negotiated.

Discharge came at the end of May. Swami was talking
more freely now and delighted to be leaving the hospital. He
put on his street clothes with great care and what seemed a little
natural pride. We had engaged one of the male nurses to stay for
eight hours a day at the apartment. My ego was definitely hurt. I
considered myself quite competent to do all that swami required.
I learned this was neither here nor there; the important thing
was the symbol of *authority*, the white uniform and the familiar
routine — important to patient and host alike. One had to learn
not to do, as much as to do — or more so. As it turned out, the
nurse's presence freed me to work at the center on things needed
there.

During this period at the apartment, Swami's system was
still in a state of shock, which compelled him to live a somewhat
immobile existence — and to sleep in the daytime more than he
really wished to, resulting in insomnia at night. All efforts to
rouse him from that mood were futile. Several times a week Mr.
Brown would visit, to put him through his walking and balance
exercises. These were interesting sessions to watch, but certainly
nothing of the kind to Swami, who had to do the work! Holding
on to the therapist, he was called upon to walk a chalk-line, bringing one foot exactly in front of the other. Again, standing still, he
was asked to raise one knee in the air, and with it the arm on the
opposite side, alternately right and left. Though very difficult at
first, this was the key to his balance.

One day when Swami Nikhilananda was present for the

therapy session he told Swami Madhavananda, "You know, I went home last night and tried to do these exercises. *I* could not do them. I just could not. See what you are accomplishing? [To the therapist:] Soon you will have him ready for Barnum and Bailey!" Swami Madhavananda once told me that for years he had always avoided swinging his arms while walking. I believe he implied that the habit was considered lowbrow in India. Now, he said, he had to do it. In all these ways, throughout his stay in this country, Swami had to do just what others told him, overturning his habit and thought patterns. It was a miracle to watch.

His relationship with Swami Nikhilananda was unlike that with anyone else. They were completely frank with each other, it appeared. The younger swami felt such a love for the older, and knew his worth so well, there was no question of taking liberties. They enjoyed banter in a way only men of detachment can know. Let me give a sample from this period.

Swami N: "Today you must go out and walk along the sidewalk; have an outing. It will do you good."

Swami M: "Saturday is inauspicious." (This is a tradition in Bengal.)

Swami N: "Forget all that auspicious business! The therapist said you were perfectly able to do it and it would be good."

Swami Madhavananda shook his head.

Swami N: "Don't you want to get well quickly? So you can go back to India?"

Swami M: "It is not up to me. Speak to Thakur [Sri Ramakrishna] about it."

Swami N (smiling): "Thakur also speaks through me, you know."

Swami M: "But also through others, like me."

Swami N: "You are in the minority. Overruled."

It was typical. And what was the outcome? Sometimes he would sigh and resign himself to walking, sometimes not. I had never seen a loving relationship between two older men comparable to this one.

One afternoon Mr. Brown asked for some books from the bookcase. These he laid on the floor in a sort of checkerboard pattern and asked Swami to step between the books, one after another. This was indeed a sign of promotion; but for the

first time Swami balked. At first no one could understand what
was the matter. Only under pressure would Swami explain that
no book should ever be put on the floor. He told the therapist
that Hindus consider words to be sacred embodiments of the
one Divine Word and therefore always to be honored. The idea
was new and took a few minutes' consideration. I, not quite catching the idea, suggested dictionaries as perhaps less objection-
able. "No, no," said Swami, "that contains *all* words." Finally we
hit upon small boxes, and at the next session we succeeded in
getting him to accept this as a compromise and proceed with the
exercise. Later, at Thousand Island Park, I sawed some rounds
of a small log for use in this exercise, and Swami actually became
fairly proficient in this hopscotch.

There was reciprocity, too, in his relation to the therapist. Swami taught Mr. Brown how to make the namaskar and
what it meant, and a Bengali phrase or two, such as "*ami jani
na,*" "I do not know." Mr. Brown enjoyed Swami's spiritual presence, more felt than expressed (for Swami said little), and behaved toward him with the utmost deference and gentle firm-
ness. It is largely to him we owe the fact that Swami
Madhavananda learned to walk again at all. Meeting him again
after Swami's passing, I asked Mr. Brown what single thing had
impressed him most about Swami Madhavananda. He thought a
moment and replied: "Inner peace. Nothing was going to disturb him. He knew he was involved in a matter of life or death;
he made up his mind to take the way to life and accepted the
consequences. I never felt that Swami was trying to resist in any
way the instruction I was giving him."

Between these visits Swami had to practice his exercises
with the assistance — often just a touch — of the nurse or myself. In addition he was to take a walk every day, of a certain
length, which at this time meant going around and around our
own block. Because of his weight and the sleepiness induced by
medication, this was a nightmare to him. It became a special
kind of game we would play, he and I, after breakfast. Reminded
that it was now time to take the walk, Swami would invent the
best reason he could to get out of it or postpone it. "I am feeling
very sleepy now," he would say, or "It looks very much like rain;
just see if it is not raining," or perhaps "I am just reading some-

thing interesting," or "Let me rest a little while first." I had to think of fresh and persuasive arguments to counter these, and it was usually fatal to let him "rest" at all or get deeply involved in the newspaper, for then the morning would go by, visitors might come and there would be no walk. Had not Swami Nikhilananda and the other swamis continually supported this policy and urged it upon him, I could not have moved him to carry it out.

Sometimes as we went around the block, a boring procedure to me, I would ask him questions about the great disciples of Sri Ramakrishna whom he had known. He never told me much. In fact, he did not care to answer "spiritual" questions, as a rule. His was a different brand of holiness, so to speak, a holiness manifesting itself at this time in sweet docility like that of an angelic child, coupled with the self-assertion of a man who is unwilling to compromise his principles. When he talked, it was about Indian customs, castes, languages; Sanskrit literature; politics; great men in public life, their virtues and foibles; and common things such as newspapers report. He never preached and I cannot remember that he even once allowed me to put him in the role of spiritual teacher.

After practicing much in this way, he was able one day to go to the center for his lunch. It seemed a great accomplishment to negotiate the two full blocks and two flights of stairs. Thereafter he ate his lunch regularly at the center. We were urged to do all we could to find diversions to occupy his time.

It was now late in June. New York city temperatures were 88 and going up, and it was humid. We were making preparations to move to Thousand Island Park and Swami was making rapid improvement. Swami Pavitrananda liked to come with a devotee in the latter's comfortable Cadillac to take Swami Madhavananda out for a drive, and to this he always agreed. He was walking farther and better now and was often jolly. Although his eyes and his teeth were giving him trouble, these repairs would have to wait.

In my bedroom just next to his I tried to sleep lightly in order to hear if he might need anything. We gave him a bell but he never rang it, nor would he call me. He was so considerate that he tried mightily to figure out a way by which he could get up at night without waking me to turn on the lights for him.

They happened to be arranged in that apartment such that one had to go through a room in the dark before reaching the switch for that room. Naturally I refused to let him try this, fearing he would stumble. So he assured me that with his flashlight he would be able to do it, and when at last he had convinced me, I told him with emphasis, on the first night, "Now, Swamiji, if you become confused, or feel lost or the 'torch' goes out..."

"Then call the Operator," he broke in.

One morning when I had used up every argument in the book to get him to go for his walk, he said he was sleepy, and wasn't it funny how sleep came over him just at this time, not while eating breakfast or reading the paper. It reminded him, he said, of the Bengali story of a notorious drunkard. This man was forever falling into the ditches of the road, after drinking at night. So one night he climbed out cursing, and said, "These rascal ditches! In the daytime they run along the side of the road perfectly all right; and at night they wander all over the middle of the road!" After we had both had a good laugh, he was ready to walk.

Present at the exercise session one day, Swami Nikhilananda said to him, about me, "This boy is more strict with you than the therapist is." Swami Madhavananda replied, "Well, you know there is a saying, 'The heat of the sun can somehow be borne; but the heat of the sand, by reflection, is unbearable!'"

III. THE OTHER PARK

Near the end of June one morning we made a scramble to get off for upper New York state, packing the car full with the overflow strapped to the top. Everyone helped to get us ready. There at the Park the old cottage of Miss Dutcher and two others used by the center awaited us as our summer retreat. Several persons had gone there in advance to open and prepare them. The half-day's journey was made without incident up the fine highways to the idyllic northern parts of the state, on to Watertown and to the International Bridge, only a few years old, which carried us over to the Thousand Islands — and the unforgettable summer already dwelt upon at length. In order to complete that account, I'll record here a few events centering around Swami

Madhavananda during the same excursion, before returning with the reader to New York the following fall.

By the Vedanta Cottage, with Attendant

He sustained the trip well. Home, for him and me for more than two months, was to be the Vedanta Cottage, a one-floor structure with four rooms and bath, situated at the foot of the hill on which perches the Vivekananda Cottage. Here the noise and bustle of the larger cottage, with its nest of bedrooms occupied by the younger swamis, by visitors coming and going and seminar students, could not penetrate. Only sounds of the forest, soothing in themselves, and the whistle of steamboats on the broad river, punctuated the stillness and serenity of our days and nights. My room faced his across a small hallway, and in the darkness, when we had not long since put out the last light for the night, a very large steamer might go up the St. Lawrence and sound its deep-throated note, resonant as from an organ pipe. Swami, waiting for sleep, would say, "Mmm! A big one!" It was as if a small child were speaking.

However, as in any ashrama, there was plenty of life

around us. Next door to the north was the cottage belonging to
Countess Colloredo. It had been given the name Sri Sarada Kutir.
Usually three or four ladies were staying there, depending on
how the devotees could arrange their vacations. Much cooking
was done in that kitchen and often Swami Nikhilananda would
take the older swami there for his meal. This was a short but
treacherous journey. What little path there was led over roots
and stones of the forest floor. Going there and back was always
attended by many precautions for our patient — a cane, and —
if the sun had set — flashlights and much solicitude. But *he* never
worried about it; he just plunged ahead, hating to have anyone
make a fuss over him or take elaborate measures for his security.
Breakfast we ate alone in our cottage. Other meals we had in the
dining room of the cottage which Swami Vivekananda's presence, even so long ago, had made an enduring shrine. The long
dining table was the only furniture known to have survived his
residence. Swami Madhavananda, sitting at its head, usually entered into the lively conversation with dry, pungent comments.

When Swami Nikhilananda's seminar began, Swami
Madhavananda was well enough to be left alone for a time. I
would attend the morning session at the upper cottage, and in
the late afternoon would join the *bhajan* (worship of God with
singing) and meditation service in the shrine room there. This
is, of course, Swamiji's bedroom of 1895 and, if I remember correctly, Swami Madhavananda once climbed the extra staircase
just to visit it. Often as we sang this vesper service we were joined
by a house wren in the tree outside. Through the opened windows came this accompaniment, unasked and unrewarded. Swami
Nikhilananda remarked once how much he appreciated it. "Perhaps," he said, "that is her *Khandana* [the song which begins the
service]." The very next day the wren came, bringing a friend,
and they sang through the whole length of that song.

The doctor's orders had been a walk of a mile-and-a-half
every day, weather permitting, and going through some of the
exercises twice a day. This was a stern regimen but Swami was
very good about it. Eventually he cared little about who saw him
or how unsteady or peculiar he might appear, and sometimes he
even nudged me to get the exercises going when I delayed. The
walk, though, was the highlight of the day, providing him with

incentive to talk, comment on the things he saw and share his insights about people, principles and scripture passages. Possibly the reason I have so little record of this is that most of it was conventional. Swami was conservative in nearly every sense of the word and the air of a gentleman born into Victorian India was ever about him. He had figured in his mind what distance a mile and a half might be, and while others might dispute his calculation, his was the walk we took. Going through the village toward the dock, he became a familiar sight to the vacationers in their cottages as he plodded along doggedly, finally spurning the cane altogether, and trying sporadically to keep his feet close together. People used to wonder why the young man carried the cane. It was good for a laugh. It was Swami Nikhilananda who insisted we take it for use on rough ground; Swami Madhavananda had his own mind in the matter and would hand it back to me. Later, back in the city, this was to be true of his overcoat and several other items.

There was a bench beyond the village library and this was our halfway station. Sitting here to rest for five or ten minutes, Swami would fall into a communicative mood and ask what games the children were playing on the lawn or what ships could be seen on the river. The Seaway to the Atlantic Ocean had recently been opened, and much larger ships were plying on the commercial routes than before. Often he could see them himself. But one day when he saw a long freighter whose name was painted on the prow, I spoke that name aloud. "What did you say?" he inquired. I repeated it.

"I am reading the name of the ship, Swamiji."

"Baba!" (It was his favorite exclamation.) "You have telescopes for eyes!" I laughed; it may have seemed so to him, plagued by the cataracts.

Questions about spiritual topics were likely to make him suddenly withdrawn. It was as if he had forsworn any assumption of the position of spiritual counselor or holy man. I wondered: Was this only for the duration of his stay in America, or had it begun much earlier? Swami talked more often of sports (he had played soccer, the Indian "football"), or political problems in many parts of the world.

When he felt ready to move on, we would go down to-

ward the steamer wharf, where Swami Vivekananda had arrived
in 1895. But Swami would not walk out upon it. Perhaps once, to
humor me, he responded to my urging and consented to approach and look into the open waiting-room. Routine was the
staff of Swami Madhavananda's life. To see the same scenes every day, to encounter the same persons, to walk the prescribed
distance — these were accepted, inevitable as breathing. I and
others who took a turn at walking with him ventured now and
then to suggest a new route, thinking perhaps that his mind, like
ours, craved variety; he was not interested. Only as the end of
our summer approached did he seize my shoulder at the start of
the walk and turn me to the left! For some days we went around
the other half of the park. On this journey there was a bench
nicely located so as to give an excellent view of the mainland, the
river and its tiny islands. Although repeatedly requested to sit
and rest here, Swami would not. After some days, curiosity got
the better of me.

"But why not, Swami!" Sincere questions usually brought
out hidden truths.

"There is a lot of grass between here and that bench."

"Well?" said I.

"Grass is not to be walked on, if it can be avoided. It is
alive, you know. You remember the Master's experience. Have
you not seen the signs in the parks," he asked. "'Keep off the
grass'?" My suggestion that this usually applies to tender new
lawns until they grow was not accepted. We kept off the grass —
and the bench.

On several consecutive mornings we now came across a
devotee who had discovered how to be in the right place at the
right time with a camera, to have the swami's darshan. The devotee also had a sanctimonious manner, a thing Swami
Madhavananda found distasteful and always shrank from. Next
morning Swami set us out on the same old walk but in the re-
verse direction, which put an end to that game.

His mood as he gained confidence in walking became
more teasing and jocular. He told me the story of someone who
came to the parson's house and, knocking at the door, was answered by the little daughter of the family. Asking if the minister
were at home this afternoon, the visitor got the reply: "Well, no

he's out just now. But if you are wanting to ask anything about salvation, *I* can tell you. I know the whole Plan of Salvation."

Swami was full of humor, as the reader can see, but it was elusive and subtle. Possibly many in India were not able to know it, alas. One day at table the swamis were talking in that mixture of Bengali and English which came readily to the tongue, and the free-ranging conversation turned to the topic of birth control. Suddenly Swami Madhavananda, seated at the head of the table, remarked, "Birth control is a very good thing." There was a stunned silence. It was a mixed group, and all eyes fixed upon him as the last person from whom one would expect such a statement. "If," he continued, "it is control of one's own birth. No more births. That is the way to practice birth control." The laughter was uproarious.

IV. INTERACTION

The weather at Thousand Island Park was perplexing. One day there would be summer lightning and torrential downpour, or so I thought. Hearing words like these from me, Swami demurred. "You have to come to India to see rain," he said. Two days later the sunshine would be too hot. The large black squirrels and the commoner gray ones, sensing the approach of autumn, would run about fearlessly harvesting mushrooms just before our feet. Swami's vision was sufficiently good now, in spite of cataract, that he could read to himself for long periods. The other swamis had been reading and discussing *Seven Sages*, a book by Van Wesep. This was a study of the development of the American school of philosophy, as the author termed it, more commonly called pragmatism. He traces the contributions made to this philosophy successively by seven great thinkers who were Americans, as defined by Professor Van Wesep: Benjamin Franklin, Ralph W. Emerson, William James, Charles S. Peirce, John Dewey, George Santayana and Alfred North Whitehead. The discussions of the book had aroused my interest. I read it appreciatively. Hoping Swami Madhavananda would interest himself in it and we might thereby be treated to his comments, I ventured to recommend it, in a casual way. There was little hope that he would consider it, because his taste in reading had run, since the operation, to much lighter material — the papers,

Reader's Digest, Time. It was a surprise, then, when he picked it up one morning while I was out and was engrossed in reading it when I returned. Amazingly, he read it straight through. While on the first chapter he said aloud, "This is a very interesting book." For Swami it seemed quite a bit to say. He read smoothly on through Franklin, Emerson, James and Dewey with appreciation but little comment.

"How is it coming along, Swamiji?" I asked proddingly one day.

"Oh…I'm in Santayana," he answered. Then grumblingly, "I can't understand a word of it." About Charles Sanders Peirce, the mathematician and philosopher, he was most enthusiastic. "Very deep," he said. "Too bad he was never appreciated. So many-sided he was." When a few days later no comment on Whitehead seemed to be forthcoming, I inquired again.

"They are all deep thinkers," said he, "but just the opposite of Sri Ramakrishna. He came to make things simple for men. These fellows only make things more complicated." That was all. But somehow it was immensely gratifying that Swami would read the book. Perhaps I had some native pride in the values of American pragmatism, few though they might seem to be from the standpoint of traditional spirituality. But his reading displayed both the depth of his mind and his hospitality to frames of thinking tangential to his own familiar ones.

It may have been on our walk next morning that he told the story of the peasant who had an oil mill. The mill was equipped with the usual grindstone, turned by an ass which walked around after a carrot on a stick. One day a philosopher of the neighborhood happened by. He noticed the bell on the ass's neck, which rang as the animal moved forward. The miller was not far away. "Why do you tie this bell around your animal's neck?" asked the philosopher.

"That should be obvious," the owner replied. "It is so that I will know that he keeps moving, and if he gets lazy and stops, I will know that."

The philosopher thought this over. "Suppose," said he, "that the ass just shakes his head, making you think he is moving?"

"He has not come here having studied philosophy, like

you," was the peasant's reply.

Swami had not only a keen memory but also a faculty unusual in those fond of anecdotes; he remembered to whom he had told which, and I do not recall that he ever told me the same one twice. One was that of a certain young novice serving his teacher. The guru had called him several times during the morning for some chore or other; at each call the disciple had replied, "I am busy with my rosary, sir." Finally the guru called him for lunch. "How many times," the disciple now thought, "should I be heedless of the guru? Let me now go and answer him." Telling the story made the swami roar with laughter, delaying the punch line for several moments.

At Thousand Island Park he began again to use the rosary. Usually he awoke early enough to sit on his bed for meditation and japa before breakfast. He would do japa again in the afternoon after his rest. Swami Madhavananda could occasionally be cross or gruff, or what we might call grouchy. But we never saw him so in the morning nor in the evening at bedtime. I shall never forget the angelic look of purity often present in his face when he said goodnight. He had taken off his glasses and from those eyes there shone such a sweetness that the very night itself seemed wrapped in that beatitude.

Swami had a number of visitors during the period he stayed in this country, including other swamis posted in the United States and devotees from elsewhere. The visit of three of the nuns from the convent in Santa Barbara, which took place at the Park, is particularly memorable. They were already known to him and with them he was especially outgoing and chatty. I thought he seemed very much like a grandfather to them, sometimes teasing and chiding. He inquired about the welfare of each member at their center, and they too were happily surprised by his jolly mood. Two of them were sannyasinis, one a brahmacharini, and all were known to me. So when the news came that these three would be arriving, I thought of a mischievous question.

"Swami," I said, "these nuns are old friends of mine. But they are also senior to me in the order. Now, what do you think I should do when we meet — touch their feet, or not?"

It seemed to pose a problem for him. Shortly, with no

change of expression, he said, "Baba! Better not. Better be on the safe side."

It was now the first week of September. Swami had been taken out on the river for the tour of the Islands, and had enjoyed it greatly within the limitations of his eyesight, and he had been taken for drives on the roads of Wellesley Island on which the Park is situated. I wished very much that he would try to hike up the difficult old trail above Vivekananda Cottage, which leads to the huge glacial rocks where Swami Vivekananda used to have deep meditation under the oak trees. The rest of us loved going there. But in this I proved too ambitious for him; it would have been very difficult. Instead I showed him some photos of the place.

The time came, alas, to fold up camp, in the intricate way necessary in a place subjected to freezing in fierce winter storms. It wrenched the heart to leave that blessed summer land for the noisy and steaming city. The trip was made in two stages by our

Vivekananda Cottage, Thousand Island Park

traveling to Amsterdam in the afternoon and putting up for the night in a high-class motel. The next day, a devotee picked us up and drove us to the to the center on 94th Street.

Swami Madhavananda always had difficulty with stairs after his operation. He now went upstairs with someone behind him and down with someone ahead of him. In this way life at the center resumed for all of us. Lectures and classes were soon to resume. On top of Swami Nikhilananda's customary responsibilities was again the heavy one of arranging more medical care for his guest. One of the first of these was a visit to Dr. Ray, who was most pleased with the progress and who discontinued the special exercises except for one which was to be done on the stairs. Now Swami had a new game to play with me.

"All right," he said, "now you count." But before I could reach twelve or whatever it was, he would say, "No, no, you lost count. You are making me do extra."

"Swamiji, I think not. I don't usually have trouble counting to twelve." And we would try again next day. In the middle of it he clapped his hands once sharply and laughed.

"Aha! You lost track again. There were two fours." And so on. It was absurd, but it was truly a compliment. He was giving me the fun and intimacy of teasing, something he did ordinarily only with his great friend, his host.

We were at a critical juncture and under considerable strain. All advice to Swami Madhavananda was to the effect that he should have his medical work on teeth and eyes done in this country. But Swami, whose self-denial was famous and unmatched, hated the thought of any more money being spent on him, any more being done to fix up "this miserable body." "After all," he would say, "when I *can* eat, I *can* see, why not wait a few years? Indian doctors perform the cataract operation all the time." There were hours and hours of this discussion.

Our walks were now in Central Park, just one block away. Here it was that I began truly to know him. It was not that Swami was communicative of his inmost thoughts, for to me he seldom was; but someone has said that the virtuous are known by their behavior in little things, and of these he was most careful. When we met anyone coming our way, Swami veered strongly to the right, even if this was sometimes more awkward than not to do

so. "That is the rule of the road," he explained. "In this country
one keeps to the right. In India it is to the left." Then I learned
that he had been given the use of a devotee's automobile in San
Francisco when he had headed the Vedanta Society there in the
'20s, and had learned to drive around the city. In Central Park
he would never walk except where the paths led. If I requested
him to take what seemed a perfectly reasonable shortcut, he would
say, "No, no. That is not a path." Grass might have to be trampled.
About the traffic lights he was meticulous. Starting an instant
before we saw the green light or delaying a moment after was
out of the question. Looking back at this now after having lived
in India, I see it as not an Indian trait and wonder how he came
to it.

Sometimes as the weather became colder the wind would
whip around the corner of a building in the way New Yorkers
well know, and would almost blow us backward. For a moment
Swami might regret he had told me not to put his overcoat on
him, nor his scarf nor gloves, but this was not long-lived. He was
adamantine in refusing these accommodations to the winter
clime. "Not necessary," was all he would say to protests. It worried the rest of us, for fear of colds, and day after day I would get
caught in the crossfire between Swami Nikhilananda's insistence
and Swami Madhavananda's refusal. Usually it ended in a glorious compromise. I carried the cold-weather gear. The swami cared
nothing for variety of routes except once in a great while, perhaps in response to some special pleading. Swami Madhavananda
had the reputation of being one of the most independent and
least suggestible of men. I found, however, that if he thought a
new proposal had some good reason behind it, or that you might
truly be made happier in some way important to you, he might
agree with a most childlike compliance. This was the face he
showed me. But to put the overcoat on merely to comply with
someone's idea that it was good for him — no!

He was much interested in language usage, pronunciation and the spelling of words, and a problem in this field might
lodge in his mind for some time. One of the signs posted on the
borders of Central Park is the warning to pet owners, "Curb your
dog." He was certain this meant simply, "Keep your dog under
control." My suggestion that it meant take the dog to the curb,

he was not ready to accept. This American use of a noun as verb was probably either new or distasteful to him. We talked about it a few minutes each time we passed the sign. "In England the noun is spelled kerb," was his final argument. I suggested a compromise, that the sign planners were punning and meant it in both senses, but he did not spark to that either.

He had some faith in astrology, a subject of which I knew nothing, and he talked of it quite often. Perhaps he believed in it more than he would admit to me. "There is some truth in it," he would say, or "It can give broad indications, not many specific details." I took the liberty of pressing my skepticism. When I reminded him of the strong ridicule Swamiji had poured upon astrology in one of his discourses, Swami Madhavananda was not moved. He also held to this faith, or whatever degree of it he possessed, in the face of many challenges from other swamis.

Squirrels abounded in Central Park. Just as common or more so were the flocks of pigeons. Swami knew my preference for the former and distaste for the latter, and teased me endlessly about this partiality. He liked to have me bring a small bag of peanuts as offering to the squirrels, and of course the fun was to see how close the squirrel would come. After a while he would say, "Why don't you offer some to the pigeons? They are also God's creatures." There was no fun if one gave in at once; so discussion was in order about the relative merits of the two. "They make such a mess, Swamiji," I would say. "Squirrels also make a mess; only you don't see it." "But pigeons spread disease." "How do you know squirrels do not spread disease?" In the end, the pigeons also got peanuts. If a squirrel appeared while he was walking in full swing, he might gesture to me to proffer the peanut. But since he did not wish to break his brisk pace, there wasn't time to coax the creature. I would finally throw the nut and run to catch up lest Swami stumble. When we arrived at a favorite bench we would sit and chat about the things around us. Swami was in a relaxed mood then. He communicated inspiration and holy fellowship through channels which appeared most ordinary. Sometimes I would wander from the bench to give a nut to a distant squirrel. At my return he might ask, "Did he take it from your hand?" If I was able to say yes, "Good!" he would exclaim, clapping his hands together sharply.

One day weeks later when he was back in the hospital, his eyes bandaged after surgery, I was reading to him various news items. "I see, Swamiji, that they are building a temple to house the Dead Sea Scrolls."

"Oh, that will make *you* happy," he commented. I did not understand why, so I asked. "Because," he said, "you are so fond of squirrels." He had heard "to house the dancing squirrels!"

We spent seemingly endless hours in the offices of doctors and dentists. Once after a two-hour wait in a doctor's office Swami said to me, "If we, who come in the train of a divine incarnation and his partners, have it like this, just think what must be the lot of ordinary people." This gave me considerable food for thought.

Most of his teeth were removed at this time. We had placed in his room a television set, hoping to divert him from the unattractive puréed diet, his various disabilities, and his entrenched desire to return to India without further expense and fuss. Swami Nikhilananda thought rightly that the television would help. Swami Madhavananda was much taken with the technology of it — its mechanism, its miracle. The set had a remote-control switch he held while sitting in an armchair. Sometimes he would invite me to come in and watch with him. Now, his propensity for changing channels was much stronger than his interest in any particular program — and it killed what little interest I might have had in watching television as he clicked the switch every two or three minutes. After a few days of this he gave his pronouncement on American TV: "The technique is marvelous, the subject-matter just nothing."

We watched the evangelist Billy Graham address a large crowd. When I asked what he thought of the speech, Swami said, "For many people this may be what they need, no doubt. But there is something higher." It was easier for him at this time to turn to the screen than to try to read. He was fond of watching trained animals, circuses and ballets. Was this partly because of his own balance impairment? Did he marvel that bodies could be trained to perform and pirouette like this?

Now he was receiving letters nearly every day, only a few of which he felt inclined or obliged to answer. He would ask me to read them, then indicate the lines along which he wanted them answered. I would submit a draft and we would go over that. Only at Thousand Island Park when some real recovery had been won did Swami begin signing his name again, and there he wrote one or two personal letters in his own hand.

In our numerous visits to doctors and dentists we raced up and down the avenues of New York in many a taxicab, I with my eyes shut more often than not. It did not seem to bother Swami; he sat back, apparently content to place his trust in the Lord. Many cab drivers (New York's are famous for their conversational talents) tried to guess his nationality, and although it was a matter of pride with them to be able to, not all succeeded. His skin was light and his nose almost Roman. One day we were speeding home from the office of a dentist whose name was Slocum. Swami was puzzled by the name, hearing it but not seeing it, and thought of it as *slokam*, the Sanskrit word for a scripture verse. So in the taxi he asked me how the dentist got a name like that. What language is it? "I feel sure it doesn't come directly from Sanskrit," was all I could say.

The day Swami had his teeth pulled was a black one. We brought him home and helped him to bed. The dentist had placed a kind of packing in his gum, which he was finding uncomfortable. He insisted on trying to remove it. I forgot my "place" completely, lost my temper and shouted at him. "No, you must *not*, Swami! The doctor has forbidden it!" He forgave me, of course. The dark cloud had its silver lining, for Swami Nikhilananda was present and it seemed to enhance his confidence in my nursing abilities.

It was now time to make a visit to the Vedanta Society on West 71st Street, deferred during the long time Swami Madhavananda's treatments were being carried out. Swami Pavitrananda had been very eager to receive him and to have the devotees meet him. One of them came to pick us up, for I was to go with him. In the ground-floor dining room of the center we were served a magnificent dinner. As dish after dish came through the swinging doors from the kitchen, I noticed that no two were carried by the same person. Evidently the eagerness to see and serve the former general secretary of the order had been keen and this was the way the problem had been solved. After dinner, 18 or 20 of their inner circle gathered in Swami

Pavitrananda's parlor and were invited by him to ask the senior swami some spiritual questions. It was the first time on this American visit that I had heard him speak at such length on specifically spiritual topics. It was gratifying that even without teeth or full control of his facial muscles he was able to make himself understood. I managed to record the following sketchy notes.

Q: "Is spiritual struggle real or apparent?"

Swami: "So long as a person thinks of himself as an individual it is real, but if one comes to experience samadhi and the world disappears, then his struggle is seen to be unreal."

Q: "Then who is liberated?"

Swami: "Whoever it was that felt bound before."

Q: "Should one remember God when doing things that are not so worthy?" (Going to a film was suggested as an example.)

Swami: "If one can, so much the better. Then that activity will itself change. And also, the Lord will not leave him long in a state where he does such things."

Q: "Does the language used for God's name matter?"

Swami: "No. If one *knows* it is God's name, that is the important thing."

Q: "Is not the natural tendency of the mind to go upward?"

Swami: "Unconsciously, perhaps you might say."

Q: "Can we exert free will to get beyond causality where we will be free?"

Swami: "Try! The point is, be consistent. Don't use free will in mundane affairs, and then put all spiritual matters into the category of God's grace."

Q: "How can we love incarnations, if they are embodiments of the God who created this hell of a world?" (Laughter.)

Swami: "In one aspect he tries to bind us, in another to free us. He plays with us thus. These [the avatars] are the benign aspects, so they can be loved."

Q: "Why doesn't the destructive aspect incarnate?"

Swami: "Maybe Hitler or Stalin was some such...but God sees it as we see a play."

Q: "Will you tell us something about Swami Turiyananda?"

Swami: "Read the books and articles. It is difficult to say much about such people. You may see the beauty of the ocean, but can you write about it like a Tagore or a Tennyson? Those who have vivid memories can recite incidents to support their statements. In our day we had no such books, we had to depend on memories. I remember one thing which the devotee Nityagopal told us Thakur had said about Maharaj [Swami Brahmananda]: 'Rakhal is like a green-looking banana which is really ripe, and like a flint brought out from under water.'"

Q: "How can one learn not to criticize others — without causing too much strain to a beginner?" (Much laughter.)

Swami: "It bespeaks a 'holier than you' attitude, to have this problem at all. Here is one idea: A person's sins are being washed off onto oneself when one criticizes that person. This is an old and familiar way of thinking to us."

On behalf of the Society, Swami was presented with a transistor radio which, as it happened, was put to good use when he returned to the hospital.

Swami had his new dentures in time to eat Thanksgiving dinner, and at the center a traditionally fine one was prepared. But now he was becoming anxious to return home and it became more difficult to make western food attractive to him. Swami Nikhilananda himself, beset with many other tasks, would go into the kitchen, don an apron and cook Indian dishes for him. It was his cooking alone that really satisfied.

The weather was cold now, much to his dislike. "It makes men so dependent on trappings," he said, meaning the gloves, muffler, overcoat and hat without which New Yorkers simply do not go out in the winter. He did like the drives on which Swami Pavitrananda would take him with his car and driver. One night after dusk we sat in the car looking out at the lights of the skyscrapers. Swami Pavitrananda told us a story about Josephine MacLeod, the celebrated friend and confidante of Swami Vivekananda. She had been taken to see an exhibit of Edison's new "lamps" — a brilliant display of electric lighting. Others in the party had been enthusiastic, while she had remarked, "But all this is man-made. It is nothing compared to the beauty of a single sunset." Swami Madhavananda listened to this. "But," he commented, "the beauty of a sunset is gone in a few minutes, whereas this beauty we can go on enjoying for hours."

The American swami and I walked with him to the Metropolitan Museum of Art in Central Park where a devotee, a graduate student in art history, was waiting for us. It was a much longer walk than usual, but on display there was the renowned Rembrandt painting of Aristotle patting the bust of Homer. Swami Nikhilananda had been talking much about it, so Swami Madhavananda had conceived a desire to see it for himself. All were discussing the fabulous sum the museum had paid, the most ever for a work of art — $2,300,000. After a guided tour of the museum by the student we stood in front of the painting for a while, Swami saying nothing. On our return we reported back to Swami Nikhilananda. Swami Madhavananda told him, pouring on the usual cold water of his inimitable candor, "It is the sale price you are enamored of, more than the picture." The two episodes were illustrative, I thought, of the swami's own strong bent for pragmatism.

V. PATIENT AGAIN

After dramatic days of consultation in doctors' offices and long discussions in Bengali, the news broke that Swami was at last resigned to have the cataracts removed here. Once he had decided, he did not look back. Yet, one felt that he was disappointed not to be able to demonstrate to his friends that his unoperated eyes would last as long as the rest of him. Much of his thought before reentering the hospital was given to the various possible routes back to India, and it was plain that he had had enough of this country. He had me bring him several airline schedules and he loved to pore over these, making alternative flight plans with due consideration for the respective weather conditions, etc.

In the second week of December he moved back to the 16th floor of New York-Cornell Hospital. Instead of his former room, not now available, he took a smaller one with no fine view; since he would be able to see little this time, it was not important. Also the male nurses who had attended him were unavailable now. Fortunately, two excellent women on private duty were found for the day shifts. Swami had become accustomed to the attendance of women nurses and he made a good friend of the evening nurse, a lady well along in years with a heart of gold. It also meant I was able to serve him in more ways than had previously been possible.

Swami's eye operations were separated by a three-day interval, as was common with cataracts. He returned from the second operation full of fun, and talking so freely that we were all surprised. It may have been partially the lingering effect of medications but possibly he was happy that these operations had been easier than he had anticipated. His conversation that afternoon was like hearing someone read from *Finnegan's Wake*.

Thus arrived for Swami Madhavananda the period in which he could not read a line for himself and had to depend on the eyes of others. In the mornings I read him the daily paper. He seldom wished to go deeply into details. We would skip from column to column as it held his interest. But unlike many older persons who have to be read to, Swami never fell asleep, leaving the reader dangling and embarrassed as to the next move. When he slept, he slept. When he listened, he was attentive even if he made no comment at all.

At other times his favorite was the *Reader's Digest*. Together, we would read the articles in an order dictated by his relative interest in the topics, sometimes until the whole issue was exhausted — even though the subjects of the last few articles might stir no flicker of familiarity in his mind. Probably a principle was involved — finishing what has been started. Swami had a Victorian approach to humor, no doubt, yet not without sophistication, and he wanted to hear every amusing remark in the *Digest*, whether the idioms were beyond his ken or not. He would be very much moved by the tragedies, something I really hadn't expected. Only a few weeks earlier there had occurred the tragic accident taking the life of Dag Hammarskjöld. The journal published a verse which had been found inserted in his family Bible. "Everyone comes into the world crying while others laugh; one should so live that when he leaves the world others may cry but he will laugh."

"That is Indian," I said to Swami.

"Yes, it comes from Tulasidas," said he.

"How typical of the Western publishers not to acknowledge its Oriental source."

"That does not matter at all," was Swami Madhavananda's reaction.

There was an article about the Bible itself, and Swami gave his opinion: "The new translations may have made many things more clear, small things mostly, but they have made a hash of all the passages we have taken the trouble to memorize." I could only agree.

He referred to the Indian Puranas as "religious novels." He liked mysteries, cared least for the science articles unless they were medical like those of Paul de Kruif, and was fond of success stories. We read about the many ways in which Henry Ford had utilized the soybean and about John Alexander Macdonald, builder of the Canadian nation — these he very much appreciated. He was not ready yet for the heavier diet of the holy books and periodicals of the Ramakrishna Order, although he did sometimes read or have read to him his Bengali *Kathamrita* (*Gospel of Sri Ramakrishna*). But he was finding divinity, I am sure, in whatever came to him, "sacred" or "secular." Sometimes I ventured to suggest that an article we proposed to read might not be as innocent in tone or content as monks would like. He would say, "You are reading for me, not for yourself — like Swamiji reading the *Ashtavakra Samhita* to the Master." One of the book supplements was the true story of Elsa, the lioness tamed and raised as their child by the Adamsons who lived in Africa. This is an engrossing story told in a graphic way, and it moved him, one could see.

The next book condensation was the biography of Ishi, "the last wild Indian in North America." The despicable capture by ignorant men of Ishi, a Yana Indian of Central California, is offset in the chronicles of California history only by his subsequent delivery into the hands of a loving and appreciative anthropologist, who saw to it that Ishi was given kind care for life as the ward of a university department. He lived many years thereafter in a museum and led a very happy life, freely demonstrating not only the skills and crafts of the Indians but also their admirable attitudes and philosophy of life. His character, as revealed in the friendships he made and in his simple pleasures and austere life, was remarkable and memorable. It showed a kinship in character between the Indians of our continent and those properly called Indians in the East. Swami did not miss one word of it, telling me afterward how inspiring he had found it — "much better than the lioness story," he said — and that Ishi was a "real man." Several years later I happened to visit another Indian museum in Sacramento where an entire room is set aside for pictures of Ishi as well as artifacts and souvenirs left behind by him or otherwise relating to his story; I wrote about it to Swami, then president of the order. He replied that he well remembered Ishi, and was much gratified to know about "his" room.

On one of the days just after the cataract operations, when Swami was asked to lie very still in his hospital bed, there came to his mind an old conundrum of the anagram type, which he asked me to try to solve. I worked on it, going to and fro in the city buses, and only after two days did I have it. Moreover, it is doubtful that I would have solved it at all had he not made one slip of the tongue while explaining the puzzle, thus revealing one of the words. (The puzzle is given at the end of this chapter.) It seemed to be Swami's delight to entertain those who were supposed to be entertaining him.

He told me the story of a man in Bengal who had a very sensitive conscience. We would probably refer to him today as a wimp. This fellow was walking on a Calcutta street when a stranger stopped him and asked, "Sir, can you tell me the way to the Star Theatre?" Our friend was prudish in such matters and thoroughly disapproved of the theater. "No, I don't know," he replied. After he had proceeded a few steps, the thought occurred to him that he had told a lie. Better go back and rectify it. So he ran back after the stranger and finally catching him said, "Yes, I know where the Star Theatre is, but I am not willing to tell you." I believe it was the same man who was once taking a train trip with his young son when suddenly, about midday, he caught hold of the conductor who was passing through the train. "Look here, my good fellow," (pulling out his own watch) "I now owe you another half-fare. My son has just passed 12 years of age." The first time this fellow traveled by train he had bought two tickets, one for himself and one for his daughter. Seeing the notice on the tickets, "Nontransferable," he had run back to ask the agent, "See here, now which ticket is for me and which for my daughter?"

It was not possible for me to stay in the hospital at night. Swami had to depend on the services of Miss B., his evening nurse, there being no alternative. She had been given the impossible instructions that no woman was to touch the swami. On the first day, finding him covered with perspiration, she set everything else aside and followed her nursing instincts. Getting up from her chair she said, "Look, Swami, let's forget now that I am a woman and you are a swami, and let me make you comfortable." She then helped him to bathe, to change his gown and bedsheets, and did all she could for him. When she had finished, Swami gave her just a grateful pat on the back of her hand. This became, she told me, his invariable "thank you" for her services from that time forth. She said she considered it the dearest kind of blessing. In whatever she did around his person she was most careful always to let him preserve his modesty completely. When about to leave the hospital Swami wanted to give Miss B. a gift. She said no king or queen could have been presented with a fortune in a more dignified manner. "Miss B.," said Swami Madhavananda, "I wish to present you with something."

"Oh, Swami," said she, "you don't need to present me with anything."

"But it is Christmas time."

"I know, Swami, but..."

"No, I wish to present this to you," and he gave her a package. She preferred to open presents at home when off duty. No, he insisted that she open it then and there. It proved to be a box of candy in the shape of a book. When she came the next day she told him, "That was a very sweet book, Swami!" And he laughed a lot at this.

I asked Miss B. what she thought was the most impressive thing about Swami Madhavananda. She replied that to her it was the fact that he was always saying his prayers. I asked how she knew that. She showed me how he had done japa on the joints of his fingers, and said she had seen his toes move with the rhythm of it also. On my way to India three years later I found that Miss B. had retired to a nurses' home, and I arranged to meet her. Her memories of Swami were vivid and it was clear that the experience of serving him had been etched into her mind. I have often wondered what her death was like; did he come to pat her hand, perhaps?

VI. SNOW AND DIVERSIONS

Christmas had indeed arrived. The streets were covered with ice and snow. In a few days Swami Madhavananda was sufficiently well to come home to the Ramakrishna-Vivekananda Center. He could see fairly well, enough to move about the house with the help of a pair of "arbitrary lenses" used while the eyes are recovering. There was doubt at first whether he could watch television. Swami Nikhilananda and others thought he should not. But there had been no ban on it by the doctors. Had there been, Swami Madhavananda would have been the firmest about observing it. But the set remained in his room and finally we heard noises coming from behind the closed door. Knocking to investigate, we found him clicking that versatile control switch. There sat Swami, like a little boy found at the cookie jar. He said at once: "I am not *looking*, just *listening*." As it turned out, the doctors had no objection, provided he did not tire his eyes.

As we have seen, Swami Madhavananda was able to surmount many difficulties with good humor. In his New York mood, he did not want serious matters. He had his "blue" moments, too, however. His 10-month ordeal was an annoying and onerous one for a man of 72 years coming to the great metropolis from a world so different. Being operated on so often, at the beck and call of nurses, attendants and teachers, having long waits, with time on his hands to spend and little of it in circumstances congenial to his use. Was it not a marvel? Fortunately he had very little physical pain throughout the experience; that is the miracle of modern medicine. On the other hand, the adjustments and indignities and sacrifices he had to undergo at every turn he bore with a sweet patience which was much more than stoicism. Heroism can be very quiet, I learned. That was the example he set, the lesson the West so badly needs.

It is no wonder, then, that we tried to do all we could to make him lose the feeling of wanting to return to India quickly, so that his medical needs might be fully taken care of. Swami Nikhilananda, particularly dedicated to this, arranged various excursions on a small scale for Swami's entertainment when he was well enough. This was the heyday of the most popular musical show of recent times, "My Fair Lady," which had now run so long that the cast had been changed several times. The convalescent swami was persuaded to see this, but he did so only after preparing himself thoroughly in a manner characteristic of him: by reading the Shaw play "Pygmalion" on which the show is based. The three of us went one afternoon to the grand theater where every seat was filled, and Swami enjoyed the performance immensely, no doubt partly due to the large role of language in the plot. It was also the only time I saw him obviously appreciating music.

Swami Pavitrananda would come, as we said, with the car in which Swami enjoyed drives. Swami Nikhilananda and I usually went along with them. In this way we went up and down Roosevelt Drive along the East River or on the other side of town, crossing the Hudson to explore the Thruway leading out into the countryside. The scenery was splendid and the trips a welcome change. Swami Pavitrananda also took him to see the film "King of Kings," the original movie version of Christ's life.

If I remember correctly, it was Swami Madhavananda himself who suggested seeing the "Threepenny Opera." in a small theater off-Broadway; it was about to close after a successful run. Adapted by Brecht from the "Beggars' Opera," a 17th-century play by John Gay, its translation was — I felt sure — spicy. Others also tried to dissuade him, thinking that a monk so ascetic and proper would not find it at all to his taste. As often happens with extraordinary personalities, he proved us all mistaken. Nothing to do but to go to the public library and borrow the "Beggars' Opera" for him to read in advance while Swami Nikhilananda bought the tickets. The three of us went on a rainy afternoon and heard those saucy ballads.

Our seats were so far up front that the little orchestra, almost under our feet, shook us with its booming beat. By the end of the first act, Swami Nikhilananda had had enough. He had arranged beforehand for our return with Swami Pavitrananda, so he now excused himself, leaving Swami Madhavananda in my care, and went home by taxi. When the show was over, Swami Madhavananda said he had found it most interesting, though greatly changed from the original. The car from the Vedanta

Society was delayed and there was nothing to do but wait in the seats. I went to tell the manager why we were staying, sitting on in the empty theater. Littered now with crumpled programs, some dim lights overhead, it created a blue atmosphere from which the actors and actresses from the "Threepenny Opera" were now emerging one-by-one into the darkening day outside, their costumes put away, their true, tired faces exposed to the open anonymity of private life. They looked with jaded curiosity at the old gentleman in strange clothing and spectacles, sitting vacantly with his young companion. In this moment, more than any other, I was overcome with a sense of the greatness of Swami Madhavananda. I was feeling ill-at-ease. But here he was, utterly unselfconscious, calm, patient, marooned in a little island world of which he had no part, yet carefree and innocent. I thought of how Sri Ramakrishna had said that one of the signs of the illumined soul is that he feels at home anywhere with anyone.

The birthday of Holy Mother was celebrated at the center with much enthusiasm. It made everyone happy that Swami Madhavananda came downstairs to attend the principal part of the worship. Lately he had not done this even in India. After the participating devotees had made their flower offerings they were allowed in turn to take the dust of Swami Madhavananda's feet. This was such a right-about-face for him it almost seemed out of character; but it was his life before he came to America as it would be when he returned home.

His eyes were healing well, permanent lenses would be fitted in India. Swami was about to go back to Belur Math and I to Sacramento. After long argument and much persuasion again, Swami Nikhilananda prevailed upon him to speak from the platform to a Sunday congregation. All were surprised that he ultimately agreed. He walked with the heavy, slightly uneven stride which had now become his standard gait, up the steps of the platform. And he delivered without the slightest hesitation — and without notes — a vigorous and well-phrased speech of nearly half-an-hour's duration. It was the first time most of us had heard him give a speech. He included in it his warm thanks to all the devotees who had helped to make him feel at home and was himself visibly moved.

On the night of his departure, a cold one in January, he

was pushed in a wheelchair down the long ramp which led to the
boarding area of the airport to save him a long walk. Swami
Nikhilananda and devotees from the center, as well as Swami
Pavitrananda with a group from the Vedanta Society, gathered
around him to have final darshan. He wore his gray round cap
and gray suit just as on his arrival, and looked quite healthy and
very distinguished. This is the way I shall perhaps best remember him. Swami Madhavananda was an example before our eyes
of what Swami Vivekananda described as the "universal man."
Swamiji wanted numbers of these to be produced in every land,
for such men could best do Sri Ramakrishna's work. Here was
one, at any rate — an Indian in America, a man whose "home"
was nowhere, yet who was everywhere at home. He had fulfilled
Holy Mother's injunction to make the whole world one's own.

VII. THE ORDER'S CHOICE

Back once more in the physical and emotional warmth
of India and the sanctuary of the great monastery, Belur Math,
Swami was prompt to write me of his joy in being again with old
friends and brothers. Swami Abhayananda, perennial Manager
of the Math, had been there with a car and large band of sadhus
right at the foot of the airplane. "I am not taking meat, but plenty
of good fish and an egg every day... The Lord was gracious to us
all that I could get away from the cold of New York." And many
other things that went with it!

When he suddenly had a fall, it terrified them. Swami
broke his right collarbone. I did not get details; perhaps he made
too quick a try for total independence. Of course it never fazed
him, nothing rippled that serenity.

Swami Madhavananda graciously sent letters frequently
— monthly at first — and I would reply. His were devoted to the
details of his physical improvement and occasionally to subjects
we had had discussions over like Le Corbusier's building designs
in Chandigarh, which Swami had just seen for the first time. I
had merely read about them and seen photos; his views were
typically conservative.

"I was tickled to death," he wrote, "at the sight of the
architecture of Chandigarh, which from the standpoint of utility
seem awful — too few openings and too thin walls. Who knows

whether some people who like the newfangled paintings of to-day may not also like the Chandigarh buildings." From there he had gone to attend the Purna Kumbha Mela, the twelve-yearly festival for pilgrims and sadhus at Allahabad. Back home at Belur he was going to the temples every day and taking additional walks in the evening. "I shall not mention the extent of the walks," he added coyly.

Swami knew that I felt certain in my own mind it would soon be time I visited India. He wrote about it, "I often think of you, and it will be a great day if the Lord makes it possible in the not too distant future."

In midsummer of that year, 1962, his brothers, under-standing how the great heat was exacerbating his eczema and other difficulties, were trying to persuade him to move to a hill station to wait it out. I could imagine how troublesome he was going to find *that*. "Fortunately the monsoon has come early," he rejoiced, "sparing me the need to move." Yet in the same season the illness of the President, Swami Visuddhananda, reached its climax and after a very short presidency, he passed away.

"Day before yesterday," wrote Swami Madhavananda, "I was given a lift to Presidentship. I have dared to accept it," he confided, "relying on the grace of our Master who has all along befriended me. Recently I made a trip up to Varanasi lasting for twenty-three days. It did not bother me to travel by rail or car" — a most important discovery for one who would now be called upon to travel all over the subcontinent.

This is what we had been shaping him for in our own way, physically, therapeutically — to provide the life structure for the destiny his own outstanding life and thought of so many years had shaped for him.

It seemed all the more urgent now that I have his com-pany again. He agreed: "I have been to America several times. Now it is your turn to come to India."

How was he getting along in his new role? A letter of September showed the same customary absence of self-impor-tance we had seen in New York.

"Yes, it would be very difficult for anyone who saw me in America to recognize me in my Indian dress here." (This was in response to my comment on the official photograph he had sent.)

"For the matter of that, I have grown rather stout during the last few years. So much so that I myself took time to recognize a photo of mine taken in 1941. Anyway, plumpness will probably add weight to the religious instruction that I am now called upon to give."

Most surprising to me was his wholesale "conversion." "By the way," his letter read, "I find the swinging of arms very helpful in walking. It would have made Mr. Brown very happy to see me take fairly long strides and that, pretty fast."

The centenary of Swami Vivekananda's birth was a year-long observance, about to commence. It fell to the fate of Swami Madhavananda to have the honor and the joy of presiding over this, the principal outward event of his presidency. I wrote to him of our plans in Sacramento to open the new temple there at the close of the festive period, if possible. "Glory to Swamiji!" he wrote. "I am sure that with Swami Ashokananda behind it, your affair will be a grand one."

The biography of Sri Ramakrishna by Christopher Isherwood, *Sri Ramakrishna and His Disciples,* now appeared. One or two passages raised doubt in my mind as to the validity or interpretation, and I wrote to Swami about it. One concerned the relationship to the Master of Swamiji and Maharaj respectively. Here is the reply.

"Isherwood is right in saying that Sri Maharaj's relationship with the Master was even closer than that of Swamiji. I myself heard Revered Shashi Maharaj say that Sri Ramakrishna had given Sri Maharaj privileges that were granted to no other disciple, e.g., the Master would take Rakhal Maharaj on his shoulders, allow him to sit on his lap as a child does with its mother and so on. But that does not take away the unique position that Swamiji occupied in the Master's estimation. The Bengali Gospel part IV at one place gives several metaphors, describing Swamiji as unparalleled. I put it this way: the Prince of Wales of England and the British Prime Minister can be cited as examples of Sri Ramakrishna's relations with his two greatest disciples. So the devotees may set their hearts at ease on this score."

He went on to give information important to me in another way: "Swami Yatiswarananda [then vice-president of the order] is here and doing well. He will fly to Madras on the 5th.

He has had to shoulder some of the burdens that should have been borne by me... By the by, Chris had his typed manuscript examined by me. Only after my brain operation, it was in abeyance for quite a while."

In another letter he recalled my query and added this to the subject: "Indians who love either Hari or Siva would understand quickly if I compare Sri Maharaj and Swamiji with them — both being superlative. Sri Ramakrishna, of course, gave the charge of his empire to Swamiji and Sri Maharaj and all cheerfully accepted that."

In June of 1963, when John XXIII had died, Swami Madhavananda wrote by way of comment that Pope John had done very great work towards mutual understanding in the world.

Swami told me his room and the portion of his veranda where he sat had been air-conditioned under the direction of Swami Nirvanananda. It had proved a great help. Monks and devotees had been urging him for some time to visit the center in Rangoon, Burma, and that autumn he actually made the visit. One of his letters read amusingly, "I am often reminded of you by any number of squirrels running about fearlessly on my veranda and sometimes going into my room. You would have fallen into samadhi at the sight of them... So you are getting pigeons there; gradually you will find that they are not obnoxious. This will broaden your outlook." He was traveling now to many places, giving initiation, opening buildings, laying cornerstones, chairing public meetings.

I wrote to ask if this swami had not had a hand in the *Life of Sri Ramakrishna*, the standard biography published by the Order.

"Your guess is right. I did the final editing, reducing the large volume of matter written by Swami Nikhilananda. He has a facile pen." Once again, the master of understatement!

Prime Minister and pivot of Indian politics, Jawaharlal Nehru left the scene in 1964. "Yes," Swami said in a passage unusually long for him, "India has lost its most celebrated gifted child and leader. As for your reference to my lack of approval to some extent, I can say only this, that no one is a hero to his valet. Probably at the transition stage a benevolent semi-dictator like him was perhaps a necessity. Certainly he had outstanding gifts of heart and intellect which the whole world is appreciating. He has no son, only a daughter and two grandchildren. His wife died long ago. India has chosen a fine man to succeed him, though not replace him. Our present Prime Minister, Mr. L. B. Shastri has risen to his eminent position steadily from a life of intense poverty; to go to school and return home, he did not have enough money. At least one day he had to swim across the Ganges while returning from school. So he feels intensely for the poor and downtrodden. As *Time* wrote the other day, 'Shastri has no enemy.' It is most fortunate that the choice of him as Prime Minister has been unanimous."

Swami included in this letter two notes concerning the life of the New York center in which we both had shared. "We shall utilize Budhananda's good qualities somewhere in India itself. Nikhilananda needed someone with good knowledge of Sanskrit, and Bhashyananda [his new assistant, later Head of the Vivekananda Vedanta Society, Chicago] is an M. A. in Sanskrit. He also is a very lovable person as well as able."

In October of 1964 Swami Madhavananda had a fall on the veranda of his residential quarters at the Math. His attendant wrote to me of his satisfactory condition following surgery. The hip had broken and a metal replacement was made for the head of the left femur. It was done by a top orthopedic surgeon of Calcutta. Swami had taken this experience in stride, and with usual dry humor, as he had so many of life's adventures.

Here is his last letter to me, dated July 7, 1965. "I was delighted to hear from your letter that you have decided to come to India. Regarding permanent visa let the matter take its own course. If you come via New York and happen to meet Swami Nikhilananda — or even otherwise — please try to bring a small quantity of eczema ointment prescribed by Dr. Lewis. I am told it is very hard to get.

"I came back from Bombay on the 7th of this month and am doing tolerably well. More when we meet. With love and best wishes, [Signature]."

But we could not meet. Swami Madhavananda filled the office of President of the Ramakrishna Math and Mission for little more than two years. The strains began to tell on his health, and even that powerful mind was unable to overcome the breakdown of internal organs and the side-effects of his medications. The news of his passing came to me through my good friend Swami Vidyatmananda of France, reporting what he had received from a brahmachari at the Training Center, Belur Math:

> Perhaps you have got the dismal news of Revered President Maharaj. The crisis was going on in the Puja time itself. But it seems he kept his vital force alive through his will power so that the Mother's puja was not hampered. He was talking with the Swami in charge of Rahara, when he coughed a bit, then called, 'Ma, Ma, Thakur,' and collapsed. The news was broadcast through All-India Radio. The time was Oct. 6, 6:50 p.m. Next day the daily puja and offering were finished at the Math before 8 a.m., the body was brought into the courtyard of the Math... There was a heavy crowd. We chanted for eight hours. A long procession began, as the remains were carried to the front of all the temples, and then to the cremation ground. Within three hours everything had been finished — Vedic chanting, kirtana, devotional songs.

I have included the details of the letter from India because it deals with final things. One would have expected this account to end there, perhaps, but in keeping with the swami's nature and sense of the just, I will let the reader in on the special puzzle he posed to me, also dealing with final things:

The following conversation took place at a funeral. The first missing word has one letter; the second has two, etc. Each blank contains all the letters of the previous blank, with one new letter added. What was said, and what was the occupation of the speaker? (See Appendix D for the solution.)

_ do not like _ _ , said the man with the black _ _ _ . The _ _ _ _ may be impressive, but when you _ _ _ _ _ a man, you _ _ _ _ _ _ a _ _ _ _ _ _ _ power of investigation. _ _ _ _ _ _ _ _ against _ _ _ _ _ _ _ _ _ will set in when the _ _ _ _ _ _ _ _ _ _ of this fact is revealed.

Swami Ghanananda, Muswell Hill, London

"LONDON IS A MAN'S TOWN - THERE'S POWER IN THE AIR..."[1]

SWAMI GHANANANDA

I. INTRODUCTION TO LONDON

"No prosaic man, I!" he used to say, a self-affirming declaration in the British manner. It barely covered the case of one around whom there was inarguably the atmosphere of "What next?" He began his work in London for the Ramakrishna Mission in 1948 and conducted it with marked success for over 20 years; no prosy person could have done that. He could be used as a textbook paradigm, I should think, for the word *paramahamsa*, a sannyasin of extraordinary and peculiar qualities.

When I reached Swami Ghanananda's monastic foundation it was late in my day. I had notebooks crammed with the pronouncements and advice of a dozen previous spiritual guides - "enough," I had said. So in London I took no notes, kept no diary, wrote down no anecdotes — and of course I am living to regret it. Memory does not serve well in supplying one with the details needed to recreate a living character. Nevertheless, I record the few reminiscences which follow as the best testimonial offering I can manage to the memory of one of the greatest souls I

---

[1] "America for Me," a poem by Henry Van Dyke.

have known.

I first saw Swami Ghanananda before he had decided to settle in London. He visited the Northern California centers on his way eastward, and in the auditorium of our Berkeley Temple he told us how Americans had impressed him with their honesty: Bottles of milk delivered by the dairy early in the morning would remain in place on the doorstep until their owners arose to claim them! Perhaps the lecture was titled "My Impressions of American Life," or the like, because the other point I recall was that all American cities look alike — "if you've seen one, you've seen them all." I remember this because I disagreed. How could anyone say that? Only years later, after seeing more of the world, did I understand.

Swami was short, slight, birdlike in movement and wore glasses that made him look like the scholar he was. He also appeared ill at that time, which he was. He was visiting the San Francisco center and was plagued, we heard, by stomach trouble, probably ulcer. Then his host, Swami Ashokananda, took him in hand, it was said, and had him examined by his own physician. The diagnosis was simply a system ravaged by fasting and undernourishment. The swami was in the habit of fasting and was now devouring his own stomach. Swami Ashokananda in candid brotherly fashion affectionately upbraided him, "Stop acting like a holy man and start eating! 'Food is Brahman!'" And he soon improved.

Naturally it would not have come to my mind at the time even to imagine I would one day be a worker in Swami Ghanananda's vineyard. But he had spent six months in our Hollywood center, helping Swami Prabhavananda by giving lectures and a weekly class. Later, when I arrived there, it was said that he had not made himself loved; some of the younger male probationers had even unkindly ridiculed him behind his back.

In fact, he was one whose image lent itself to that sort of thing. At close range Swami Ghanananda had an attractive face; his expression was insightful, genial and often smiling. From a distance, however, and with his glasses on he looked cross. There was strabismus and the glasses did little to correct that appearance. Swami's voice, too, tended to put people off. High, a little thin and dry, pronouncing excellent English in precise tones, it gave the impression that here was another fussy schoolmaster.

In other words he had what today we would call an image problem. As the reader will see, it was undeserved. Yet he himself may have preferred it that way; one can't be sure.

It was as his guest for two or three days that I met him next. That is, though I was at the London center for that period, such was his condition that I saw him for only half an hour. I was on my way to India at the end of 1965, and he had written to Sacramento saying that I was welcome at his center for as long as I liked — they would arrange a tour of London for me. As we didn't know each other, the person meeting me would identify himself by holding a copy of their journal, *Vedanta for East and West* — an unwitting portent of things to come.

Swami Ghanananda in five years had reached the point where he was able, with the help of a generous donor, to purchase a house in which to establish the center's work. It was one of those semi-detached rowhouses (known in the United States as a duplex) of which whole neighborhoods in London are constituted. This was in Muswell Hill, well in the north of the metropolis, beyond Highgate. The house was unmarked by any sign or ensign and thus indistinguishable from others around it, except for those who knew. The left half of the building, it was clear as we approached, was the focus of activity. Here we entered and went upstairs. The other half had remained as it was, a family house with bedrooms, parlor, etc., and was used by women devotees for overnights and retreats.

A quick bow in the sanctuary, and I was shown into the presence of Swami Ghanananda. I would hardly have known him, so much older he appeared. Though I had been informed on my arrival that he was not at all well, diabetes having been discovered in 1957, I was still inadequately prepared. Swami was having difficulty with breathing, plagued by cough and wheeze; there was great economy in his words. He sat in an armchair in his bedroom, which was near the shrine room, with literary work on his lap and surrounded by stacks of papers, books and journals, all in glorious disarray. Or so it seemed. People of his type often have their own filing system at another level. Swami Ghanananda hoarsely repeated the welcome he had written, including the fact that I would be housed at Holland Park, the new branch of the Ramakrishna Vedanta Centre of London, as this was known. I think he apologized for his unsocial condition. I asked a few questions. The interview was over.

Dusk was long past. I was now shown into the ground-floor dining room where a core devotee, the center's treasurer in fact, waited to serve me supper. It was she, a teacher in the primary schools, who unknowingly taught me the meaning of the word "sterling." In her warm, respectful service the best in the English nature shone forth, rescued the day for hospitality and put me onto the scent of what Vedanta in London was all about.

Although I met the two young men living there with Swami, one Indian and the other, to my delight, like myself a former member of the Society of Friends, I was to have little more of their company now. This was all I could know of Muswell Hill until later, when I moved to England from India.

Through circumstances to be recounted later, Swami Ghanananda had been enabled, only the previous year, to acquire a huge new house in the Borough of Kensington, the very heart of residential London, at 54 Holland Park. With it came the expectation of a larger scope for the public work — lectures and classes reaching more people, growth of the monastery and easier access for travelers from abroad. Ceremonies inaugurating this second home, this mansion of five floors, had been held in conjunction with the Swami Vivekananda Centenary of 1963-64. It was already late at night when I arrived at the place and was warmly greeted by Swami Parahitananda — English, Swami's longtime student and monastic trainee, recently become a sannyasin and assistant minister for the center. Close in age, we two soon established rapport. There also lived in the house a devotee, an Indian boy employed in a business firm.

Sixteen high-ceilinged rooms at 54 Holland Park sat in solid splendor from the beginning of the century, most of them empty just now. The shrine room, where we first proceeded, still bore the carved scrolls and gracious ambiance of the onetime music room of some great family of years past. The room given me on the third floor was number 10. I went to bed.

How can one explain what happens at those times in one's life when the veil that covers us is lifted? The pall of ordinariness which blankets our nights and days, making us seek ever-fresh

variety and permutation of forms and feelings? We suppose that
we will, through distraction and variation, somehow enhance the
quality of our consciousness — not being aware that "enhance-
ment" itself is the ghost we do not believe in, the shadow we can
never embrace, projected beside us. I went to bed in that room,
but in place of sleep there came upon me an experience of power,
rare in my life, before or since. The room — no, the whole house
— was as if charged with a higher force. That power was a *sattvik*
one — bright, light, intelligent. It broke through the clouds of
hoping, struggling, frustrating waiting. And because I was no
longer a novice in Vedanta, a host of questions poured through
the lower layers of my mind. How had this "new" building acquired so quickly an atmosphere like this one? Would all transient travelers who put up here now be able to feel it? Was it
accomplished in one great *prana-pratishta*, the life-giving ritual
of dedication? Or was it, in my case, the gift of that
crotchety-looking old man eight miles away on the hill — in spite
of such illness? And if that be so, does he scuttle the barriers of
space, just now; or the barriers of time, by having planted a seed
when I was in his presence? There are what Swami Ashokananda
used to call, somewhat irreverently, the tricks of the trade. Moreover, our minds never seem to tire of asking explanations from
the Great Inexplicable.

Eventually we learn to give little significance to such
puzzles. Some people think they can find answers. I doubted
whether I would ever know, and attempted to concentrate on
this new light and strength instead. "Remember," Swami
Prabhavananda had told us, "all help, whether from inside or
outside, comes from God." Had I been a saint, surely the whole
night would have passed in contemplation. But sleep came, and
with it, resumption of the commonplace and "the old Adam."
Next day I took a tour of the scenes, sounds and historic sites of
the city; managed to get Swami Ghanananda on the phone for
my adieu and thanks; then boarded the plane for Calcutta.

We met again in Belur Math, over two years later. Swami
Ghanananda visited India in 1968 to have his last sight of old
friends and contemporaries and to discuss at the headquarters
the future of the London center. He had been living away from
the country for so many years — about 20 — that he was known

to many of our monks only by reputation, and although he stayed
very quietly by special arrangement in the guest house for Westerners situated near the rear gate of the monastery, people were
curious to have a glimpse of him. He had brought a few devotees
with him, including his new attendant, a tall boy from the Mid-
lands who had joined him at the Muswell Hill household. Gentle,
affable Tarak was attuned to his every move and need. Swami
Ghanananda was the disciple of Swami Shivananda whom he
greatly revered. That must be the reason he liked to name his
attendant Tarak — Swami Shivananda's personal name.
Parahitananda, at Holland Park, had also been "Tarak."

I remember, one afternoon at the Math, being part of a
gathering around the swami as he discoursed, in his impromptu
and peppery fashion, on the work in England and the state of
affairs in the world at large. For a man broken in body he had
astounding mental energy and vehemence of expression. I was
present also one afternoon in the veranda of Swami
Vireswarananda, our president, where he received the London
swami for a friendly chat. I was so caught up in the rarified atmosphere of old times generated there that I do not recall making any mental notes of what was said. Partly it was the fault of
my being ill still, for recovery from hepatitis had been slow. I had
told my superiors I felt I could not remain in India and desired
reassignment to the West, without waiting several years to take
final vows. Just where I would go I left to them, probably unaware of how much of a problem it posed for them.

It was a matter of some surprise, therefore, when during
Swami Ghanananda's last few days at Belur, the general secretary came up to me and said, pointing in the direction of the
guest house, "Here is a swami who will take you!" I tried to digest
this news, for there were problems to ponder: a new land, an
unfamiliar climate (though unquestionably an improvement over
the Indian), different associates, a new abbot. Nearly everyone
thought of this monk as "odd" to say the least. How would it all
sit with me? These are big junctures, externally, in monastic life.
The "little people" in a big institution cannot see how the strings
are being pulled behind the scenes by those who have to make
the decisions. Every monk, novice or professed, feels the tossing
of this ship and struggles for balance and serenity of mind to

accomplish smooth passage.

A boat trip, as a matter of fact, was just what Swami Ghanananda had in mind! There were meetings between us. He wanted me to go to England by ship "to save money." "You will also recoup your health," he declared, tossing his head and pursing his lips in that funny way he had, "and gain weight on the long journey." It was final. My books and personal effects would be crated and sent to Bombay, from where I would board ship and sail for London — like Alice, coming to Wonderland. And that reminds me of an article written from my post in Narendrapur, Bengal, on Lewis Carroll's book studied Vedantically, an article submitted to *Vedanta for East and West*. The editors, Swamis Ghanananda and Parahitananda, had liked and published it. It may have been a factor in the swami's thinking me useful to him.

He was right — my health did improve on the sea voyage, and a long one it surely was. I went on the French line Messageries Maritimes, and due to closure of the Suez Canal and a national train strike in France, it took nearly five weeks. June had begun when the train from Dover delivered me at Victoria Station and I stepped into the life at Muswell Hill. I wrote promptly to my former superior, Swami Lokeswarananda at Narendrapur, to inform him of my delayed but safe arrival.

"I have never had much contact," he responded at once, "with Swami Ghananandaji except when both he and I lived together at Belur Math in the thirties. He was very nice to me then and I too liked him very much. What I liked best about him was his simplicity. I am glad to hear that you like him too and you think that even when you know him very closely, you will go on liking him. Where there is genuine love and affection minor conflicts of misunderstanding can do no harm. Unfortunately, we tend to overlook the many good points that the other man has; we seem to be too much concerned about his weaknesses." It was a message I needed and to which I have had to refer throughout

II. CRYPT AND CRUCIBLE

It must be clear from the very fact of their venturing here that there was an element of the unorthodox in monks who came to the West to plant the seedling of Vedanta. In some there was a

Ramakrishna-Vedanta Centre, 54 Holland Park

heavy dose of orthodoxy mixed in, producing bizarre combinations. This is seen in Swami Ghanananda who, with a background
of a Brahmin family of South India, retained many vestiges of
the traditions of that inheritance. He had constructed the prayer
hall and shrine on the pattern of a theater, with "audience" squatting on the lower portion, facing west, and "stage" occupied by
all that was holy. Throughout the order the shrine area receives
special attention as regards its purity and sanctity, sometimes to
an extraordinary degree, but I was hardly prepared to find that
here it was completely separated from the worshipers and medi-
tators by a solid sheet of glass the width of the room. At least ¾"
thick and perfectly transparent, it wasn't immediately visible. It
extended almost to the ceiling, leaving just enough of a gap for
the passage of air — and this was a large room. Behind the partition was one of the largest pictures of Sri Ramakrishna I'd ever
seen; it was a photographic enlargement of one of the original
prints. Beside and behind him on the spacious shrine table, and
on the mantelpiece against the wall, was arranged a large assort-
ment of the various deities: Kali, Krishna, Buddha, Siva, Christ.
Through the side door into the shrine room no one passed save
Swami himself and the boy serving as priest and — on occasion
— those to be initiated, but that only after a complete bath and

fresh clothes. Shades of San Francisco — but this seemed designed to defend a sterile laboratory. It was only much later that I learned that the glass wall had not been part of Swami's original design, but had been necessitated by an act of vandalism some years before.

What role does such external ritual purity play in the building up of a store of psychic and mystical power? I have often pondered it. I was struck with admiration for Swami's zeal regarding ritual purity, for as I came to know him better and saw the influence he wielded, the sources of which could not be discerned simply by reckoning the visible factors, the more I felt that in his life and work such a connection was being demonstrated. I believe he attempted also at one point to regiment the prayer hall visitors and users by insisting on their having a bath before coming, a proposal found — not surprisingly — unfeasible.

At major celebrations Swami Ghanananda would perform the puja himself just as he often did the vesper service when feeling well enough. He was meticulous in the extreme about the arrangements and purity of the offerings. In the ceremony itself he would become like one lost. A current of uplifting spiritual consciousness would be initiated, which hardly anyone could avoid noticing and being affected by in one way or another. As one devotee remarked, it was strange and moving to see one who was at times so masterful and full of fire become patently humble as he sat there surrounded by banks of flowers. He did something else I had never seen others do. He would linger around the door of his room after worship was over, evidently scrutinizing the effects it had had on the various devotees as they emerged from the prayer hall. It was not something I read into it; he admitted it to at least one person.

Most of his day Swami spent in his own room, which served as bedroom, living room and office and has already been described. There he gave himself the necessary twice-daily injections of insulin. There he read his mail, the material and proofs for the magazine and prepared his lectures. There too he spent a great deal of time in bed. It had surely preserved him to this age of seventy years, the amount of bed rest he had taken over so many of those years. Who knows whether he was asleep? It was a great matter for speculation for the novices. What we do know is that he would come to the tea table after one of those long "naps" and say to a secretary, "Have you heard from M. lately? No? Write to her. She is ill." Or "Go and call on N. and you can take her some prasad," or "Send a little money to S. He needs it." This information did not come from the mail. Once he told a devotee who was feeling over-pressed with work and worries, "It will be easier when you reach my age. You can shut your eyes and everybody will think you are sleeping, and they will not disturb you; but really you will be meditating and you will gain spiritual strength." Reducing his metabolic needs undoubtedly helped Swami Ghanananda to undertake the fasting for which he was famous. I did not see it in my time, which was characterized by his eating each meal precisely as prescribed by his medical regimen, down to the half-ounce, but I heard that he used to fast on the slightest excuse; he was known to live on nothing but fruit juice or milk for as many as nine days before a major festival such as the Durga Puja.

Speaking of food, I was released from the strict rule of vegetarianism enveloping 68 Dukes Avenue, Muswell Hill, in a most interesting way. Still recuperating and on doctor's advice, I ate fish. Swami told me to buy it at the market and take it into the little-used kitchen of No. 66, the women's retreat house next door, and cook it there, which I did.

The ashrama's atmosphere of spiritual intensity, engendered by the meditation periods and the ritual scrupulosity, Swami knew how to preserve even in the relaxation and recreation of the dining hall. It was here we all gathered, brahmacharis and devotees alike, to have — with our coffee, tea, etc. — his jokes, told with twinkling eyes and a giddy laugh, and his outlandish stories. One of his favorites was that of the flying serpents of Sargacchi, near Murshidabad, Bengal. He had lived there, writing letters in English for Swami Akhandananda, one of the disciples of Sri Ramakrishna, so when the latter pressed him to remain there with him, there was the expectation that the young monk would wish to avail himself of such an opportunity. Swami Ghanananda, however, had seen, in the dusk, a snake jump over a well. This and the prevalence of dysentery in the area persuaded him to forego the privilege.

At the meal or tea table Swami often rose above himself, so to speak, in brilliance of wit, brightness of spirit, sweetness of expression and personal inspiration. That humor of his cannot be quoted or exemplified; it verged on the zany and took time to get accustomed to. "blithe spirit" was an expression of the time, and often came to my mind. At other moments there was a vibrant silence, no void, but a silence filled to the brim, bringing inwardness and peace. Not seldom there were depth charges — pungent personal comments comprehended by the party targeted, if not by others present. One never knew what to expect. Nowhere was "the guru" more in evidence than here at the table, and probably nowhere better received.

There were good windows in the kitchen from which one could view the roomy back yard and the squirrel living in the big shade tree. It, too, had found the secret of Swami's heart and occupied a good niche there. Swami would see that his friend the squirrel had respectable food offerings, intimately tendered, and would come and report to us its antics. I was a fool not to have noted down on paper or in mind these and many other seemingly trivial transient things, for they are the very stuff of biography. But I was still dazed by having moved, still puzzling over whether I could live with this strange man!

Swami Ghanananda had been a good walker in healthier days in his early years in London. He had been an intrepid explorer and in this way had seen many parts of the city. He told us to walk. We usually did not go far, but it was a joy in good weather to stroll in the company of a brother, or alone up to the hilltop, religiously to circumambulate grand old Alexandra Palace, and speculate on that Queen's personal martyrdom and other wisps of British history of which the fog and crisp air were redolent.

Going out was hedged, however, by certain important strictures, especially for Swami Ghanananda. He asserted them to be astrological. Thursday afternoon was inauspicious as a matter of course. "Well, hadn't the Master observed all these things?" he would say. One came to feel that, after the *sruti*, the primary scripture of revelation, it was the *Panjika*, the almanac prescribing the various auspicious hours and days as well as those not so, that held sway over our life. Swami kept in his room a chalkboard with various cautions and reminders written there:

"Sat. morning, don't go out.," "Don't write letters next Wed.,"
"See that B.F. doesn't arrive Mon. morning." Not only that, it
was possible for the auspiciousness to change within the course
of the day. Abrupt decisions would be made, sudden changes of
plan. We might be all set to make a visit to Holland Park ashrama
and Swami would call down the stairs, "No, we can't go today."
There were some who suspected all this was designed to make us
flexible. Aside from its possible perversity, that was not, I think,
true. I cannot demonstrate what dire catastrophes were obviated
by all this, but Swami Ghanananda *believed* in the *Panjika*. He was
a strong-willed man, not given to fear, one whose tone of voice
or stare was sufficient to settle promptly any dispute. Yet if the
question of astrology's validity was raised with him, he would
discuss it coolly, rationally, and if you still had doubts he would
toss the whole thing off with a rising inflection of excitement,
"But these things do work, you know!" Or "Sri Ramakrishna himself paid attention to all this!" Yet his dealing was individual with
the various students, and he told at least one, "Astrology is not

Taken on a Visit to Greece

for you. For you — meditation."
        A number of his students supported Swami Ghanananda
in his dedication to astrological niceties. One particularly dear

and unusual soul was Tillie, a widow who lived nearby and did most of the gardening for the ashrama. Tillie was a good gardener, but that alone cannot account for the relation that Swami had with her; it was unique, beyond the comprehension of anyone else. He shared her private world — lived in the dreams and visions she cherished of the past and for the future. Sri Ramakrishna was in the habit of visiting Tillie, as were Swamiji and many other astral entities. What she would say about her visions, as if it happened to everyone all the time, would shock and bemuse me into embarrassed silence. But not Swami; he would accept her and her ingenuous assertions, a bit self-flattering, just as they came. Tillie usually wore an ample white gown and wide-brimmed floppy white hat as she did her pottering about the flowers and shrubs. Swami Ghanananda had placed a framed photo of her, dressed in just that way, prominently on the wall of the dining room. She considered herself the denizen of a heavenly world, on loan to Earth for assisting in the Master's play, and Swami said yes. She was an "alien" long before we became acquainted with the term. This devotee took a special liking to me and wrote me letters at least annually for the rest of her long life.

There were at that time two girls, his disciples, of whom Swami was taking particular care. It was as if he thought of these two as candidates for monastic life. He took special pains to teach them scriptural wisdom and to guide the pattern and style of their life and thought. They were working girls, but as there was no convent (I believe Swami had attempted to get one sanctioned by the headquarters in India but had been turned down) Swami made do as best he could, and with these two devoted young women had an affectionate, very humorous and lively-witted, almost motherly, relationship. At the very end of his life, before his successor had arrived, they lived in No. 68 for a period of months and helped to take care of their teacher.

The effect and influence of the labor of these swamis who worked at deeper levels, quietly in their own corner of the world, is easily overlooked or minimized. Those who came as I did, in the last phase of Muswell Hill center, could have no comprehension of what had taken place there. It is a story one has to doubt will ever be written or could be. The aura of peace and goodwill, the intensity of aspiration in its level of vibration, were the fruit of years of careful tending and of heartrending self-denial on the part of his workers and disciples. It is a record to be found only in the lives of those he reached and touched. He tended the fire of the furnace in which those lives were forged, and without them it is easy to lose in the dry dust of time all trace of the testimony, of the consummate contribution to Vedanta in the West, made at the house on Dukes Avenue. I do not exaggerate. Because such persons do not talk about themselves as the ones we all know are wont to do, this early stage of a spiritual foundation always remains veiled; I have seen it in every chapter of this book. As one who chanced upon Muswell Hill wrote, "The immediate environment was not particularly lavish, one might almost say it was more than a trifle dilapidated, but... the impact was such that one of our party remarked, 'This is the place for us,' and from that moment our search had ended." Swami Ghanananda's students were impressive.

How pulseless he could be, like cold steel! And if the blade of that disapproval pried between your ribs, take care. I remember once I stood in a room examining, a little uneasily, something I realized was not exactly my business. His footsteps creaked the floorboards outside and I supposed he was bound elsewhere. Soon I became aware that the footsteps were going forth and back not far from the slightly open door. Then he abruptly entered the office where I stood, looked me up and down and asked crisply, "May we help you?" I found some lame excuse to drop the matter in hand — it was the official list of the journal subscribers. "That is not your concern yet; that will come in time," he said. The edge of his voice had gone straight through me and I can never forget it. Had he been watching through the crack of the door? He didn't always need eyes to see, as we well knew. Swami Ghanananda could use a tone, a wink, a gesture, a guffaw, a slanted word, to marvelous effect. "A cat under ashes," as a monastic disciple used to describe him.

Yet the house on Dukes Avenue was permeated by love. I would go to bed and feel blissfully carried off to sleep. A feeling of nearness, of the saturating presence of affection, would steal over me at unexpected times. It was something I had not experienced since my days with Swami Ashokananda. I think now of

Swami Ghanananda as a fulfiller of desires, odd as it may sound. Like the fabled Kalpataru, the tree of Indian lore, supposed to bear as fruit whatever is desired by the one who finds it and stands under it, he could make dreams come true. He made many come true for me, and it seemed to be his joy to do so, though he seldom allowed anyone to catch him in that enjoyment. How many times we saw him hiding that sweet grin which made his eyes seem to dance, behind a paper or book! As if to say, "I know that you have appreciated what I have given you, but let us not speak of it." It was difficult to thank him for anything: He was too humble for that. Not that he turned deferentially away from thanks — something in his manner forestalled it. It was some years later that I remembered in this connection the confession of Sri Maharaj, Swami Brahmananda; "If I love a man, I never let him know of it."

It was Swami Ghanananda who initiated public work for me. It was then I realized why he had been willing to bring me to England. He had other plans for Swami Parahitananda, his English assistant, and I, though but a brahmachari, would have to assume most of the latter's tasks: editing, giving discourses, interviews. So a tryout was held. Swami told me, "Prepare a talk, and Edna (the treasurer mentioned above) and I will come and listen." Choosing the title "Vedanta: a Strength-Giving Religion," I tried to model my thoughts and their development on those of Swami Ashokananda, my ideal lecturer. It was delivered one evening in the lecture hall (made, as usual, by the throwing together of two large rooms on the ground floor) and, sure enough, I had an audience of two. Both liked the lecture and gave appropriate suggestions; at least Swami said it was satisfactory and this pronouncement opened a whole new direction for my monastic labors.

It was disturbing, however, suddenly to be asked to "preach," even though we carefully cultivate the underlying realization that it is Brahman in the speaker, who is in the act of worshipping Brahman in the listener. It was sufficiently disturbing that I believed I had to write a letter to the vice-president of the order at Belur Math, a senior swami known to me, asking him how I could deliver lectures in view of what the Master had said about the blind leading the blind; I had no divine command. Swami Nirvanananda wrote back at once in a loving and understanding vein. "Certainly you are not going to preach of your own accord," he reminded me. "You have been asked to do so by the authority there and he is deputed by the order, and I think that is the badge of authority. You are not going to give talks with the idea of preaching. You will do it as the service of the Lord and as a part of your sadhana. Work is worship, and any work can be looked upon as worship. Work done in the proper spirit will become worship and that helps the aspirant to march onward. You can serve the Lord and humanity with whatever you have and simply do your best." Soon I was sent to speak outside the city as well, in answer to requests made to Swami by various groups.

He sent me now to live at Holland Park. From among the many empty rooms, I chose No. 10 where I had stayed on my brief visit. We went to and fro, the one house to the other, and not always in the car. When one took the "tube" (subway), the usual terminal north was Highgate. This means a confrontation with the famous Highgate Cemetery. One had to walk alongside it for some distance, and as it was often in the news, either for current dire happenings or for some ancient mischief, I would try to keep high thoughts in mind and whistle a tune.

III. IN THE BOROUGH OF KENSINGTON

Smaller than Kensington Park, the *grande plaisance* of the West End, Holland Park was the newest of the city's large acquisitions. The dignified mansion which had played host to the political Fox family of Stuart times, and the palace intrigue of their royal patrons, had suffered severe bomb damage in the war. Together with its surrounding gardens, lawns and forest, 55 acres in extent, it was made over to the care of the Greater London Council, which rebuilt the house and refurbished the estate, adding a stunning gem of a park to the city's already ample collection.

Soon Swami announced that the new house at 54 Holland Park, one of the many great ones all built together near the Park in the nineties, was now to be considered and spoken of as the Centre itself, no longer a "branch," and that he would be moving there to live, returning to Muswell Hill from time to time.

The house, standing five floors and built on the wing plan, with its large rooms placed on either side of a central passage and staircase, stood on a street simply called Holland Park. Holland Park Avenue, an east-west arterial only one block north, busied itself with bus lines, corner pubs, betting offices and family greengrocers. Refuge from all that, and from nearly everything a city signifies save certain sounds, was achieved by taking the five-minute walk south to the Park entrance. There one lost one-self in the long avenues of lime trees or the groves of rhododen-drons or by taking a seat in the formal gardens of annuals and lavender, or standing at the fenced yard where ducks, guinea fowl and peacocks screamed as they scratched for food. I sup-pose each of us paid the Park a daily visit in fair weather, either singly or together, except Swami Ghanananda himself, for those days he had left behind him.

At first he came down for a day, sometimes two, to the new ashrama, using two of the second-floor rooms as bedroom and library/office. Though life was on much the same pattern as at Muswell Hill, it was the English swami who was looking after this place as required and according to his fashion. The strained relations between master and assistant were soon apparent — reaching at last the note writing phase, replacing direct address — but I had no inkling of what was about to transpire. Swami Ghanananda one day called me in to announce that Swami Parahitananda, who was officially Assistant Editor of *Vedanta for East and West* would soon be leaving for India, and therefore would be showing me how to do that work. By this time one had learned not to be unduly impressed with every dramatic pronouncement. Plans often changed. I kept hoping that this one would not ma-terialize. But when Swami Parahitananda and I had sat together, discussed the principles of editing the journal and the mechan-ics of its production, he confirmed that he was indeed packing and would be away for "a year of austerities." Although the new work would be stimulating, my disappointment was keen. I liked this young British swami, respected the acuity of his logic and the courtliness of his manners; I had hoped to learn, too, from his store of specialized knowledge and had expected we would live there compatibly. A person in the "middle" would serve a sort of cushioning function, I had anticipated. Very soon he had gone and new events took place.

There had already been a fresh arrival. A young man from Germany, well-educated and artistic, who had corresponded with both swamis, put in an appearance. He was liked and appreciated by all and was duly initiated and enlisted as a monastic candidate at Holland Park. Swami Ghanananda actually made the move now, to the newer house; but there was too little time left for him to feel at home there. For Tarak, his attendant, it was a whirlwind, this getting together of Swami's things, and his own, and bundling and transporting them to the other end of town. Attendants have their special ways with their abbots. Arguing, even at length, may be necessary to protect them from "blind spots" which even abbots have. This boy was not the only one who could or would do this for Swami, but he did it best. Although exasperated by his tenacity, the boy had a love for him that encompassed one situation after another. I think we all helped in the moving, and in due course the other brahmachari also made the move. With its full complement of five monastics and one lay resident, the official life of Holland Park as a Vedanta center began.

Some words need to be said about the acquisition of this enormous establishment. It was one of the master strokes of the wizardry of Swami Ghanananda. In one great thunderclap, so to speak, there appeared upon the scene a 16-room townhouse in acceptable condition and the endowment of funds to support the work for years to come. One may prefer to say, as Swami did, that this took place through the grace of the Master, Sri Ramakrishna, and no one doubts it; the question will still remain, why such grace to this monk and not another; why at that time and in that place? This is what I mean by his magic. I am certain that it was as a result of his own austerity and intensity of spiritual practice that it came about, but even more as a result of his absolute faith in Sri Ramakrishna. The sequence of events was itself astonishing, not to say miraculous. Not party to any of those incidents, I can only report what I remember having heard, hoping this record will be reasonably accurate. Here again are all the elements of surprise and unconnectedness with which life around Swami was replete. An Englishman, never referred to by name but only as The Donor, a recluse wishing no public notice, had one day telephoned the Muswell Hill center, reached the swami, and declared himself willing to make two substantial donations (several hundred thousand pounds), one to Vedanta and the other to the Buddhists. This person we never saw, nor did he attend services or visit the swami. I am not sure that the latter ever met him, but he did send Swami Parahitananda to the recluse's abode to discuss and receive the donation and it was he who made any necessary contacts with The Donor thereafter. We never pressed him on the matter. With this money the search for a new building in a better location was begun, resulting in the purchase of the prime property and the establishing of investments for the center's maintenance. Swami Ghanananda would be able to take his leave of London peacefully, with all this behind him. The day was not far off.

Two superb rooms on the first floor, surely dining or ballrooms in another day, separated by a removable partition, made up the lecture hall. On a raised platform at the south end stood a large plain table. Swami Ghanananda was the scheduled speaker every Sunday at five in the afternoon. To me it was curious, having the public there at that hour; he had the idea that the English were faithful churchgoers and would resent competition with their habitual observance. But did anyone come who had been at church that morning? It was doubtful, and of course once it had begun it was, in a way, enshrined and difficult to alter. However ill he might feel or weak he might appear, Swami would unfailingly present himself, mount to the platform, seat himself behind the table and give some account of the subject. It was still on occasion a glowing affair. He gave an invocational chant and spoke for about an hour, sometimes ending by a call for questions. Late in the year, when he seemed very short of breath, I asked him one Sunday if it didn't tire him much to give the lecture. "Oh, no," he reassured me, "on the contrary, I feel *stronger* after lecturing."

There was little about the talks that could be predicted, save that they would be concise, well illustrated with anecdotes, stories and his own experiences, and though language-perfect, possibly for the beginner difficult to follow. The development of his thought could be subject to sudden interjections of regret, surprise, complaint or humorous comment. In a lecture on

"Yearning for God," for example, he gave his explanation of *dama*, second of the "six treasures" of sadhana. He added dramatic effect by saying, "... dama, control of the senses. Some people say, 'I close my eyes and even then I see things I should not!' That is because the mind is not controlled. Horrible! And who is responsible for all this? If God is responsible, then you must pray, 'Lead us not into temptation.'" One learned to enjoy this abruptness as the flavor of the dish. Other of his statements in the lecture could be startlingly original. "The light which is Atman is always shining. But in deep sleep the mind has become so tired, it turns away from that Light." No one, I think, has said this in just that way.

This is what the casual visitor would see and hear. Was not a deeper drama taking place? Such a phenomenon I had observed in some other teachers; the passing of instructions or advice to particular individuals during an address to an audience was often patent in Swami Ghanananda's discourses. It is a special form of the guru's love. Many a student reported the feeling of being pinned down from time to time throughout the hour as the swami's dancing eyes would light on her or him and hold that person in a burst of personal message. Unknown to other listeners he would use these "one-on-one" contacts to thank or comfort or criticize or even praise, as if only you and he were present.

A disciple told me that in the early days in Kingsway Hall near Aldwych, where for 15 years Swami gave his Thursday evening lectures, there was one rainy evening an audience of one — or two, I don't recall now. Most speakers, surely, would have called it off. Swami Ghanananda went about it in his usual businesslike manner, presenting his faithful devotee with the compliment of a topnotch, intimately personal, ringing rendition of the message of the evening. On the effect of those nights at Kingsway Hall another has written, "Although his manner was quiet and unassuming, one felt that the swami had deep personal experience of what he was speaking about and one sensed a hidden power. In the West, philosophy and religion have often been opposed, and I was on the side of the philosophers where they seemed to be more honestly seeking the truth than were the religious dogmatists. But what a new insight the Vedanta philosophy and the life of Sri Ramakrishna gave into Christianity and religion as a whole."

But we were discussing life at Holland Park. The lowest portion of the Park mansion lay halfway below the ground, a floor consisting of dining room, furnace and utility room and a set of bedrooms evidently originally for servants. The kitchen was crowded narrowly under the house's entrance staircase. Swami came down to the dining hall once a day to have his noon meal with us, unless — as happened more often now — he did not feel up to negotiating the two long flights of stairs. Often he would use the lunchtime to educate. He loved the epics, particularly the *Ramayana*, and the tales it spins were his favorites. He would repeat them to us and could repeat them over and over to the same audience, feeling he was relating them for the first time, so much did he put himself into the telling. The more outlandish the story the better it seemed to come off and the more he enjoyed it. His laugh was one of the odder things about him and many loved him for it. He could laugh at you, certainly, and he did so now and then — but in such a sympathetic vein, so filled with ill-concealed love, that one simply sat back and laughed at oneself, an object in a painting. This was a perennial trick with him, as with all expert spiritual teachers: to use his own nonattachment to push one into detachment as the only possible response.

Occasionally he came to lunch in somber mood. Thinking to stimulate him to scintillating conversation, I might chatter a bit, only to be told "keep quiet!" The meal was then taken in silence.

Besides the national sagas, another of Swami's great loves was Mother Kali. Her festival was for him a high point of the year. In the hallway at Holland Park we had framed colored photographs of the eloquent images used at Belur Math for worship of Kali, Durga, Jagaddhatri and Saraswati. I cannot now remember the context, but one day he asked some of us, "Have you ever thought about the effect on a man's baser desires of the vision of Ma Kali?" Women would not be body, he meant, but spirit, thereafter. Topping all his predilections, possibly, was his dedication to Shankara. His own birthplace was not far from that of the great acharya of whom he was a lifelong champion. The flavor of his writing and his speaking was in the panoply of Vedantic *darshanas* definitely Shankaran.

He would tell us sometimes of his dreams, the strikingly spiritual ones. There were two in particular in which Swami Brahmananda and Swami Shivananda, respectively, had visited him. How I wish now that I had recorded those! I did ask him if he often dreamed of his guru (Swami Shivananda). He answered that he did not. "Rather," he said, "I dream more often of Maharaj [Swami Brahmananda]." He told an anecdote about him, new to me and unusual. One time Maharaj, while in Madras, wanted a picture of temple dancing girls, to see in detail what the bracelets, anklets, etc., looked like — all this in connection with the staging of Girish Ghosh's play, "Vilwamangal." He asked the devotee Ramanujachariar to procure such a picture for him. While bringing it to Maharaj, Ramanujachariar had to pass Sashi Maharaj, Swami Ramakrishnananda, who was flabbergasted to see the seductive picture. "What is that? What is that?" he cried, rushing into Maharaj's room. But Maharaj would not give any reply. It was Sashi Maharaj's habit to make pranam to Maharaj daily. For the next three days Maharaj refused to look at him when he was doing it. On the third day he burst out laughing and then gave the whole explanation.

Referring to the passing, a few years before, of the president, Swami Madhavananda, and the poll taken by the senior monks on their choice to fill the post, Swami Ghanananda told me of the great regard he had for my guru, Swami Yatiswarananda. "I voted for Suresh Maharaj and no one else!"

Conscious as he was of his primary mission, conveyer to the Western world of the spiritual and cultural treasures of India, he was also concerned to see that the Indian devotees were catered to in various ways, and he had many Indian students. After Indian independence and the general breakup of the empire, the Commonwealth was formed, an association through mutual interest, financial, historical, diplomatic and sentimental, of its former parts. Citizens of the previous colonies, migrating to the British Isles, were given citizenship there. A vast throng of Indians in London swelled daily in number. Only a slim fraction of these came to the doors of Holland Park or Muswell Hill, but many who did so found in Swami Ghanananda a helping hand, a canny advisor, a brother or a teacher. Naturally there were whole families who were devoted, and although the Indians who participated in the center's daily or weekly functions were in the minority, on special occasions they would come in scores, even hundreds, for festive celebrations. If he were so inclined, Swami could let them see his joy and intimacy and loving concern, even for their smallest children — something they rarely encountered in contact with the busy monks in the larger centers of India. They told us how much they appreciated this warmth. To some, newly arrived and insecure, he would outright give or lend money; for others he would seek a contact possibly leading to a job; others received psychological counseling to help overcome the stress of the new culture; yet others were encouraged to establish a shrine to the Master and a holy atmosphere in the home. Not a few received full discipleship.

One of the ways Swami served them was unique, I believe, at least for a center in the West up until that time. On request he had started performing the *annaprasana*, the celebration of a baby's first solid-food taking. In the shrine room at Holland Park this was carried out at first by himself and then, as time went by, by the novices. As I observed and then officiated at this intimately Indian ritual, I often wondered how the families were feeling about having me do it — for I was still a "foreigner" in their eyes. I wondered at my own migration from ritual-eschewing Quaker to performer as Hindu priest. But no doubt this too was a part of Swami Ghanananda's magic.

Seeing that the swami allowed the weaning ritual, families would be moved occasionally to request the *sraddha*, or funeral rite (not done by monks in India). Such petitions he handled sympathetically but in a manner which cleverly avoided blurring our traditional boundaries. The family would be told that flowers and fruits might be brought and offered *to Sri Ramakrishna* (instead of the deceased); they were to pray to him for the soul of the relative, and to read aloud in the shrine room the second chapter of the *Gita*. It was difficult to say which the Indians found more surprising — the fact that they could make an observance here at all, or what it was they were asked to do.

The magazine *Vedanta for East and West* was a project close to Swami's heart. He had begun publishing articles as pamphlets even before the establishment of the Muswell Hill center, having observed the production of the Hollywood journal, *Vedanta and the West*. As Swami came into touch with some of the notables in English literary circles, he was quick to make friends. He would subsequently ask them for articles. Of course some came forward of themselves, seeing the high standard in content and language constantly employed. In the editorial work he gave me freedom, then went over everything with his own eyes. For me there were the British spellings and usages to master. Swami's standards in English grammar, usage and punctuation were exemplary. He had taken his M.A. in English and in India his proficiency was well known. Shakespeare quotations would pop out anytime they would help his point.

Swami seemed to take it for granted that once the assistant editor had shown me the procedures everything would go smoothly, and I appreciated that trust. Still, there were minor matters over which we sat together. For example, in the United States we considered it correct to follow the impersonal pronoun "one" with the masculine possessive "his," as in "one should repeat his mantra." Swami Ghanananda ridiculed it. He would have only "one should repeat one's mantra." (It had nothing to do with gender in that era.) Policies for procuring material, correspondence with authors, monetary and other matters concerning the printer, all were explained from his experience. Like most small magazines today, this one did not at all pay for itself; that was not the primary consideration in his eyes. *Vedanta for East and West* was a vital organ of the London center and a hallmark of its contribution to the mission of the order.

One day as we sat in his room discussing such affairs he made a sort of prophecy I found awesome. He said, "In the long run so far as history is concerned, of all the persons making up our movement, only two names will go down: Sri Ramakrishna and Swami Vivekananda."

We were busy that first year at Holland Park. No sooner had the book *Swami Vivekananda in East and West* — a compilation of articles by Indians and Westerners from the journal — arrived from the printer, ready for distribution, than we began work on a third edition of his own opus, *Sri Ramakrishna and His Unique Message*. This was his last literary production, one that still wins plaudits. By that time, his body was truly worn out and he had more and more to rely on others for proofreading and decision making. He lived to see it through to publication. What many consider his finest book had come out in 1956 to commemorate the Centenary Anniversary of the Holy Mother. *Women Saints of East and West* was a "first" in surveying this field world-wide, representative of the great faiths; the essays were by various hands, many of them women. His own account of Sri Sarada Devi is widely regarded as particularly apt in introducing her life and thought to new readers in the West.

Considering how regulated the life of the monastery was by the routines of shrine and housework, book and journal business and the astrological calculations, Swami Ghanananda granted remarkable freedom in certain respects. In a sense I found his regime more liberal, more truly in the spirit of Vedanta as I conceived it, than those of abbots in America. If, for example, anyone wished to attend church on Sunday mornings, one was free to do so. The Hare Krishna movement descended on the city that year, opening with a gala Rathayatra festival and employing for the first time a live elephant in its parade. Swami was tickled by the idea. Several of the boys wanted to go and see the fun, and he encouraged them. Two other offbeat organizations of the many gracing the London scene — for it was, after all, the heyday of the mystical sixties — came to mind: one, the exciting boy guru, just over from India; the other, an extraordinary musical outfit, Quintessence, forming itself around dedicated ashramites espousing sadhana. We were permitted to sample the gatherings of both of these. When the Sufis wished to begin their London work in the same year and invited us to take part in their first Inter-Religious Congress, he encouraged them and sent me to represent Hinduism at the convocation.

One day Swami Ghanananda said, "Those who join this monastery know that they will be provided with sufficient food, clothing and a roof over their heads; opportunities for prayer, meditation, study and work; if in spite of all this they cannot remain, they must know it is their own doing, the fault of their own minds." On another occasion, I think in front of two of us, there came from him a confession that I found the most astonishing of many surprises: "Even I have to struggle to stay in the monastery," he said. Now if he, at his age — well, what could one say? What a lesson on the ceaseless tossing of the human mind!

Playful as he was with the devotees, Swami was not often so with us monastics. Yet there were times when he teased for fun. How touched I was when, as he went out the front door for a two or three-day visit to the other house, he would embrace me, saying, "Be of good cheer, Swami!" — and I but a brahmachari. At one such time he had been pulling my leg over some matter or other and now, "You may let *me* play in this way with you," he tossed off gaily, "but don't allow others to do so! Heh, heh, heh!" And away he went.

Jokes on himself he hardly ever had occasion to experience, but when he did he handled them with aplomb. When a senior swami from Bombay arrived for a visit, it was surprising that he greeted our swami in a very playful way. "Look out, look out!" exclaimed Swami Ghanananda, "I am a sick man!" The young Bengali devotee residing in the ashrama was full of fun and mischief. Around the old swami, however, his face was straight and he minded all the signals. One evening he was sitting in the large reception room downstairs with us, the brahmacharis. All were engaged in some sort of verbal frivolity. The sound of a key in the front door suddenly heralded the presence of the revered swami, unexpectedly returned from Muswell Hill. This boy, not wanting for some reason to be found there, on impulse took a dive behind a large sofa. Everyone was expecting Swami to go on up the stairs to his room, but alas, the folly of guessing where he was concerned! He found it convenient now to rest between floors, came in, sat down on that sofa and began to chat. As time passed, of course it became more and more difficult to keep a straight face, especially for our boy who began to snicker behind the sofa. The game was up and the swami, genuinely astonished, joined in the general glee.

One of the last persons to make a friend of Swami Ghanananda and to have the privilege of his interest and counsel was a young student whose parents were Chinese immigrants. It was a joy to see these two together; Swami's love for him was thinly veiled. I am sure he wished to mute it, always, for it was Swami Ghanananda who had told us that a young monk once said to Swami Shivananda, "Oh, Maharaj, you love us so much!"

and the great swami had replied, "If you have understood that I love you, then that is no love at all."

This phase of life at Holland Park came to a close in 1969 with Swami's decision to send to India his second monastic disciple also, to be enlisted in the training center. He, master of all the contacts and mechanics of book sales and mailings, also a professional hotelier, etc., would be sorely missed, however eager and ready for the adventure he might have been. Yet I suspect that this man inwardly realized he would not see his teacher again in the flesh. Now, except for the occasional stays of boys who were flirting with monastic life, the residents had been reduced to five.

IV. ENGAGEMENT

I wonder if there is something about living on an island that gives people special qualities and special needs. Perhaps it produces a sort of compensatory anti-provincialism, a broadening of horizons and an education of the heart toward receptivity to those outside. If so, Swami Ghanananda was an ideal island man. Before coming to the West he had carried out, with significant success, assignments for the order on Sri Lanka and then on Mauritius. Gradually the talent for reflecting and expressing the spiritual needs of the people of England must have grown in him. For although Swami did not have, by comparison with some monks in other large Western cities, a sizable following, he was remarkably successful with those attracted by his work and thought, both in helping to develop their spiritual faculties and in seeing that they developed a lifelong commitment to sadhana.

His Indian students we have already taken note of. It is time to mention what other sorts of persons came into his orbit and the means and methods he used in serving them. Prominent in the first issues of the journal are the names of the writers Sir John Stewart-Wallace and Kenneth Walker; early friends, they helped Swami in editorial, business and public relations matters, both directly and through their own contacts. It was before my time but well-remembered that Mr. Walker, a surgeon, teacher and philosopher, had been of outstanding help and usefulness to Swami and to Vedanta in Britain.

Most of the devotees came from ordinary walks of life —

middle- and lower-middle-income people. They were secretaries, teachers, civil servants, accountants and housewives. On the board of management of the center were, among others, two physicians, a professor and a man who ran a bicycle shop. Geoffrey Watkins, of London's famous bookshop, was a trustee whom it was often necessary to consult — and, unfailingly, a friend to all of us. One of Swami's most interesting and fruitful connections was with an author who was also a housewife — writing plays for the BBC and articles for the magazine, making retreats from time to time at Muswell Hill while running her home in the west of England. I met the political and academic figure, Lord Soper; Marcus Braybrooke, an ecumenically inspired clergyman; and the classicist Norman Marlow who taught at Manchester University.

During this period I pondered on why a thinker like Swami Vivekananda, so much lionized in his own day, whose teachings had received both publicity and appreciation at the time he worked in England, should seemingly have been buried in the ensuing 70 years, at least so far as penetrating into British thought and society is concerned. I do not feel I have all the answers as yet but I have realized it is not merely a British phenomenon; it has happened worldwide, and even in India itself to some extent. The times have changed. One recalls the work of Meister Eckhart and of many others, "lost" and rediscovered.

Some of Swami Ghanananda's occidental students and friends were not British but simply resident in England, having come — like so many Londoners — from the continent, and contributing to the cosmopolitan complexion of the life of the great city. Some would fly in from Europe to see him, others would invite him to visit them. Swami made in this way a total of eight trips abroad, which included a remarkable meeting in Athens attended by 1,000 people and a visit to C. G. Jung in Zurich in 1952.

Swami told us on several occasions about this visit. The superconscious state had been their topic of discussion in an atmosphere of friendly exchange. Jung was looking for an authoritative and rational explanation of it — had been, it seems, for years — and Swami Ghanananda offered the remark that it transcended the distinctions of knower, known and knowledge. The state being indescribable, even for one who has experienced it, Swami said, it was not surprising that Dr. Jung's requirements of definition had been difficult to satisfy. Jung then asked that question so difficult for Westerners to forego: "What does it do for one? What gain is there from samadhi?" "It gives supreme peace and light," was Swami's reply. "But is it worth it?" Jung suggested with a slight smile. The remainder of this conversation is not recorded, but the very asking of such a question belies that enlightenment we seem to see in some of Jung's published work.

Few could imagine Swami's facility and expertise in business and financial matters, it seemed so improbable. But the members of the board spoke of his quick grasp of the issues and a store of administrative acumen beneath his deceptive surface of almost naive simplicity. There was a board member who, retired from business, had served Swami many years as a kind of confessor figure, to whom he could confide much and whose opinion was asked and valued. This man occupied that advisory role for the center as long as he lived, which was not for long after the swami's passing. Though he had on a number of occasions to trim Swami Ghanananda's designs to a more practical cut, he nevertheless had a high opinion of the swami's judgment in everything. As Sri Ramakrishna used to say, "One who can measure salt can also measure sugar." And as I remarked at the beginning of these memoirs, common to all the monks of the order well known to me was a large measure of common sense with which their idealism was usually seasoned.

Swami kept everybody busy, visitors and ashramites alike. "Some employment would be found," as a devotee described it, "in the kitchen, the garden, the mail-order books department, in the office, typing letters and articles and especially in preparation for the festivals, for all your known talents and those you never knew you had." Swami had a quaint way of dealing with complaints about others. If one came to him in high dudgeon over the shortcomings of a fellow worker, or about how irritated one felt by the slights or slurs of different persons, he would spread a wide grin, cock his head a bit on one side and say, "Yes! People are like that!," cluck his tongue and then laugh. It was as much as to say, you are right, to be sure, but then what can be done about it? It was Sri Ramakrishna's "endure, endure, endure," not preached but shared.

Classic was the description given by our playwright in the Memorial Edition of *Vedanta for East and West* (No. 116), of the precise balances in Swami Ghanananda's teaching method:

"To those of us whose work reached and might influence, the general public outside the Centre, he taught the duty of listening to the *ishta* within, rather than to comment and criticism from outside, and he himself refused, I found in my own case, to interfere or to make suggestions. His method here was always to give help indirectly, by what one learned simply from being with him, though he always answered direct questions patiently and in great detail. Although he gave his blessing to the work and watched over it with concern and attention, he always taught me to turn to the ishta as the ultimate guide; the work must 'come from within.' Had I not known him, I should never have believed it possible for strong authority and the giving of freedom to be so perfectly blended in one and the same person." I, from my own experience and recollection, can heartily endorse her statement.

Swami used different means to effect his ends. He often took great pains, using even harsh measures to help one see one's weaknesses. But the evidence of his utter detachment in the midst of all his guruship was the fact that his attitude, mood, expression and tone of voice could change radically, toward several different persons in succession. Someone said she saw him change mood three times on the way upstairs, to match the mood of the three persons he met on the way. He seemed to catch the vibrational state, so to speak, of a person, as if he were like a mirror held up to each. Meeting yourself that way, so to speak, gave you a certain power of self-monitoring. Actually I said it all when I spoke of his "magic." Disciples testify to his speaking of events apart from his sense knowledge, in other times and places, and of how he warded off dangers for them and averted looming disasters without impinging on their freedom to make mistakes if they were bent on it. Someone, doubting these powers, asked him point-blank, "Swamiji, is it true that you can read our thoughts? If so, would you answer this question I am asking now?" And he at once answered it aloud. He told another that he read thoughts only when it helped someone or when he felt it was the right moment. These capacities made Swami a very unusual monk, but what I treasure more, now that the years have gone by, are the great paradoxes: mystery and simplicity; scholarship and innocence; authority and humility; fearlessness and sweetness.

"He didn't lead," said a seasoned disciple, "he pushed." True, and yet in other cases people felt that he neither led nor pushed, but simply "was." Just being with him, even if he was talking about the proper way to cook rice, carried them somehow toward the chosen aspect of Deity, providing the link which was so difficult to establish for oneself. Nor did he need to be present to do this. As I hinted at the beginning of the chapter, he appears to have possessed a power of spiritual psychokinesis.

V. ROUGH GOING

It was not much of a secret that one of the chief reasons Swami had made his recent trip to India was to arrange for an assistant who would be his successor as well. There was no need for us, the novices, to have any information about, or part in, these negotiations. As I was the only one who had been among the monks in India recently, the name chosen would not have much meaning for the others, perhaps. At last, however, word was passed that Belur Math was considering two of the present heads of Indian centers, and I offered the brothers whatever I knew of each of these. What in England is called backstairs talk now commenced and speculation had its day. It would appear that Swami Ghanananda had agreed to accept the choice of headquarters and also to retire from the active running of the center as soon as the new swami could get his bearings.

In late summer Swami Bhavyananda arrived and was in many ways a surprise. To us the two swamis appeared to have but one feature in common, *i.e.* possession of a sense of humor — and the expression of that was totally different in each. The new swami was large of build, physically robust and apparently extroverted in temperament. For the first three days with us at Holland Park he reeled off such a continuous stream of jokes and humorous stories we were quite bowled over; that may or may not have been his conscious intention. The older swami was living now at Muswell Hill. His new assistant visited him in the daytime, and was suitably deferential and restrained. Swami himself was quiet and watchful as he tentatively weighed a successor he had never known or met. The situation was fascinating and instructive.

As indicated, although the monastics were all in the new ashrama now, Swami Ghanananda was being well attended and cared for by the devotees close to him these many years, as well as by the two young ladies mentioned above. From them we learned of his heart attack near dawn one morning early in October. He was taken at once to a hospital nearby where he remained for five weeks. One or more of us went every day to see him. For me it was strange to find him occupying just another bed in a row of the twenty or more making up the ward, for I was accustomed in America to attending on our swamis in private rooms. The British medical system was different, I realized, but surely there had been offers to engage a room for him, and at the end he had it. Though I do not remember hearing so, it must have been Swami's own choice, remaining so long in a public ward. Perhaps he really did not wish to put the center, now no longer "his," under the extra expense. At any rate, Swami used the opportunity to make friends, as everywhere he did. Whenever we came we found him either talking with a crony from another bed, or ready to tell us about the sad problems of someone who had just left or just arrived as a patient — anyone's problems but his own. He was quickly on good terms with the staff and was a popular resident in the public ward. The place had a more informal atmosphere, too, than hospitals of that day in the United States. Visitors seemed welcome most of the day. This was the time when those closest to Swami Ghanananda who were still in the area, such as Phyllis, the vice-president of the center, moved into position as his "family." She was keeping virtually constant vigil and did so to his last, labored breath. She seemed always to be there. Other board members and longtime devotees too had their opportunities for personal service.

As mentioned earlier, Swami had sent his monastic disciples to India and his attendant to Holland Park. I had been there only a year; his assistant had just arrived; the functions of the center were already largely in the hands of a new crew. Did it have an effect on his will to live? Had Swami already concluded that the future of the work had no need, now, for his flagging energies? The doctors reported that his condition went up and then down, as they monitored the cardiometer's zigs and zags. There was not only the cardiac attack, but the basic diabetic constitution and severe emphysema as well. I went one evening and talked a little with him, holding his hand and watching helplessly as the color of his flesh seemed to grow ashen before my eyes. Going home, I reported to Swami Bhavyananda that I felt for the first time that he really was about to go, after all.

Swami's last hours were, at least from the human standpoint, full of suffering. I was on that floor and could hear — but would not see — his passing. Only Phyllis — faithful, cherishing him as her very own life — ministered to him in those moments.

We were all in shock, for even with the possibility of death hovering over us from day to day, it had come, in a way, suddenly. Two very modest and moving services were held. The first was in the hall at Muswell Hill, with no more than thirty-some persons in attendance. Swami Ritajananda had come over from Paris to lead the ceremony. Around Swami Ghanananda's open coffin we chanted, made our salutations and sang. It seemed as if a child were lying there. The second service took place at the cremation, done the same day at a cemetery chapel. My picture is hazy now, for there was shock and mental stress. Swami Bhavyananda and I did some readings and probably some words were said. The ashes were sent to India, where they arrived in February. In front of Holy Mother's temple at Belur Math his brahmachari disciple consigned them to the river Ganges. So, the one who had sent him away from his presence came again right into his hands.

From Swami Vireswarananda, president of the order, I received the following acknowledgment of my letter of report to him: "Yes, Ghanananda has passed away and not only London but the organization is poorer by his leaving us. He was such a rare good soul. But Sri Ramakrishna thought to take him away and so we have to say 'Amen.'"

Within a very short time, at least a portion of his legacy to the movement became evident. Undoubtedly that legacy is an unfolding blossom, some petals of which are yet to open. This much, however, was visible within weeks: he had raised and trained a body of devotees constituting the core of the Ramakrishna Vedanta Centre, who, in spite of Swami's strong and distinctive personality, were oriented to the principle of the Impersonal. He had filled them with a spirit of adherence to Spirit and not to flesh or form. Scarcely a single member of that core drifted away during the months of transition following his death. Those who have experience in groups of this kind must know the odds, on such occasions, when the passing of a powerful leader, the bumping and shifting of new management and the personal loss to many individuals all too often result in disarray for an organization. Some communities never recover. In the smooth and quick rebalancing of the London center several factors no doubt played their part, including the expertise of his successor, but the central factor, the deep root of continuing vitality, was the cohesion of the students in their commitment to the solid and illuminating principles of the Vedanta taught and embodied for them by Swami Ghanananda himself.

Swami Ghanananda had the ability to make you feel that the land of the Spirit was a very real place, and that he was, in fact, living in it. What Barbara Foxe says, in her *Long Journey Home* about Vivekananda, that "other people could draw maps," but he obviously lived in the land they described, applies in this case. He would make us see, if for only a brief moment, that this marvelous state of being exists; like the first disciples of the Master, as Swami Pavitrananda once put it, who "made you feel that God-realization was so easy and inevitable," Swami Ghanananda was living testimony to that, communicating to his students the feeling that if they would only plod on a little further they would reach the goal of life, just around the corner.

APPENDIX A

Addendum on the Philadelphia Center

The following are memoirs by other American students, Elizabeth Mowers and Mary Corson, included with their kind permission.

* * * *

I taught children in a primary school. When a good friend of mine there learned that I was looking for a spiritual guide, she brought me the church notices from a Sunday newspaper. She had found a Vedanta Center headed by a Swami. I went. For about a year I attended the lectures and was so absorbed in the teachings I just never spoke to the Swami. One day Swami Yatiswarananda said to me, "Why don't you come and see me?" It startled me and I was silent. He said, "You are not ready yet." Later someone told me casually that Swami might return to India. That woke me up to a need to visit him; I think it was in 1945.

I remember when he had received a couple of poems from a German devotee. She had written them in English for his sake. As they had no meter he requested me to put them into poetic meter. One of these poems was about Sri Ramakrishna and the other about the meaning of OM. I chose the latter. To accomplish it I had to meditate on the meaning of each line and try to realize her thought. The only time available to me was before retiring each night. It was my private experience. It took over a month. It was, I realized, a form of meditation and I always went to sleep following each effort; so I believe it entered

my subconscious. When I took the work back to him expecting
some response, he merely said, "Put it over there," indicating a
spot. I learned the lesson too.

  E. M.

* * * *

  We were only a few members in the Philadelphia center
in the 1940s — a handful of really dedicated devotees, Swami
called us. The meeting room had seats for perhaps forty persons. On class nights sometimes only five to eight persons would
turn up, but the Swami carried on with just as much earnestness
as if the room were packed.

  The Center was in what had previously been a medical
or dental office, consisting of two Siamese-twin rooms, walls and
woodwork all nicely painted cream color, floor intense brown,
no formal shrine as such, but incense and flowers were placed on
a mantle before a picture of Sri Ramakrishna. The lectern was
on a handmade wooden rectangular platform. Under it and covering the central part of the back room was a very gay-colored
natural-fibre rug from India. It seemed to set up quickened vibrations throughout the otherwise plain interior and even ran a
line of life between it and the Swami's eyes. As I remember, the
central picture of Sri Ramakrishna on the wall facing the members was the color reproduction of the painting by Dvorak. The
rear side door opened into the hallway which led back to the
Swami's apartment. We felt quite free to come and go there during or after a service or party. Yes, we did have parties and they
often included other centers, especially the New York centers
because they were the nearest, no doubt. But Swami always in-
stilled into us the more important idea of nearness to our Vedanta
brothers and sisters wherever they be.

  Early in my acquaintance with Vedanta he gave me a note
of introduction to hand to the Swamis Bodhananda and
Nikhilananda when I wished to go on a "pilgrimage" to New
York to meet my new relatives. Swami Akhilananda used to visit
us at intervals. Though stationed at the Boston center, it was he
who first attracted the Philadelphia group. Not yet organized
into a true center at that time, the group must have met in mem-

bers' homes.

Swami Yatiswarananda once loaned me his umbrella, which was soon broken at the stem by heavy winds. He asked for it the next time we met and reporting this to him I told him it was being repaired. He asked how I found out where to repair it and how much it was to cost. I gave the information but also mentioned that the repairman had opined that it had broken because the metal was fatigued as well. Swami put forth the idea that he should not have loaned something not able to hold up in service; thus did he take all the sting out of it.

Often after the evening class was over the Swami would walk me home, which was quite a few blocks and which took us through the dark Philadelphia railroad underpass. It was quite a brisk walk and he never said a word the entire way, not even upon reaching our destination.

A stranger took a seat in our midst on one occasion. When the Swami was talking, this individual stood up and began proselytizing. Whereupon the Swami got up and came forward, took him by the back of the neck and ousted him by force, saying: "Go rent your own hall!"

I recall a mother telling me Swami wrestled on their floor with her young son to prove to him that sannyasins are not sissies.

Another lady and myself had the privilege of cleaning the chapel and Swami's apartment for awhile. Swami would seem to be occupied somehow, but often moved from room to room to see how things were coming along. At times he would sit at his desk in the living room and shave with an electric shaver. I would sometimes watch him out of the corner of my eye. The little intimacy of it has become more and more pleasing to me through the years. I couldn't realize then his graciousness. I was watching for something to be proven in him, for he had been described to me before I met him, as though he were God Himself — very holy and too sacred, so I thought, for one like me to be allowed to look upon. It therefore required some reconciliation on my part to accept the rather normal actions in such a one and recognize his spiritual leadership and help. I never did in those days. But fortunately we do not need to be aware of blessings that come upon us. When we finished cleaning, the Swami would give us each a dish of ice cream or rice pudding.

He dressed as a well-to-do American would have dressed, for he didn't believe in looking shabby or poor, especially in his particular position as head of our center. In spite of this, he was turned away from a better class cafeteria-style restaurant one time because he was thought to be a black. He never said one word about the it. He just left.

Once he invited the devotees to dinner. We met in his apartment and then walked to a neighborhood restaurant together with him and Swami Akhilananda. It bothered me that he asked what I had had for lunch that day because I had ordered the same for this dinner. Whatever he discovered through the answer, it seemed to please him very much.

Personal interviews were given by the Swami in the living room of his apartment with the door ajar. He sat in a chair across from the tea table.

Looking back through a visit to India and many experiences in life since the Philadelphia days in Vedanta, I marvel at the wonderful orientation of Swami Yatiswarananda. He brought the truths of Vedanta to our hearts on an American tray, shorn for the most part of Eastern culture. It was a masterful bit, shaded exactly with the right amount of light for our individual place in our individual corner of the world.

- M.C.

APPENDIX B

Notes from a 1950 monastery class of Swami Prabhavananda on the meaning and performing of the daily worship of Sri Ramakrishna.

1. Purification. (a) Think of Vishnu, the all-pervading presence of God. (b) Touch all the senses — shutting their doors — of the organs of both perception and action. (c) Recall the truth that others have seen God just as a person sees the sky overhead: this gives us confidence.

2. Vessels. Each represents the substance or material cause of the universe. The Five elements: the symbol of earth represents the smell sense; of water, the taste sense; of fire, sight; of cloth, air (touch); of sound of the bell, ether (hearing). They have come from Him and so they represent Him. Everything is made up of Brahman and Sakti; we are to see this. Establishing the vessel: a yantra is made, of triangle within circle within square. Triangle = Mother power, circle = universe, square = Brahman, the covering of everything. The large spoon represents the power of protection. Astraya phat = God's weapon. Three petals of vilwa leaf — why? Control of sense, renunciation, knowledge of God. Kurma = tortoise, conceived as bearer of the earth ("I don't know exactly what that means," said Swami). From the sun you draw the water of the sacred rivers. When you say Om over these things, you are invoking the presence of Brahman. A river is barren without fish, so fish mudra is used. This also symbolizes the joy of living in the Impersonal.

3. Obstacles. These are created by gods who are jealous because you are trying to surpass them. The obstacles come in very subtle ways (you might suddenly lose interest in meditation, etc.). Also they come from evil influences.

4. Seat. You worship everything you use. These things do

work. If the seat is firm, auspicious, you may be able to sit for three hours straight.

5. Guru worship. For us, here, it is Guru, Sri Maharaj, then Master and Mother, Totapuri and Bhairavi Brahmani, Siva and Durga. You can think that all are Master and Mother. (a) Salute Ganesha, the doorkeeper. (b) "astraya phat" is always invoking the power of protection.

6. Purification of elements. This is the meditation prescribed for the believer in the Impersonal. Here there is no universe. This happens in nirvikalpa samadhi, which occurs when the kundalini reaches the sahasrara. So you dissolve all these things in turn till all is dissolved in Brahman. All karmas are dissolved too, in Prakriti and Prakriti into Brahman. And I am He. The "burning of the black figure with red eyes" is optional. (a) Make a full pranayama — left, right, left. (b) Now to worship you must have a body; so you get a new body made of the name of Ramakrishna. This is Nyasa.

7. Now you can worship. With flowers, for all sorts of gods and goddesses so that no one will be jealous. Repeat nyasa as a reminder.

8. Mental worship. Do the general things — bathing, clothing, perfume, incense — you needn't try to follow all the written details. This is true also of the offering of mental flowers.

9. Special offering. In the conch shell. This is like the Christian Mass. It is more sacred than that with the big spoon. The circle of fire, circle of sun and circle of moon — these symbolize the lotus of the heart.

This we have to understand: creation is the degeneration and distraction of the mind. We are to get rid of it.

Symbolism of the aratrika: earth element = flower; water = water; fire = light; air = cloth; space = sound of bell.

Food offering. When you are spiritually advanced you will see that a light from the picture is being shed on the food; the Lord eats with his eyes! The prana mudras symbolize the relation of food to our life.

APPENDIX C

Notes on worship from Swami Ashokananda's morning class.

Ceremonial Worship consists of five stages: Preparation, Purification, Mental Worship, External Worship and Concluding Practices. The purpose of worship is to pay homage to the Deity, and to generate a feeling of oneness — these are the formal elements. Then, too, it is an act of service; a spontaneous feeling of love arises and increases as it is mutually reactive, the worshiper on the Deity and the Deity on the worshiper. The principle goal is the participation of our whole being — physical, emotional, intellectual, psychic and spiritual.

(1) Our physical being participates for its own purification. To participate in the offerings our body as a whole is used. All our senses become purified.

(2) Our emotional being is satisfied in the devotion, our human nature finding expression through love. These things are universal. Some practices in the worship, such as foot-washing, are of local significance. Some of the universal ones are the offering of food, flowers, candles, lights, incense and perfume. Is this not too anthropomorphic, is the question often asked. That need not concern us; the important question is, is He pleased with our devotion and does He respond? Since God is inextricably bound with human nature, does He not respond greatly to its needs? God does actually respond (as can be seen in very high states of consciousness), whatever the explanation.

(3) Our intellectual being is manifested in the mental worship, since all the things in the process are to be conceived symbolically.

(4) Our psychic being finds its satisfaction in the preliminary purification practices. Purity, both internal and external, is

closely related to psychic sensitivity.

(5) Our spiritual being: you are losing yourself in the spirit of the thing if your worship is thorough and successful. You will feel yourself as Spirit.

Whom do we worship? We worship Saguna Brahman. God-with-attributes may be (1) without form. He can have many aspects — love, power, truth, etc. and combinations of these. He may be worshiped as lover, friend, parent, child, etc. Or (2) with form. Some are not manifested on the physical plane, e.g., Siva, Kali, Vishnu. Some are Incarnations. Here again various relationships are possible: "servant of Christ," "Buddha of Peace." We are never to worship Sri Ramakrishna as just a saint who lived in Bengal. Note here the Catholic conception of the Madonna who intercedes, and saints who are never identified with Deity. Thus it is with Holy Mother and Swamiji. But we worship the Incarnation as God Himself. Why? Because they usually reveal themselves to their disciples during their lifetimes, as such. It is, then, not just a device for spiritual growth. Do we then forget his human aspects? No, for the reasons mentioned before. We can approach him with real feeling which will grow. Stages of the worship (simple type) preparation:

(1) Cleaning the shrine room. Since God is everywhere, why is he more in the shrine room? Isn't this a limitation? No. If he is everywhere, he is also in the shrine room; the state of mind is what counts. It is very beneficial to feel this in our present state. Purity is a very strong idea in worship; the main purpose of ceremonial purity is psychic purity and sensitivity. Real devotees succeed in seeing all these things. This is apart from the spiritual growth and training in carefulness also attendant on purification. It is productive of great sanctity, as in Orthodox Judaism, Catholicism, Hinduism.

(2) Bathing ourselves before worship. The entire body is to be washed.

(3) Cleaning the shrine itself, the holy-of-holies. Why must we approach the shrine with great reverence? First, God may be displeased otherwise. Second, we can damage ourselves; third, we draw out what we bring.

(4) Offering plants and flowers. These are Sri Ramakrishna's and are to be treated as such. They must not be

cankered, improperly blown or very imperfect, or have insects or cobwebs. Preparation of both flowers and vases is to be done carefully.

(5) Offering of food. It is put here on two plates (for Sri Ramakrishna and Divine Mother) and a tumbler of water prepared for Sri Ramakrishna.

(6) Candles are lit and incense offered; thus begins the ceremony of worship.

APPENDIX D

Solution to Swami Madhavananda's puzzle

"I do not like it," said the man with the black tie. "The rite may be impressive, but when you inter a man, you retain a certain power of investigation. Reaction against cremation will set in when the importance of this is revealed."

The speaker was a coroner.

REFERENCES
& BIBLIOGRAPHY

References to further material on the swamis' lives and works.

Swami Yatiswarananda

ORIGINAL WORKS:
> *Adventures in Religious Life*
> *Meditation and Spiritual Life*
>> Well-organized compendium of his talks and writings.

TRANSLATIONS:
> *The Divine Life*
>> Collection of scripture passages for chanting and meditating.
> *Universal Prayers*
>> Collected from many (Indian) sources.

Swami Prabhavananda

> *Vedanta for the West* (periodical)

ORIGINAL WORKS:
> *The Eternal Companion*
>> Life and teachings of Swami Brahmananda.
> *Memories of a Loving Soul* (Swami Premananda)
> *Yoga and Mysticism*
> *The Sermon on the Mount according to Vedanta*
> *The Spiritual Heritage of India*
> *Religion in Practice*

TRANSLATIONS:

The Wisdom of God
     Excerpts from the Srimad Bhagavatam
The Upanishads, with Frederick Manchester
Crest-Jewel of Discrimination, with Christopher Isherwood
The Song of God (Bhagavad Gita), with Christopher
     Isherwood
How to Know God, with Christopher Isherwood
     Yoga Aphorisms of Patanjali
Narada's Way of Divine Love

Swami Ashokananda

ORIGINAL WORKS:

Worship of the Spirit by the Spirit and Spiritualizing
Everyday Life
Swami Vivekananda in San Francisco
When the Many Become the One
Swami Brahmananda
Swami Premananda
Memories of Swami Shivananda
Meditation, Ecstasy and Illumination
The Soul's Journey to Its Destiny

TRANSLATION:

Avadhuta Gita

Swami Nikhilananda

ORIGINAL WORKS:

Vivekananda, a Biography
Holy Mother
Hinduism

TRANSLATIONS:
> *The Gospel of Sri Ramakrishna*
> *Vedantasara*
> *Drg-drsya-viveka*
> *Atmabodha*
> *Bhagavad-Gita*
> *The Upanishads*
> *Mandukya Upanishad with Gaudapada's Karika*

Swami Madhavananda

TRANSLATIONS:
> *Vivekacudamani*
> *Brhadaranyaka Upanishad*
> *Minor Upanishads*
> *Bhagavata Purana*

Swami Ghanananda

> *Vedanta for East and West*, Memorial Issue, (#116)

ORIGINAL WORKS:
> *Sri Ramakrishna and His Unique Message*
> *Vedanta for East and West*, periodical, many articles (from 1951 to 1969).

EDITED:
> *Swami Vivekananda in East and West*,
>   Essays collected from around the world.
> *Women Saints of East and West*, with Geoffrey Parrinder